Awesome Puppy

Activities & Training to Make Your Pup An Awesome Dog

By Ray & Emma Lincoln

Awesome Puppy
Activities & Training to Make Every Pup an Awesome Dog

By Ray & Emma Lincoln
Copyright 2011 by Ray & Emma Lincoln

Published by:
Awesome Book Publishing
P.O. Box 1157
Roseland, FL 32957

ISBN: 978-0-9840538-3-4
Library of Congress Control Number: 2010934525

Other Books by Ray & Emma Lincoln:

The Cure for Useless Dog Syndrome
Dogs Hate Crates
Dog In a Box
1 Month Cure for "Useless" Dogs

This book is dedicated to the rescue of pups suffering in puppy mills and other abusive situations here and around the world. They are also Awesome Puppies.

Table of Contents

PART 1:

Introduction

"Show me your dog and I will tell you what manner of a man you are"
-Max Von Stephanitz

Chapter 1:

What Your Puppy Learns Now, He'll Do for the Rest of His Life

The activities and training methods in this book are designed to change your entire future with your dog.

Each week of development in your pup's first year, especially during his first six months, will have huge impact on his future personality and behavior. And dogs learn most of their crucial life skills in the period between birth and twenty weeks, as well as learning most of their good and bad habits, whether you consciously teach them or not. Before twenty weeks is also the crucial time to introduce your pup to all the people, places and things you plan for him to encounter later in life to prevent reactive behavior later on.

Every single interaction with your young puppy will have a lasting effect, and we wrote this book to help new pet parents get exactly the results they want. Achieving powerful lifelong effects from seemingly small interventions is the cornerstone of how we train dogs. And this book teaches you how to make everyday activities with your pup work for you, shaping his character while you have fun together.

In the average home, good, or bad, habits may get reinforced hundreds or thousands of times a day, quickly making your pup's behaviors deeply ingrained. And every little thing you do around him matters. So we created realistic activities to occupy your pup whenever you have a few free minutes, along with enjoyable and easy games, mental games and practical ways your pup can help your family, rather than some of the impractical tricks you may find in other books.

It's imperative to start teaching your pup good habits the very first day you bring him home because patterns of relating set down in your pup's very first day in your home can influence his behavior for the rest of his life. And what you do with your pup in the first six or eight months of his life, especially during the first hours, days and weeks, can have as much effect on his behavior as all you do in the coming years.

Caring owners can certainly train and shape their dogs to be better at any age (as we've found rehabilitating adult and senior dogs with serious issues). And dogs have almost unlimited potential. But you can never recapture the powerful and far-ranging influence of a pup's early weeks when the littlest adjustments make the biggest difference. For this reason, you should start actively shaping your pup's behavior, personality, mental health and intelligence from the very first second you welcome him into your home. **Unfortunately, by the time most owners bring pups to formal obedience classes, the pups have already lost much of their potential to be the great dogs they could have been.**

We believe a committed pet parent can accomplish a lot more at home, with a surprisingly small amount of work, than you can by confining your puppy's training to formal classes. By enjoying specific games and activities, like the 45 activities described in detail in the "Activities" section, or by introducing important stimuli like new people, places and things based on the various "Lists" in this book you can strengthen the bond with your puppy and build his potential.

There's no need for harsh corrections. Loving pet parents can easily get the exact dog of your desires, with no strain for owner or dog. And puppies can actually become more intelligent if they experience the right stimuli and learning from a very young age.

One perk of selecting a young puppy is the unique opportunity to dial in the exact personality you want for the creature who will be your close companion for a big part of your life. But, even if you acted on impulse when you bought or adopted your pup, even if he's older and even if he shows some minor behavioral problems or seems hard to control, you can still shape him to show more of the behaviors you want- starting with an investment of just a few minutes at a time for some of the activities in this book.

Your dog's potential can be as individual as that of a child you raise. And much of his "value" system- the choices he makes and the personality he develops depends on your "parenting". *Awesome Puppy* gives pet parents the full picture- all the obedience commands and the most important games, activities and ways of interacting to create truly Awesome Dogs- exquisite dogs that transform life in a higher sense for their families.

In addition to detailed instructions and insider's hints for training all the basic commands to pups in every state of mind, *Awesome Puppy* also includes 45 enjoyable games and exercises designed to shape your pup's psychology while building physical and emotional fitness. These activities help teach vital attitudes and habits and vital skills (listed in Chapter 2, Sections A & B).

And they also help you avoid the "40 Bad Behaviors & Thought Patterns You Should Never Teach Your Puppy" listed in Chapter 3. Just reading these lists can provide insights for you to immediately start improving your relationship with your dog.

These days, dogs live longer than ever, with fifteen years a common lifespan. We believe your dog will be a central member of your family for all those years, defining an entire era in your family's life. And pet parents and their dogs have a right to actively enjoy their bond every day, in a manner that's practical and integrated with family life. **Dogs also provide emotional, and even spiritual, fulfillment, allowing us to enjoy our inborn bond with nature and our sense of our higher selves.** And we can, on some level, return the favor to them by bringing out their highest potential.

Once owners understand the basics of canine psychology that underlie the training techniques, activities and games described in this book, they will have a greater in-depth understanding of dogs. And this can act as a comfortable jumping off point for a lifetime of better communication and influence, so you'll always know what to do with your dog and you'll never have misunderstandings.

Pet parents never have to raise their voices or use harsh physical corrections to get obedience and respect. **We personally don't use choke or prong collars, we don't physically push puppies into position to train obedience and we never lock pups in crates for training or any other purpose.** We know you get better results training with positive reinforcement, changes in lifestyle and an understanding of canine psychology.

How to use this book:

Start anywhere in the book based on your needs. You can start with the quick reference lists of the most vital things to teach a puppy, including lists of specific people, places and things to expose your puppy to during his first six months to make him a better dog for the rest of his life. Use these checklists whenever you have a free moment and want to do something quick, interesting and productive with your pup.

You can start at the beginning of the Obedience Training Section for general tips to make all training easier and more effective, and then work through the commands. Or skip ahead to start with any of the individual commands you need at the moment.

Other pet parents will want to immediately try some activities and games in Part 3. You can scan the standardized descriptions of each activity to choose the ones that fit best with your lifestyle and your pup's needs at the moment.

Or you may first want to read the Housetraining section for in-depth instructions on how to housetrain your pup and teach him good house manners without crates or cages.

The Obedience Training Section shows you gentle methods to train your pup all the basic commands. The section also includes instructions for teaching him how to go to a specific place where he won't disturb guests; how to drop items on command and how to walk politely on a leash and never pull you.

The 45 Activities in this book teach your puppy a wide variety of skills he'll need in life, including physical, mental, emotional and social skills. For example, activities like "Umbilical Cord" and "Heeling Without a Leash" teach your pup that the best place to be is by his owner's side and that he shouldn't make trouble in the home. The mental games "Follow My Eyes" and "The Finger Pointing Game" teach your pup the vital skill of looking to you for information in life, rather than just reacting on his own. And this one habit alone can improve your entire future with your dog.

"Nosework" and "Find Hidden Rewards" sharpen your pup's senses and his mind. "Explore a Tunnel" works on coordination and emotional confidence. "Use a Soft Mouth" teaches a puppy not to bite humans and "Mock Veterinary Exam" is essential practice to make your pup a better citizen at the vet. Special games like "The Gate Test Game" teach your pup to think and solve problems while actually building his IQ. Your pup can also learn to "Identify Family Members" by name, to "Learn to Come to Everyone", to find a person that is out of sight and to "Give Kisses" or "Use a Soft Mouth" to greet guests, rather than nipping or jumping up on people. These skills will make him much more welcome whenever people gather.

So that pups can burn off physical energy, the book also includes easy games like "Play Soccer", "Play Basketball", "Toy on a Line", "Jump Over/Crawl Under a Bar" and multiple activities that work just as well indoors as outdoors- even for toy and teacup breeds.

Puppy games like these do more than just prevent behavior problems. If you stimulate your puppy's mind and body when he's young, he will become a healthier, happier and more intelligent dog. And a dog that practices decision-making early in life, through games, will learn to make better choices later in life in every situation.

Even if you are reading *Awesome Puppy* six months after getting your pup- and even if he is showing some behavior difficulties- you will still benefit from all the activities and principles of canine psychology in this book. Starting right this moment, you and your pup can enjoy some of the games and activities. Pretend today is the first day you're bringing your new fur baby home and start shaping his behavior for the positive right now.

We are proud to help pet parents and their puppies at this critical time in their journey...

Chapter 2:

What Every Puppy Needs to Learn in Life

Section A: List of Attitudes & Habits Every Well-Behaved Puppy Should Learn

You'll find activities & training tips throughout *Awesome Puppy* to help teach all these vital attitudes and habits. Your pup should grow up to believe:

1. I always think before I act
2. I'll only get attention & affection when I perform activities my owners want
3. I'll never get attention, or anything positive, if I jump up on people
4. I never put my mouth on a human harshly, even in play
5. I look to my human leader for guidance in the face of any new or intense stimulus- I constantly "check in" with my people for direction
6. I accept delayed gratification & tolerate frustration, knowing this brings reward
7. I always come every time my owners call. It's like a reflex for me to want to follow my owners rather than running off by myself
8. Human touch is a good thing, not something to be afraid of
9. I never push past a human; all humans get the "right-of-way" over dogs in every situation

10. Friendly new people are likeable and harmless. It feels natural acting calm & polite in public places, rather than crazy

11. There's no need to get overexcited about other dogs. I always meet them properly

12. It's easy to communicate my needs to my owners and vice versa. We speak the same language, so there's no need to force what I want

13. The only way I'll get what I want in life is by doing the things my humans want

14. I'm comfortable with my body & feel balanced & stable moving in different situations, so I'm less prone to injury

14. I always treat all family members, including children and elders, with full respect

15. I'm human-oriented; even though I enjoy playing with other dogs, I'd rather be with humans than alone or with dogs

16. I respect and act gentle towards my owners' visitors, including children and infants

17. I respect my owners' small pets, including cats and livestock, because this is what my owners want.

18. I respect my owners' possessions and every item in their home, and I never damage anything, even when they go away

19. Mealtime is calm time. My owners are the only way I get food and I know they're fair, so all I have to do is stay calm and pleasant to get the nutrition I need.

20. I only urinate and defecate outside of the house. My owners' house- including every room- is my house and it doesn't feel natural to soil it.

21. I'm familiar with the "outside world" because my owners take me out all the time. When I encounter new things in the world I feel pleasantly alert and interested, not nervous, hyperactive or aggressive.

22. I know how to learn; if I make an error, I know I can learn to do better next time to gain rewards.

23. I can be empathetic with humans about important things, even when their ways are different than dogs' ways. For example, I understand that human skin is more tender than dogs', so I treat it gently.

24. I stay calmly and happily in the home to wait for my owners whenever they go away. I never feel overly stressed, never damage items, never hurt myself, never bark excessively and I never require crating.

25. I enjoy pleasant walks in the neighborhood with my owner and the only way I know how to walk is heeling softly at my owner's side. I'd never try to pull, but, if I ever did, I know my owner would immediately stop walking, turn around or terminate the walk entirely.

26. I know my owners are fair. They show leadership, which I naturally follow rather than cruelty, inconsistency or overly domineering discipline.

Section B: List of 15 Skills Every Puppy Should Learn to Reach His Potential

You will find instructions and activities to promote these necessary skills throughout *Awesome Puppy*. By the time he grows up, every puppy should learn these skills:

1. Using his nose properly, as dogs were bred for
2. "Bounce-back", the ability to return to a calm, inquisitive state, even after being startled by something new.
3. Meeting other dogs properly
4. Meeting new people properly
5. Greeting new stimuli with caution but not fear. Pups should be unafraid to follow their owner up steps, riding in a car, walking through shallow water, snow, etc.
6. Tolerating grooming & veterinary exams
7. Tolerating human touch on every part of the body, including touch by children
8. Tolerating touch to sensitive body parts- specifically paws/nails, ears, tail and inside mouth
9. "Heeling" or walking properly beside every family member on a leash.

10. Walking at his owner's side on command while not on a leash

11. Controlling his own body; no spinning, jumping or bouncing off walls when it's time to act calm. At any time a pup should feel able to "stay" or "wait" on command.

12. Dropping an item he's holding in his mouth whenever his owners say so with no hesitation.

13. Excelling in exercise and sports. Dogs are natural athletes and young dogs should have reasonable exercise to develop their bodies and center their minds.

14. Learning a large working vocabulary of words and verbal commands (at least 100)

15. Coming willingly to people whenever they call

Chapter 3:

List of 40 Bad Behaviors & Thought Patterns to Never Teach Puppies

You'll find instructions and activities throughout *Awesome Puppy* to help change most of these bad behaviors and thought patterns. Your pup should *never* think:

1. It's okay to jump on people; I get attention for jumping on people.

2. I can "tune-out" or act autistic towards people, as though I don't deeply notice or even care about them, and yet I can still obtain the things I want.

3. I don't lose privileges, attention or what's important to me even if I growl at, snap at or bite people.

4. I nip people's hands (or heels) so hard it draws blood, but my owners laugh at it because I'm just a puppy…

5. I like dogs better than people. I've grown up during my formative weeks constantly running and playfighting with other dogs, and I take all my guidance from dogs. Because I've spent more time with dogs than alone with people, I can't bear to be away from dogs for an instant & I feel humans are secondary

6. I've learned the place for a dog is in a crate, not with a family, because my owners (or breeders) left me in a crate all the time. Now, I feel more natural isolated in a cage than free in the house with the people.

11

7. It's okay to go from zero to sixty in two seconds- either I'm not relating to people at all, or I act completely wild, pushing myself on them insistently.

8. I have strange cravings. I feel compelled to consume inedible objects that make me sick and cost huge vet bills. My owners downplay my condition, calling it normal puppy chewing, which it is not.

9. I, and only I, control mealtime. My owners leave my food down all day and I eat whenever I please. I also demand human food and aggressively steal from other dogs. If people try to stop me, I might bite them, too.

10. Being around food makes me crazy and I've learned to get food by stealing & counter-surfing

11. I can "split" my owners against each other. After I disrespect one spouse, the other indulges me. So, when one spouse refuses my whims I try the other. They start yelling at each other and I get anything I want.

12. The first way I learned to play was with my teeth and my owners encouraged me to bite their hands when I was a tiny puppy. Now I'll always bite them.

13. I play tug of war with my owners and they encourage it, even though they always lose. So, if I want, I can also bite on and tug their clothing, the leash, etc…

14. Every time I go on a walk it's a pulling contest. My owner keeps pulling on me, but I pull harder.

15. The "outside world" is a novel place for me because my owners rarely take me out. On the rare occasions they did, I went nuts the second I saw new things. And this created a pattern where my owners take me out even less.

16. I act fearful around thunder, the vacuum cleaner, loud noises and a hundred other strange things. Rather than staying calm and/or getting me professional help, my owners nervously pet me, which reinforces my fears.

17. When I act inappropriately, my owners narrow the world to live with my bad behavior. For example, because of my separation anxiety, they've stopped going out to dinner.

18. I don't like my owner's spouse or romantic partner, so I bite them, growl at them, etc, and my owner allows it.

19. My owners are very busy and ignore me when I act calm or do what I'm supposed to. But when I'm bad everything stops and they give me attention. This makes me want to act bad more often.

20. My family encourages me to jump on them. Now I jump on all people, even though in the dog world is very rude behavior.

21. I don't like people touching me. I grew up in my early weeks without this kind of stimulus, and now I'll either turn away, or act nasty if a human tries to touch me.

22. I'm grown now, and physically old enough to be capable of holding my bladder and bowels. But I despise my owners and/or their other pets so I intentionally mark the house with my urine (and feces) to make it clear who owns this place.

23. I enjoy games that give me the physical, or height, advantage on humans so I can show them who's boss.

24. I go where I want to go and run out the second a door is left open. If the humans want to follow me when I run away, fine, but I've got things to do and I'm not looking back.

25. My instinct tells me to chase and hunt, so I'll chase and hunt when I want to. Lucky for me, my owners provided a cat, a hamster and/or a smaller dog.

26. And, if that gets boring, I can chase their children.

27. I have no respect for children, even my owner's children, because they are small and weaker than me in every way. I barely notice them except as an annoyance.

28. If I want to take something that belongs to my owners' kids, I do especially like all their little snacks and their stuffed toys, which I tug out of their hands. My owners don't seem to mind when I bother the children- they don't show leadership or take time to teach me alternate behaviors

29. My human parents act inconsistent with discipline. One is overly soft, the other overly temperamental and cruel. Both ways harm my behavior.

30. My owner followed a dog trainer who told them to "alpha roll" me or use a shock collar, prong collar or other cruel method of discipline when I was very young. So I learned to be timid and afraid of everything.

31. My owner used those same overly harsh methods when I was very young, and now I've become the bully, attempting to use dominance/aggression on anything weaker than I, including my owner's timid wife!

32. I'm a little afraid of other new dogs because I never experienced them young. Now I've learned that if I lunge at dogs and act angry my owner will soothe and pet me and make the scary dogs go away.

33. I'm a little dog, and my owner pets me if I snap or growl at people who approach when I'm in her arms. Since she pets me, I guess she's okay with my aggression.

34. I'm a small dog and my owners don't seem to realize I'm a dog. They cuddle me or hold me all the time and never let me walk on the floor. They also don't ask me to show any manners or obedience, even though I wouldn't mind some structure.

35. I have nothing to do all day. I'm left in a blank room or crate.

36. Sometimes I'm so bored that barking is the most enjoyable thing I do all day.

37. My owners were stressed when I was a young pup and they've always acted unpredictable in response to all my actions. Now that I act stressed all the time, too, they almost seem more comfortable.

38. To get rid of stress, I've learned to chew on myself. I've licked and bitten some spots raw.

39. I am a victim of no exercise. I let out this bodily frustration the minute my owners come home by immediately bouncing off walls and running around like a tornado.

40. My entire world that I know is my backyard or, even worse, a tiny crate. Like any wild animal left 24/7 in a tiny cage, I am a disaster waiting to happen.

PART 2:

Training

Chapter 4:

How to Make Every Puppy an Awesome Puppy with New Learning Every Day

"If your pup's not learning something new every day, then he can't achieve his full potential"

Why not write a wish list of all the different things you'd love your dog to accomplish in his life? And then, over the course of his lifetime, spend time with him and make the wishes come true day by day. To make it easy, all of the activities in *Awesome Puppy* are more than just fun parlor tricks. These enjoyable activities also build your pup's character, obedience, good manners and sensitivity to your needs.

Each activity and game in *Awesome Puppy* is specifically designed to build different traits of a puppy's character and good behavior, such as bonding with his owners, using his mouth gently, staying calm, reacting properly to guests and thinking before getting into mischief. Other activities and games in the book build a pup's body, senses and intelligence. **And most of the activities are designed to take only minutes at a time so you can do something productive and pleasant whenever you and your pup have a spare moment.**

The book also teaches other important skills- to potty outside, to walk beside you nicely on leash and to seek your attention by doing things you want instead of pestering you. Viewing it this way, one new task a day isn't much- in fact, your pup is capable of learning *many* new things each day.

Unfortunately, if you don't make a conscious effort to teach your puppy the things you *want* him to learn, he'll learn things you'd *never* want him to learn, like how to climb up onto your countertop, how to bark for attention or how to open your refrigerator door. **One of the most important things we teach dog owners is that a pup learns from every single interaction with the family and the environment.** Each time your pup repeats a negative behavior that's not extinguished, it becomes more ingrained. But the solution doesn't need to be punishment. Instead, by teaching your pup all the new skills that are important to you, he'll easily forget bad behaviors and instead he'll naturally fill his hours doing the things you *want* him to do!

In addition to teaching owners foolproof methods for training obedience, *Awesome Puppy* **also includes a broad variety of activities and games to develop your pup's potential. And shaping a pup's behavior and future personality through real-life activities, while enjoyable, can be more effective than formal training in a class.**

Each new learning experience you share with your pup builds understanding and respect and makes your relationship richer and fuller. While your neighbors may struggle every day with an unruly new puppy, just by sharing some simple activities you can easily enjoy fun and fulfillment with yours.

Dogs are intelligent sentient beings and you likely already know impressive personal stories about their intelligence. And, of course, the lifesaving accomplishments of service, rescue and police dogs clearly demonstrate dogs' abilities. Yet many people still leave developing pups alone- sometimes locked in cramped wire crates for eight to twelve hours each weekday with nothing to engage their minds.

These pups never go out into the world when they are young and their only chance to move for a few hours is in a small blank yard with nothing to stimulate their senses. And lack of adequate mental and sensory stimulation like this during critical weeks in puppyhood can stunt the development of a pup's mind, senses, emotions and his ability to socialize with dogs and people in the world at large.

Don't were originally bred for intense activity including hunting, herding, guarding, rescuing people and helping their owners in a variety of daily activities. So it's not surprising that if we give them absolutely nothing to do and no way to learn about the world, they can develop problems like destructiveness, anxiety and depression.

Pups that grow up with minimal things to do and to think about (for example pups that are raised in puppy mills or routinely crated for long periods while their owners work) develop less useful intelligence and less effective senses. The fire may go out of young dog's eyes and his owners may never realize what he could have been. Other pups may react to frustration and boredom with destructive behavior- like barking, marking or chewing on furniture. But when you give your pup adequate physical and mental stimulation each day, he can fulfill his potential and manifest as regally as a show dog.

We believe beautiful and hardworking show dogs rather than some of the badly behaved dogs you may see on your street or on popular television dog training shows should serve as your benchmark for what your pup is capable of. Just meeting a few show dogs (which you can easily do by attending the next large-scale all-breed AKC show in your area) may change your entire perception of what life with your dog can be. You'll notice that these gorgeous show dogs act friendly to dogs and people and excel at obedience, even under demanding conditions. A good number also work in careers as farm dogs or therapy dogs. And even though the average pet owner may believe it's difficult to train a puppy to be an extraordinary companion- equal to the most impressive dogs you've ever seen- we know it's actually easier to shape a puppy to be well-behaved than badly behaved.

We treat our personal dogs with so much affection and indulgence that people might call them spoiled if they weren't so mannerly. In our lifestyle we constantly interact with dogs in real world situations rather than just doing repetitive formal training. And, from the time our dogs are pups, they can expect every day to be different. We often take dogs on real-life outings with us. We always reward them with love and attention when they act nicely and we build on their mental, sensory and social skills. It might seem difficult to give a pup this much feedback, yet it's actually easier than what many owners go through chasing after their dogs and constantly correcting.

We also never crate dogs. We expect perfect house manners with our dogs always free in our home. And we've never been disappointed, even with adult dogs we've rescued from extreme conditions.

Since we've never lost the enthusiasm we had for dogs as children, we enjoy teaching dogs hundreds of words, skills and games. (See our activity book *The Cure for Useless Dog Syndrome,* print or Kindle version, for many suggestions for dogs of every age and life situation).

Pups are probably much more intelligent, in more ways, than people can imagine. Not only are dogs smart in terms of IQ, they are also psychic in practical, bankable ways. And their senses of smell and hearing are so much stronger and more precise than ours that their abilities seem almost magical. **Your pup could be a little genius and could develop into a helpful, considerate and obedient dog to exceed all your wildest dreams. But, unfortunately, if you leave him bored and if he feels you don't care what he does, he may just channel all his natural brain power into mischief!**

If you shape your dog's habits during his puppyhood, he will never learn bad behaviors and you will set the stage for an ideal life with him for many years to come. **One method for raising a smarter and more nuanced dog is to teach him something new every single day.**

Of course almost every puppy owner knows about basic obedience training. And training is safe to start as young as 8 weeks if you use gentle methods like those described in this book.

Awesome Puppy also gives valuable hints on how to integrate obedience into everyday life to make the commands really useful as well as instructions to teach additional helpful commands like "Look" and "Go to Your Place". (Find in-depth instructions for training all the obedience commands in this Part).

Socializing your young puppy to interact properly with humans and animals in diverse situations is another important form of learning. (See "Socializing Your Pup to People and Dogs" in Part 4, including a list of people and situations every pup should encounter early in life.) **If you use each day to properly introduce your young pup to one new person, animal, object or situation at a time, he will come to recognize these stimuli as natural and you shouldn't have to worry about him acting aggressive towards people or dogs out in public in future.**

Teaching your pup to distinguish scents and track down different family members is another important, and possibly lifesaving, skill covered in the book. (See "#13 Nosework" and "#15 Identify Family Members" in Part 3.) And take one day to teach your pup the vital commands "Drop It" and "Leave It". (See instructions in Chapter 5 in this Part.) Learning to give up items he's holding on command could save your pup from ingesting dangerous items, and it's also the basis for many games and activities, from basic to advanced.

Learning proper house manners (like not barking excessively, not chewing on human possessions and not jumping on furniture) is also beneficial for your pup as well as for your family. If your pup could talk, he'd thank you every time you politely communicate your desires and house rules to him, for it gives him a needed sense of structure. This sense of continuity reduces stress and makes a canine feel safer. Other important activities like " #40 Learn to Come to Everyone" are fun for families to practice anytime. And a skill like coming when you call can make your dog infinitely easier to live with and possibly save his life.

Taking your pup for pleasant, bonding walks with you is also a form of learning, especially when you introduce your pup to new terrain and new stimuli. (Find general instructions for heeling in this Part.) You should base the level of exercise on your pup's physical needs and condition. You can try different routes, walk in snow, sand or leaves or even weave through obstacles together. (See #37 "Weave Through Poles".)

When your family members have some free time and feel like trying something new and enjoyable, you can #18 "Play Soccer" or #25 "Play Hide & Seek" outdoors with your pup according to our safe instructions.

Or you can vary your pup's physical experiences by playing or swimming in the water together, or taking a walk on the beach on a mild day if it's permitted in your community. You could also participate in formal dog sports or activities, such as joining an obedience or agility club, joining in one of the other AKC dog sports for particular types of dogs (such as herding, tracking or earthdog) or showing your dog in the AKC ring. And if you don't want to participate in competition agility you could teach your pups to conquer homemade agility obstacles that you can easily create in your yard. (See #17 Explore a Tunnel" and "#37 Weave Through Poles" in Part 3.)

Other unique games in Part 3 of *Awesome Puppy* such as "#1 Follow My Eyes" and "#9 The Finger Pointing Game" teach a puppy the vital skill of looking for direction and working with his owner and the requirement of time effort and equipment is minimal.

You will find 45 enjoyable games, activities and exercises to try with your puppy described in Part 3, along with complete instructions. You can also expand your pup's learning by using the "List of 100 Different Surfaces & Novel Items to Introduce Your Puppy To" (in Part 4, Chapter 9). Introducing your pup to any of these 100 items is one of the most productive uses of just a few moments and it's also a lot of fun.

The activities described in depth in *Awesome Puppy* can be enough to keep your pup busy every day for years. And if you are interested in additional games and activities, for pups as well as mature dogs in every walk of life, consult our comprehensive activity book *The Cure for Useless Dog Syndrome*. You will find activities ranging from walking over different surfaces, racing with owners, searching for hidden treats in cardboard boxes, distinguishing different color toys, barking "yes" or "no", performing adorable tricks and even jumping rope as well as activities specifically for multiple dog households. *The Cure* also focuses on creative alternatives for owners with limited mobility, trouble bending, standing or walking, households with children and high-energy dogs.

Pet parents can get creative, and each owner and their dog will discover their own personal favorite activities. Kids can select structured games and activities from this book or they can use our games as jumping off points for their own new games. Instructions for all activities and commands include specific cautions for children where applicable. Teaching your puppy structured games and activities will make everyone in the family smile. And it's more productive, more engaging and safer than the "standard" games of tug, chase, wrestle or nip- which can sometimes create serious behavior problems.

Throughout your dog's life, you will have the opportunity to introduce him to literally thousands of new learning experiences- at least one new concept or opportunity a day.

We recommend that you write down a new game, activity, exercise, obedience command or socialization experience that you wish to practice with your pup each day and then check it off when he completes it. One line in your appointment book or smartphone can keep other demands from constantly crowding out healthy fulfilling time with your puppy during his critical developmental periods. And practicing some of the easy and engaging choices in this book can take away stress, even if you get home in the evening too tired for a long walk or an exhausting game of Fetch. When you think just a little differently, you'll be surprised at how much you can accomplish with your pup.

Chapter 5:

Obedience Training

Section A: Overview-General Training Tips & Troubleshooting Based on Canine Psychology

Good obedience training vs. bad obedience training:

Obedience is more than just a few standard commands taught in a class, leaving owners and their dogs with no insight how to use the skills in everyday life. **In its truest sense, obedience is the language through which dogs and their owners learn to communicate with each other. The moment your dog first "gets" his first verbal command means you have mastered a shared language you can build on. And this feels almost miraculous.**

The time to start teaching your puppy "obedience" is the moment you bring him home. And unfortunately, if you fail to teach him desired behaviors, you'll reinforce undesired behavior with every interaction. For example, if you pet your puppy when he jumps on you when he's young, he'll learn to jump on people as an adult. But you can easily prevent this by teaching him an incompatible positive alternative, like sitting when he first greets people.

The reason the standard obedience commands, "sit", "down", "stay", "heel" and "come" (with instructions in this chapter) have been around so long is that they can be highly useful.

For example, "sit" is usually the easiest command to teach and it's a handy alternative to many undesired behaviors. And "down" helps dogs act more compliant and less aggressive or reactive. **Commands like "Look", "Wait", "Leave it", "Drop It" and "Go to your place" (with instructions in this chapter) are also important for an easy-to-live-with dog.** Your whole family should practice all the commands with your pup in real-life situations throughout the day, not just in formal practice sessions or formal obedience classes.

In addition to keeping commands fresh in your pup's mind, a little spontaneous obedience practice every day reminds your puppy that he enjoys pleasing you. And practicing certain commands, such as heeling by your side around obstacles or running to you from a far distance at a fast pace can burn off excess energy. **The mental exercise of performing obedience commands actually intensifies physical exercise, so adding obedience to walks or play sessions makes exercise more efficient. And obedience practice teaches pups that act "antsy" or wild how to calm and center themselves- a vital skill for successful adulthood.**

There are different methods of teaching obedience, so you should choose what feels best for you and your pup *as long as you use gentle methods, gentle equipment and a patient and loving attitude.* Most owners can teach obedience on their own at home; and this is often the best choice for naturally patient and light-handed owners with gentle friendly pups.

The only time families will need professional help is if your pup has serious problems like fear or aggression. In this case, we recommend you consult a high-level trainer or behaviorist with advanced college background (as opposed to dog trainers with simple "certifications" which can vary widely in quality).

Even if your pup doesn't have any dangerous issues, some families may also want to enroll their pup in group classes so he can practice obedience around other dogs, or you may want a dog trainer to demonstrate specific techniques. But make your choice of dog trainer very carefully. Pups can sometimes be terrified by a rough or insensitive dog trainer they encounter during early life, just like they'll be positively shaped by a good trainer. And abusive training at an early age can cause lifelong bad behavior in a dog.

If you feel you need professional dog training help, be cautious about the words "gentle" and "positive". Although you definitely want a positive and gentle trainer to work with your pup, many dog trainers today are using these popular catchwords interchangeably with the term "behavior-modification training". Training by behavior modification does not, in itself, guarantee that the particular trainer is a kind and gentle person, or that they won't scare your puppy.

And, even though today many dog owners are rejecting harsh correction/ compulsion methods that used to be the norm years ago, a number of well-paid, well connected dog trainers still use violent methods that can physically injure, and emotionally scar, pups.

For example in some popular classes, trainers demonstrate yanking the leash and jacking pups up, often using choke or prong collars that are known to be dangerous for pups under 6 months. Other trainers "alpha roll" pups to dominate them, throwing a pup to the floor on his back or side and holding him by the throat and not releasing him until he goes limp and passive. Then they teach owners to duplicate these methods. And then we are called to treat the dogs as adults when they cringe from their owners' hands or try to bite.

True "positive" training methods are deeply kind and humane- an obvious contrast to collar yanking and alpha rolling. But unfortunately some trainers, including a number with impressive sounding certifications and affiliations, advertise themselves as "positive" and "gentle" to attract business regardless of how they actually treat dogs. Some of these trainers don't realize themselves that they are being overly rough- or that a pup's doting parents might prefer them to be gentler.

Just for example, we've witnessed well-liked "positive" trainers handling pups roughly, yelling at and cursing pups, leash-jerking pups under 6 months on choke and prong collars and deliberately forcing hysterical pups to lie in their own filth in crates to "teach them a lesson". We've also heard groomers boast about how they routinely physically overpower panicked young dogs with hard physical corrections. This frequently leads to injury with clippers and scissors, and we've sometimes had to treat adult dogs for life-destroying neuroses after repeated visits to these groomers. Yet all these dog professionals had convinced their customers that their practices, and their theories that puppies needed to be "dominated", were "positive" and beneficial to dogs.

Customers whose dogs we've treated for serious emotional and behavior problems have also told us trainers and breeders have "schooled" them to: alpha roll toy breed pups; pinch pups' ears; squeeze pups' snouts and shake them; handle pups with welding gloves, knee pups in the chest and step down on leashes, knocking pups off their feet and pinning their faces to the concrete to teach them to lie down.

We also treated several small breed adult dogs that had been injured and terrorized by electric fence collars applied too early and too intensely when they were puppies. One traumatized Lhasa mix had grown up to slink along the ground and cringe as though she expected to be attacked from above at any moment- she couldn't even walk upright!

Unbelievably, some trainers who advertise themselves as "positive", including some who belong to well-respected training organizations- proudly use electric shock collars (or e-collars) for behavioral training- even on puppies under 1 year. Other trainers who call themselves "positive" use prong collars and teach their customers to use them, even though prong collars are considered dangerous for pups under 6 months old.

A good number of trainers who say they love dogs tell owners to lock their pups in small wire crates almost every moment when they are growing up. And some trainers instruct owners to slam metal pot lids down on a crate to scare a pup into silence if he cries and screams to be released. These trainers also instruct owners to leave pups crated lying in their own urine and feces for hours each day to housetrain them. And they instruct owners to leave their pups (and adult dogs) locked up in his crate even if the animal panics and hurts himself to the point of bleeding trying to get out. You can easily find recommendations like these in many dog training books- and all over the Internet. And many respected contemporary dog trainers, dog authors and other professionals consider them *good* ideas. Unfortunately, whenever advice comes from professionals like these, it can make families try the same techniques.

However each of the training methods described above can cause serious- often crippling-behavior problems in adult dogs- problems much worse than what the owners initially hired the trainer to cure. And the earlier in his life a pup experiences harsh treatment at the hands of a breeder, groomer or trainer, the worse the effects will be.

Even though dog trainers can pay for a variety of different certifications which may sound impressive, the truth is that the dog-training industry is completely unregulated by the government and there's no official licensure and no consistent certification. Some certifications are no more than 2 week classes; others are just short-term Internet study. Generally, advanced college degrees (master's or doctoral) in related fields are a good sign that we tend to respect. But even a quality college degree doesn't guarantee the professional will have an instinctual connection with your pup, or will prescribe the safest and best training program.

Likewise, experience is important for dog trainers. Yet some trainers have spent the past 20 years training thousands of dogs with harsh methods, so experience alone cannot guarantee kind and expert training for your puppy. The truth is, in the current unregulated industry, the information a dog trainer studies, the training methods they use and their standards are largely up to their own conscience- and the same is true for the businesses that train and certify them.

There are some very kind, talented and dedicated dog trainers out there, at every level of experience and education, just like there are some others that take advantage of the system. So, if you wish to hire a trainer, in addition to checking their educational credentials and references we suggest that you interview them on the telephone and in person. Ask in-depth questions about their training philosophy, examples of their exact methods rather than just words like "positive", and books they've read and the reasons they liked each. If detailed questions make the trainer flare up and act impatient, angry or rude towards you, it's a red flag that they'll also treat your pup harshly and impatiently.

Rough training methods can sometimes intimidate pups enough to make them obey in the short run- but they don't teach a pup to *want* to obey. If a trainer is too harsh with a young pup, the pup may learn to obey that person out of fear. Yet the training may not generalize and, even though the pup knows the commands, he may act disrespectful and wild with his family.

If you want to use a professional dog trainer, you should choose the best, and choose a nice person just like you'd want as a teacher or coach for your children. Training sessions for your puppy, just like schoolwork or sports for your child, should definitely feel like effort- but training should never cause stress or pain. You, your family and your pup should all like your dog trainer. And if you choose the right trainer for your pup, this person can be an inspiration and an influence for your pup's entire life. So we also recommend not hiring a trainer, or choosing a group class, solely based on price in the immediate sense.

Most readers of this book will likely want to try training their pup at home rather than hiring a professional. (And this is why we wrote this professional level, yet easy to use, book as a comprehensive resource for pet parents like you.) **One of the most important benefits of training at home is that it's safe to start as early as 8 weeks. You can train all the commands right away, without having to wait to teach any and every family member can learn to reinforce the commands in everyday situations. You will also integrate the commands along with socialization and exposure to real-world stimuli.**

To train basic obedience on your own, use the detailed hints and training instructions for all the commands in this chapter. *Unless your pup shows any dangerous behavior*, you should be able to train him much more quickly than a professional without the expense.

Also practice a number of the 45 Activities in Section 3 to shape your pup's behavior and increase his obedience while spending quality time and having fun. Each activity is designed to shape dog behavior, psychology and/or physical development in critical ways. By reading the standardized bolded captions at the start of each activity, you can select those that address your biggest priorities.

Whether you train your dog on your own, or with expert assistance, the most powerful thing you can do to improve his adult behavior is to teach him right as a puppy! And the best time to start gentle training is when your pup is as young as possible. As long as you stay gentle, you can begin training most of the commands and activities in this book today.

Training Tips & Troubleshooting:

The hints in the sections that follow answer common questions about training and make it easier and more effective to train the 9 basic commands described later in the chapter and will help if you have trouble training any command. This section includes:

1. Training around distractions
2. Ending training sessions on a high note
3. "Real world" rewards
4. Using treats for positive training
5. Troubleshooting if training commands doesn't work

1.Training around distractions:

You'll notice we often suggest that you "increase distractions as tolerated" when training obedience commands. The ultimate goal is that your adult dog should obey all commands no matter if he's walking with you on a busy city street, through an event with 2,000 strange dogs or on a morning walk when a squirrel suddenly runs by…

The way to get your pup to be reliable under demanding conditions is to first make him obey the commands perfectly under less challenging circumstances and then slowly add

increasingly challenging distractions. Your pup can most easily learn a command when he's home alone with his owner. Adding people or other animals makes concentrating harder. Guests are more distracting than family, and strange visitors the pups has never met are the most distracting. Stimuli at closer distances are always more distracting than those seen at farther distances and performing commands off-leash is harder than on leash. And your dog will have the most challenges in an unfamiliar outdoor locale with many new people and dogs at close proximity.

You should first teach your pup to master each command at the easiest, least distracting, level. Once he is performing perfectly at that level for a while, add a single distraction- such as practicing the command while a second family member is present. Work at that level until your pup's performing perfectly, and then add your next distraction. Once your pup's perfect at that level, you can increase the difficulty by adding yet another person or a more stressful distraction like another dog.

Add one distraction at a time, master difficulty at that level and then add one more distraction. Success at the new level could take hours, days, weeks or longer. If your pup fails at the new level of difficulty, drop back to the previous level and build up gradually. Your pup should always fully master one level of difficulty before moving to the next. Practicing the same commands under different challenges and in different locales means your dog will adapt better in real life situations. And it also keeps obedience practice fresh and interesting for the dog and the handler.

2.Ending training sessions on a high note:
Don't make formal training sessions for young pups overly long, and always end on a positive note. You can almost sense when your pup is getting ready to burn out, fall asleep or start acting flaky as his attention span wanes. For some reason many people feel compelled to push obedience practice beyond this point. In our experience, when something negative happens in an obedience session, 99% of the time it happens in that period of time after your gut instinct already told you it was time to pack it in.

Unfortunately, if a session ends with stress, your pup can generalize this bad feeling to all obedience. If you notice your pup slacking toward the end of the session, try to gently coax him into one more successful repetition of any command. Then praise him and break for rest or a fun play session together. If your pup picks this moment to fail at a newly learned command, the best strategy is to "step down" to a command he already knows perfectly and get one good repetition of that one. This still counts as the positive ending you need. **Pushing too hard to get a response that just isn't working may make your pup resistant about obedience practice the next day. But if you end on a high note, your "student" will be eager to try again.**

3. Using "real-world" rewards

Alternating food rewards with "real-world" rewards is an important cornerstone of how we train. Treats are not the only way to change a dog's behavior. Real world activities such as going for a long walk, going out the door, playing with a new toy, being petted, going for a car ride, having a ball thrown for him to fetch and many others are also highly rewarding for dogs. And activities or privileges like these are powerful motivators to influence dogs' behavior. You should teach your pup that, whenever he performs an obedience command or any everyday action you ask of him, this is the way to get the real world rewards he wants.

For example, we train dogs to automatically (without verbal command) lower themselves into a relaxed "down" position before we throw a ball. We simply wait long enough that the dog lies down on his own and, when he does, we throw. We also teach dogs to automatically "wait" calmly before we will open a door for them. The opening of the door becomes a very simple real-world reward that the dog values at the moment, and it doesn't take long for him to understand that obedient behavior benefits him because it's the only way he can get what he wants. This mindset then generalizes to good behavior in every aspect of life, because the pup realizes that he must please his humans, rather than struggling with them, to get all the things he wants.

Unfortunately, real-world rewards work just as strongly as learning tools in a negative sense. By giving in to your pup's demands, you may teach him that you'll let him in if he barks rudely at the back door; that you'll share your food with him if he begs at the dinner table; you'll speed up your pace if he pulls on the leash and that you'll hurry up and take him on walks if he mauls you at the door every time you lift his leash. But you can change everything by changing your responses: wait for your pup to stop barking for at least 2 seconds before you let him inside; wait to feed him until he sits calmly and patiently; stop walking whenever he starts to pull and put the leash away and cancel the walk if he acts crazy at the door. **When you create a world where all the good things your pup wants are dependent upon the good behavior you want, you eliminate the need for constant correction.** And real-world rewards easily create a 100% win-win scenario for dog and family.

Hint: "Four on the Floor" is one of the best examples of a real-world concept every new pet parent should teach their pup. The concept is simple- never reward, pet or give your pup any type of attention unless he has all four paws on the ground. Petting your cute little pup (or even giving him attention by trying to push him off) whenever he jumps on people reinforces jumping, and this can become a real problem when the dog grows up. **From the very first hour your pup comes home, you should always wait for him to put all four paws down before you give him any attention, praise or petting.** And make everyone in the home, including guests, act consistent about this, too. **Just doing this one small thing when your pup's young will make him infinitely better behaved when he's older with no corrections and no strain or stress for**

anyone. (It could also save you hundreds of dollars that you might have to pay a trainer if your dog becomes a jumper.)

4. Using Treats for Positive Training:

We recommend using treats (or other positive reinforcers like toys or praise) to train all the obedience commands described later in this chapter, rather than physically pushing, pulling or correcting your puppy.

Below are some general instructions about using treats for training based on the questions most new puppy parents ask us:

a. Why use treats for training?

Positive or reward-based training- such as training with treats as reward- is now generally accepted as the kindest and most effective dog training philosophy. Rather than a dog complying with training because he's physically manipulated by his handler or fears his handler, instead he *wants* to do the right things, even when the handler isn't around, because he's learned to associate obedience with reward. These behavior changes can last for life, even when no treats are offered.

Food treats are *not* intended as the sole motivator for a dog to do things for you. But small tasty treats are usually the quickest and easiest way to mark desired behaviors so your pup associates doing the things you want with a pleasant reward.

You cannot always rely on treats to change behavior in every situation with every dog. And you should not use them exclusively (as we will explain). **But you should always keep treats on hand when training, especially when leash walking or doing any exercise out in public.** And treats are not just for formal obedience practice; they can help you change your pup's behavior in many real-world situations, rather than having to resort to much tougher interventions. Any animal lover with perfect timing can use treats to shape almost any behavior, not only in dogs, but in other large wild animals (unless the animal is in a high state of aggression).

Wherever you go with your dog, you should also take treats. A leash is certainly a tool for managing dogs, and it makes good sense to use one in certain situations. But, for us, a leash comes into play very little when we work to change dogs' behavior. For us, the most important tools are our senses, our minds and how we present ourselves to influence dogs' emotions, mental state and reactions. We also use rewards (usually, but not always treats) to quickly establish communication and to make everything go smoothly without a struggle.

You'd never forget a leash when you take your pup for a walk, nor would you forget to put on your clothing. Yet carrying rewards to influence your pup's behavior might make the biggest difference of all, so you should pack them first. When your dog grows to 100 lbs. and an unexpected encounter with other animals happens in a public place, having treats available can sometimes save the day.

b. <u>What treats should I use for training?</u>

The first rule of using treats to shape your dog's behavior is to stop giving treats out at other times. Never give your pup treats just because he looks cute or because he pushes on you or barks at you demanding food. Only use treats as a reward for a specific behavior you want, whether it is coming when you call, obeying obedience commands, acting proper as the neighbor's dog passes by or dropping an item when you tell him to. If you give out treats casually all the time, the treats won't hold much value for your pup and he'll be confused about what behaviors you want. Using the wrong treats make training your pup harder, while the right treats make training easier.

The best treats for training are:

1.) not allergenic 2.) safe for digestion 3.) great tasting and smelling
4.) soft and chewy, not crunchy 5.) small, or can be broken into smaller bits

When training, rip each treat it into small (even tiny) pieces. Each treat should mark a single success, and shouldn't be large enough to fill your dog up or represent a sizable reward on its own. If a large dry biscuit takes a long time for your pup to crunch on, this will distract him from your next command.

Many positive trainers sometimes give the wrong idea that treats mean more to dogs than anything else. In contrast, we believe dogs are noble by nature and that they care more about people than they do about food.

Just shoving treats at a pup indiscriminately could make him act pushy and only obey commands for treats. But in the majority of typical situations (with some exceptions for serious fear, aggression or disorders with nervous system or other physical involvement) we still tell pet parents to use treats or other rewards to start shaping behavior when commands are new to their dog. **Treats are a helpful marker for desired new behaviors- and the physical reward is not the deeper reason a dog will work with you.**

Our philosophy on this point is in direct contradiction to the ideas of some the past decades' most popular dog authors/experts who take behavior modification theory for dogs to its literal extreme. We are personally familiar with strict behavior modification theories- especially because of Emma's background in psychology/mental health. But this is all the more reason **we refuse to believe that behavioral decisions and motivation in dogs- or humans- can be explained as pure stimulus-response. And we refuse to discount the aspect of the soul in motivation- in humans- or dogs. Dogs, just like humans, won't always respond as experimental design suggests. Motives like altruism, which exist in canines as well as humans, can't be charted.**

And motives like this often inspire behavior, even when there's apparently nothing tangible for the subject to gain.

Never forget that your pup is not just a machine that will always respond to treats, or to certain training techniques. He is a thoughtful personality with motives similar to his human family members.

Treats are used primarily to facilitate communication in general, and to introduce your pup to new commands, and we've noticed the food value of treats is not really the main motivation for most dogs. For example, many of our clients "spoil" their dogs on gourmet home-cooked diets. These pups that dine on prime cuts of steak and fresh vegetables whenever they want really aren't starving hungry for the store-bought treats we offer during training, yet they still work diligently to receive these treats as rewards. This is because dogs primarily want to do right. **Dogs enjoy working just for the sake of achievement, and the treats serve as a powerful marker of when they do something right to please their humans.**

Our belief that dogs enjoy working to please their Moms and Dads does *not,* **however, mean we agree with dominance theories of training! A dog working to please a person is completely different from a dog working because he is afraid of a person. And many still-popular old-school training techniques are based on fear and/or physical distress.** This includes painful collar corrections, choke collars, pinch collars and electric shock collars- harsh corrections that aren't necessary to get optimum performance from your dog.

There's never a need to frighten a dog or pup to get him to do what you want. We believe that physically and emotionally healthy dogs are genuinely social animals that want to please Mommy and Daddy in exactly the same way your children might. Your kids don't strive for good grades because they're afraid of you, or because you offer them a trip to Disney or a tasty dinner on the table. Instead your children make the effort to excel at schoolwork because they feel proud of themselves when they can make you proud of them. This is the reason your child smiles when he receives a straight "A" report card. And achievement has the same meaning for your pup, only with him it is treats, rather than good grades, that symbolize when he's going in the right direction.

c. How frequently should I offer treats?

1. Don't offer treats every time:

Once your pup learns what a command means, you shouldn't offer a treat every single time he performs it. Instead, once you're sure the pup knows the command by heart, start giving treats intermittently, only every few repetitions or only when he performs most quickly or perfectly. An intermittent schedule of reinforcement is actually more motivating than constant rewards and better represents real-life, where you won't always have treats available.

2. Your pup should also learn to work for non-food rewards:

As described above, you will eventually want to phase out treats to where you only give them rarely. And, in real life, every dog should be able to obey commands successfully without expecting treats even if weeks or months go by without any.

Always alternate food reinforcers with praise and petting as reward. But don't get over exuberant and ruffle your pup up, especially if you want success with commands like "stay" that require calm.

3. Some pups just don't like treats.

For these pups, being handed a favorite toy for a brief chew, or having a ball thrown for fetch can substitute for food rewards. Some dogs respond incredibly strongly to toys as reward, so always pack a nice squeak toy, as well as treats, on walks in case you want to refocus your pup. Sometimes a favorite toy, rather than a food treat, can pull a pup's attention away from a distraction like another dog, and focus him back onto you and your commands.

d. Why it could be a sign of trouble if a pup refuses treats:

If, during training, your pup with a normally good appetite suddenly refuses to take food at all, or if he seems to choke on it, this may be a sign that he is physically ill or injured, highly stressed in some way, or exhausted or overexcited to the point where he cannot even digest. Or he could be getting ready to bite. ALWAYS IMMEDIATELY CONSULT A LOCAL PROFESSIONAL IF A DOG OR PUP SHOWS EVEN THE SLIGHTEST SIGN OF AGGRESSION or if you have any reason to suspect the dog or pup might harm you or your children. All information in this book, including advice about spotting dogs that may bite and dealing with angry dogs is intended as general theory only, and is not intended to replace the help of a local professional in individual cases.

1) If your pup suddenly refuses treats during an obedience session, he may be in physical distress:

Avoid exercising your pup excessively in hot sun and/or hot summer weather. (Also use care because some group classes or day care/day camp facilities encourage lots of exercise in summer sun.) Inability to swallow treats or vomiting treats up might indicate that your pup is overheated. Or he could possibly already be suffering heatstroke. If you know you've been working the pup vigorously in hot sun or hot weather, check him for the signs of heatstroke. (You can find this information online or through your veterinarian's office). If his temperature is high, cool him appropriately according to instructions and get him immediate veterinary care. (Even if he appears to recover, any dog that suffers heatstroke needs treatment to prevent serious long term health effects.)

If heat isn't a factor, check your pup's other vital signs, visually examine him and run your hands over his body for signs of injury. It's a good idea to pack a good home veterinary manual in your vehicle so you can refer to it on outings.

If your pup doesn't appear to be in any real physical distress, but just appears somewhat hot or physically exhausted, give him a little water (not too much or too cold) and a cool out-of-the-way place to rest and recuperate. Young pups need frequent rest breaks and in a few minutes he should be himself again. Don't push so hard next session and always train and exercise young pups in the shade. (Here in Florida we do a lot of training and games inside.) To stay safe, make vigorous outdoor exercise and obedience sessions brief- especially in extreme weather- and always consult your veterinarian about how to safely exercise your particular pup.

2) If your pup stops taking treats during a long obedience session, he may be mentally exhausted:

After too much training some pups feel mentally and emotionally tired and need to reboot. Others just might be bored with the training or the treats. To be safe, cease attempting to train the pup, don't try forcing any more treats on the pup and don't go anywhere near his mouth with your face until he relaxes. Don't do anything further to stress or agitate him. Take him to quiet place with no stress, rest awhile and then try again using a toy or praise as reward, or try again the next day.

3) A pup that snaps too hard to take treats make be overexcited, terrified or highly stressed:

If your pup takes treats so hard and violently that he nips your fingers or so quickly that he literally almost chokes, or foams at the mouth, this is evidence of serious stress. First rule out physical causes, such as heatstroke or seizure and make sure there are no signs the pup is ready to bite. Then follow the same advice as for the pup that won't take treats because he is tired. Give your highly stressed pup physical and psychological rest and time to reboot with no further commands. Stop trying to force treats on him. Then assess when (and if) he recovers sufficiently to resume training based on his behavior and your instinct as his owner.

Do not allow a pup in this state of overexcitation or stress to be near young children until his stress lessens, because excessive stress or fear often leads dogs to bite. If your success with training doesn't improve, or if the pup's whole body ever goes stiff while you are training or petting him, stop immediately. Stiffness is a serious sign that a pup will potentially bite. Read #5, below and don't attempt more training until you consult a high-level behaviorist. Then report the exact symptoms and allow the professional to assess whether there's a serious problem or whether you are safe to continue "do it yourself" training.

4) A pup that refuses treats may be dominant:

If your pup isn't physically or mentally burnt out from prolonged obedience, but he just seems irked at you wanting him to work for treats, this could become a serious problem. When a pup rudely and painfully pushes past treats in your hand without looking into your eyes and, especially if he "bumps" you hard with his shoulder, it could indicate that he's challenging you and he lacks sufficient "pack drive" or concern for getting along with his human family. A pup like this may also take treats so hard from you that he not only hurts you, but actually draws blood! And dominant pups *will* someday bite when they don't get things exactly their way, unless they learn better ways of interacting with people. But there's still hope if you read your pup's behavior properly and resume training with more caution and different motivators.

You can easily tell the difference between a pup that's just stressed, overexcited, silly or "hoppy" and a pup that's annoyed with humans and doesn't *like* to work with them. A pup that doesn't respect humans or their commands prefers to overpower people rather than do what they want in every aspect of life. A pup with dominance issues may scratch your children's faces, pull so hard on leash that he injures you, mark your pillow with urine and feces, mount on guests, hurt other pets and consistently refuse to come when you call him. A pup with true dominance issues will chew violently on his empty food bowl or chase off your cats and eat food from their bowls, while still refusing to look in your eyes or eat food offered from your hand.

Most pups aren't actually dominant and aren't really trying to challenge people even when their behavior is problematic. More often pups just haven't learned what their owners want and it's relatively easy to open the lines of communication. If you want an example of a Labrador that loved people but was challenged by an excess of energy and many "learning disabilities", read the charming megabestseller *Marley & Me* by John Grogan. Marley, as described in the book, wasn't a dominant dog; rather he was the quintessential goodhearted dog with a few emotional issues that just needed the right training.

But some pups must be worked with carefully to prevent serious dominance of people (*not* just puppy playfulness like Marley's) from blossoming into aggression. If your pup acts dominant, as long as he doesn't show any of the signs of physically dangerous aggression described in the next section, adults can still proceed with training (and you must!) You can also practice some of the Activities in Part 3 designed for increasing a pup's reliance on humans (for example #1 "Follow My Eyes" and #9 "The Finger Pointing Game") to change the dog's priorities.

When you train obedience to a dominant pup that won't take treats, you can also offer toys or real-world rewards (described in detail in this chapter) rather than the food treats as reinforcement. Or you can train dominant pups before mealtime when they're more motivated by appetite, or offer some kibble as reward during training exercises rather than serving it all at mealtimes. **Keep young children away from a seriously dominant pup during training until all signs of dominance vanish and/or a qualified behaviorist clears him for safety.**

5.) Danger- how to recognize signs of a pup acting truly aggressive when you try to train him:

Some puppies of 8 or 9 months can weigh 100 lbs or more, and even a minor bite from a dog like this can seriously injure a person. Recently, we've also seen increasingly frequent incidents where pups as young as 8 or 10 weeks aggressively attack people, aiming for the face and leaving bleeding and scarring. (These actual *attacks* by young puppies are completely different from playfully nipping hands or "herding" by lightly nipping heels. Nipping, mouthing or herding are relatively normal puppy behaviors that easily extinguish with behavior shaping like that described in Activities like "#20 Use a Soft Mouth" in this book.)

True canine aggression is highly complex, and we cannot attempt to adequately cover the topic in this general puppy obedience and activity book. Our best advice is that owners who observe any signs of true aggression in their pup should consult with a local behaviorist, applied animal behaviorist or veterinary behaviorist with advanced qualifications for advice on how to proceed, and should not attempt further training (especially with children present) until they get the green light for safety from the expert.

Many of the signs of aggression- such as snapping, snarling and growling are obvious but there is one red flag for aggression that owners often miss. **Sometimes the only sign a dog or pup is about to bite is if the dog's body goes stiff. This can happen when you first attempt to get a dominant or fearful dog to do something he doesn't want to do.**

If you understand canine body language, and if you modify your training in the right ways after an incident where a young puppy goes stiff, you may be able to diffuse any future aggression and teach the pup to comfortably take direction from humans so he'll never bite in future. Or you may require a professional to help you achieve this result. But, **the moment a dog stiffens, you must first react properly to keep everyone safe until you can obtain professional advice.**

You will recognize a stiff dog because his body suddenly feels so hard and unnatural that it seems frightening. If you've ever observed two dogs-or two wolves on film- just before they attack each other, you will know what this stiffness looks like. If you haven't, the first time you feel a stiff dog's body it will make your blood freeze. People's natural instincts make us uneasy when we feel this- as we should be for our self-preservation. Unfortunately, young children aren't yet mature enough to sense possible threats in the same way, so they may continue touching a dog in this state- which can prove dangerous.

A stiff dog is *always* a dog that will bite; it's just a question of when. In some cases it might not happen immediately. But in other cases, you have just a few seconds to diffuse the situation and do the right thing to make the dog relax, rather than attacking.

Dogs can stiffen during training, but it can also happen when an adult- or a child-tries to pull away a toy or hug a dog in a way he doesn't like.

Don't confront the dog or grab him by the collar. For optimal safety, if the dog is no immediate threat to anyone or to himself, smoothly take your hands off him, allow him to "cool off" and reevaluate your training strategies later once he's calm. Trying to confront him and "show him who's boss" or "break" him when he's stiff might cause him to bite. But if you simply take the stiffness as a warning sign you still have an opportunity to change everything for better in the future.

If the stiff dog *is* a threat to any people, you may be able to either calmly call him away or calmly walk him away on leash and there's a good chance the tension will dissipate. You could also give a command like "Back", "Down" or "Sit" and this may snap the dog out of the defiant state and return him to a more obedient state.

If a child is in danger and the dog won't come away when you call, you can get him away from the child by calmly inserting your body between dog and child and confidently and assertively backing the dog away. If this cannot work and you have to lift a small child or baby to keep them safe from the potentially angry dog, do it smoothly and confidently rather than abruptly, then turn your body to shield the child and calmly walk away, without allowing the child to panic. And don't show any nervousness yourself.

How you immediately deal with any potential aggression is up to your personal judgment in the situation and the general suggestions above may not be appropriate in every case. But we strongly suggest that once your dog shows any unpleasantness towards people, including stiffening, you consult a local high level behaviorist before again allowing children to train, cuddle or play with him.

6.Troubleshooting if training commands doesn't work right immediately

Read this troubleshooting section to start training all commands in the quickest most effective style and avoid the most common problems dog owners experience. Obviously, pups can't learn some of the more complex commands perfectly without some practice. But if your pup doesn't show progress of any kind after you work with him, return to this section before repeating the actions that aren't working.

This troubleshooting section can also help if you learned training methods somewhere else but your pup is still having problems in the home. Often when we meet owners with the worst problems training their pups, we find they learned the ineffective methods from a trainer or class they paid for. Once we work past these methods, these dogs start responding better.

The authors are always surprised when dog owners tell us about attending group obedience classes where it took an entire one-hour session- or more- to teach dogs to sit. We feel like spending an hour on just one command is boring to the point of being counterproductive- it certainly would be with the dogs we train. One-on-one we can usually train a solid "sit" in minutes (using only positive methods and no physical placing) with a clientele of dogs aged 8 weeks to 15 years, most of which suffer from emotional disturbances and/or physical challenges.

The "sit" command is one of the simplest. And yet it's not always to get a pup to obey "sit" or any command if he has underlying problems. Cookie cutter training doesn't work with every dog, so to get the attention and trust of your pup you must find the tone and body language that work best for him. Almost any dog can become an obedient dog with the right knowledge and sensitivity on the part of the owner/handler. This section covers solutions for the problems that come up most often when training the obedience commands detailed later in the chapter. If, after trying these suggestions, you still have major problems controlling your pup, getting his attention or getting him to obey commands, you may need an expert dog trainer with a kind personality to diagnose the problem and demonstrate exactly how to communicate with your pup in his language. Once you've opened the lines of communication, in the future you should be able to quickly and effectively teach your pup anything you want him to learn.

How to use the right style for effective training:

If teaching your puppy a command takes much longer than it should, *and if your pup does not have any serious problems such as illness, aggression or clinical hyperactivity*, you are probably doing something wrong in body language or style. And this problem will likely bleed over into other areas of relating with your pup, making training or controlling him in future more difficult. If you're having difficulty, try the following:

1. **Give up the attempt for a moment and give your pup some appropriate exercise**
2. **Remove all distractions from the scene, including: television, children & other pets**
3. **This time, when you give the command:**
    -use a straight, confident stance
    -use a confident, yet conversational, tone. No shouting
    -focus completely on your pup
    -believe that, by focusing your energy, you can get your pup to obey perfectly
    -Don't repeat yourself twice. Instead, if the pup doesn't obey, either wait, or walk
him around a few steps. (Or you can position him according to instructions in this section, but this is not the preferred method.)

It never helps to shout or snap at a pup while training (even if you've witnessed "professional" obedience instructors training this way). Prepare to **command your pup in a confident, businesslike tone. Don't beg or plead with your dog helplessly. For example, don't tell him "sit?" as though it has a question mark.**

But never act sharp or harsh. If you want your pup to grow into a trustworthy companion as an adult, you must never allow him to be trained harshly as a pup, even by the most experienced or most popular dog trainer in the world- or the most popular trainer in your town. If you ever observe a professional training pups this way, don't allow that man or woman to train your pup and don't imitate their methods.

Always act like a lady or gentleman around your pup and he should reward you with that same level of respect when he grows up. **Show 100% confidence and consistency. This will make your pup naturally follow your leadership with no need for you to struggle to exert "dominance".**

For most occasions you should always command your dog in a totally focused, yet conversational, voice. You should save loudness and intensity for rare occasions when your pup is about to do something that can get him killed. And teaching basic obedience commands is *not* one of those rare life-threatening occasions (no matter how loud or intent you may have seen other dog trainers or obedience instructors act). The only possible exceptions are the "Leave It" and "Drop It" commands.

In most cases, when a dog owner does something wrong during training, they are usually acting too rough, too loud or too impatient with their pup. Pulling or pushing on a pup to try to teach him commands is also a bad idea (although we've witnessed it in many popular obedience classes). Struggling with your pup can make it take hours to teach commands that he could have learned in minutes. And constantly trying to overcome a pup can damage your potential for an extraordinary dog/owner bond so that your pup loses his deeper impulses to *want* to be obedient.

Although we usually train most new commands off leash inside the home, sometimes using a leash can make it easier to train new commands. If your pup has problems concentrating, or jumps around constantly, leash him when first teaching a new command. Then walk him around in a little circle and bring him to face you so that you have his attention.

You can lure your pup and focus him by letting him know you're holding a treat. But if he becomes overly focused on the treat or if he snaps or jumps at you, hide the treat away until he calms down. **Usually the easiest way to teach commands is to offer a soft, hypoallergenic treat broken into tiny pieces as reinforcement. But some pups can't or won't take treats.** Others may go out of control completely and try to leap at you and slaver all over you to get the food treat. In these cases you could substitute a favorite toy as a reward, which you allow the pup to hold for a few minutes after each successful repetition. (Squeaky toys are usually good to get dog's attention, but they are dangerous. To prevent your pup ingesting the dangerous squeaker, only allow him to play with squeaky toys while you carefully supervise).

As soon as your pup is facing you and you have his attention, take a deep centering breath, blank out the rest of the world one hundred percent and envision that he will obey your commands perfectly. Once you learn to do this, teaching all commands becomes infinitely faster and easier. Now begin.

Section B: Instructions for Training Basic Commands

1. Training "Heel" (or how to walk on leash)

Why this is important: start out leash walking right and it will always be easy; start out wrong, and problems with heeling will not only affect leash walking, but every other area of life with your dog

Difficulty level: When a dog doesn't "heel" properly, it can cause a hundred times more problems than disobedience to all other commands put together. Considering the level of physical and emotional agony a dog that pulls will cause in his lifetime, it's surprisingly easy to teach a pup to heel when you follow our advice. But if, rather than using the tricks of body language and canine psychology, you constantly try to force your dog to heel by pulling back on his collar, every single walk will continue to feel bad.

Instructions:

Dogs should be able to easily walk on leash as light as a feather. Yet problems pulling on leash are extremely common, causing some owners to suffer a lifetime of distress whenever they have to walk their dogs, and other owners to stop walking their dogs entirely. But **there are two simple keys to good leash walking:**

1. Keep a general healthy balance in your relationship with your dog and

2. Accustom your pup to leash walking properly when he is young

If you do these two things, leash walking should always be easy.

You should never train a puppy under six months using force, "correction" or "compulsion" methods. In fact, it's debatable whether dogs of any age should be trained by these methods. But owners should be aware that compulsion used to be widely accepted and is still taught in many classes. If you hire a trainer for your puppy, ask him about his methods, and look out for mention of "leash corrections" or "training collars". And then observe. The trainer should use positive methods, luring your puppy with treats and handling him like the delicate little treasure he is. It is the nature of dogs to want to follow when leadership is shown correctly. So if a trainer jerks or shoves your young puppy or uses any harsh leash corrections, this is unacceptable.

To avoid possible serious injury, never use a choke or a prong collar on pups under 6 months and never let a trainer use one! We don't recommend these for adult dogs either. Used wrong, these types of collars can also bring out pulling; panic on leash or dog aggression- the very behaviors you want to avoid. Instead, use an appropriately sized harness or buckle collar. Never pull hard. Instead, you will lead your dog by stopping and changes in speed and direction.

The extremely good news is that an eight or ten week-old puppy cannot pull you off your feet, no matter what his breed (including some of the large guardian breeds that have been our "babies"). So the time to lay the groundwork for walking him correctly is now.

a. Acclimating your pup to collar and leash:

From the first moment you get your pup home you should start teaching him to enjoy wearing a collar or a harness and having people guide him on a leash. Learning to accept a collar and leash as natural and pleasant parts of life is a critical milestone for a pup- and learning to dislike these items can cause tremendous problems.

Every time you walk your dog you should feel as comfortable as if you were walking hand-in-hand with your sweetheart along a seaside boardwalk on a perfect summer evening. Having your dog connected to you on leash is just a gentle non-verbal way to establish security, connection and communication. So you should never rush collar and leash training and never use these items in any way that hurts your pup or causes him to panic.

Pups that are afraid or hate the collar or leash may attempt to roll and spin, halt and refuse to walk or compulsively bite on the leash. And when these pups quickly grow to 90 pounds or more they may pull so badly their owners can't walk them or take them to the veterinarian. Sometimes owners are seriously injured by pulling dogs. To avoid these problems, you must make your pup's attitude positive toward leash and collar starting from the youngest age possible.

First, choose safe equipment. A well-fitting harness that a pup can't slip out of is especially good with toy and teacup pups. Or use a nylon or leather buckle or clip style collar, but no choke or prong collars, which can be dangerous for pups under 6 months. Frequently check the fit because pups grow fast; and don't leave a collar on your pup in a crate or around hazards that he could snag on.

To acclimate your pup to collar and leash if he's never used them before start by "casually" leaving the items lying on the floor with some treats laid on top of them. This should lure the pup to take the treats and sniff around the collar and leash. If he remains near the leash and collar long enough to calmly investigate them, reward him with more treats and praise.

After sniffing around a little and taking a few treats, many puppies will stay calm enough that they will allow you to simply put the collar around their neck. Even if the pup acts just a little bit nervous and tries to twist around to bite at the collar, as long as he doesn't appear deeply distressed, you may be able to distract him with treats and play so you can put the collar on and he will forget he's wearing it. Once the pup calmly walks around wearing the new collar for a few minutes, take it off. Then put it on again, rewarding him with treats and encouragement each time he wears it. Soon he should be wearing the collar full time.

While accustoming your pup to collar and leash be careful to read his body language correctly. If your puppy acts extremely wiggly, and/or frightened or freezes stiffly when you first put on his collar, you can enlist the aid of a helper to distract him with toys or treats. Or, if you're alone, you can start by simply laying the collar over his neck the first few times to get him more comfortable with it.

Irresponsible breeders don't bother to introduce pups to collars and leashes. So many people bring home a 5 month old puppy from a pet store that's never encountered these items and his first response to them may be craze and terror. But allowing a dog like this to avoid collar and leash for additional months creates unimaginable trouble. Trying to grab a year-old 90 pound dog barehanded to prevent him from trampling a visiting 3-year-old can feel like trying to stop a greased rhino. And the dog will act more stressed and uncooperative every time a person painfully scruffs him on his bare neck attempting to catch him. Unfortunately, if your dog reaches this size and age feeling he's the kind of animal that doesn't naturally wear leash and collar, he may never easily tolerate human control again without in-depth professional rehabilitation.

But if you are unlucky enough to have obtained your pup came from a breeder or former owner who never introduced him to leash and collar, you could make the problem even worse if you almost strangle him with leash and collar the first time he resists - this can easily happen when a puppy panics. Instead, take your time and use gentle-reward based methods to accustom him to these items at whatever pace works best for him.

Practice gently in 5-minute increments throughout the day, with hundreds of repetitions if necessary. Associate giving your pup anything he wants with him having to tolerate the leash and collar calmly. For example, keep the items on your leg when you cuddle the pup and present his food and toys on top of them to desensitize him.

Teaching the pup to love collar and leash as natural and wonderful rather than just clipping them on and letting the pup freeze in terror or roll, scratch and pant until he's tired sometimes requires a lot of time, patience and gentle repetitions - so a loving pet parent is the best person to do it. For many pet parents, getting your new puppy comfortable with collar and leash will be the first exercise in gentleness, patience and trust between you.

b. While your puppy is getting comfortable with his collar for a few days, you should also start training him to walk properly off-leash at your side:

The first step to teaching your pup to walk well beside you on-leash is first teaching him to walk well beside you off leash. First, when the pup is off-leash in your home, call him to you on and off throughout the day, encouraging him with kissing sounds, running backward or clapping your hands. Puppies under 16 weeks are hard-wired to desperately want to follow their "parents", so they'll *want* to come to you. *Capitalize on this tendency now* and lavishly reward your pup with praise and/or treats whenever he comes willingly when you call him. The time to start calling your pup like this is as soon as he is old enough to walk.

Next, start calling the pup to you as you walk around the house. Make him follow, luring with treats if necessary. Praise and encourage with loads of excited baby talk! Next imitate heeling on leash by having your pup walk alongside you as close to your left side as possible *off leash*. Some trainers stick a treat onto the end of a small dowel or stick to lure the dog (this can help with small breeds). Or you can hold a treat or toy in your hand, hung down at your left side. Make your pup stay by your left side, walking near you for as long as possible, and practice this type of walking together in the house whenever you get a chance. Encourage him with praise and smiles as you walk. You can also say "Good heel".

Wind around obstacles, speed up and slow down and make staying by your side a challenge. Take this game into your enclosed yard if you wish, and have different family members try it. This is a great way to "play" with your puppy. If you, or your children, ever feel at a loss for how to play with your puppy, this can replace some of the popular, but potentially dangerous games like tug-of-war or wrestling.

When practicing with your puppy walking by your side, keep individual training sessions short and end on a high note. Try 5 or 10 minute sessions frequently throughout the day. And as your pup grows, he will be able to tolerate longer sessions. **Continue playing this "game" for the life of your dog at least a few times a week.** Try "heeling" off the leash like this everywhere in your house and yard, and get your kids in the habit of moving around with the pup in this fashion. Having him walk calmly by their side is safer than if he chases or jumps at them. And it establishes a precedent for the future, so that as the pup grows and the children stay small, they can still keep control of him while walking. What's important is that your pup will want to stay close to his human's side, so no one in the family ever has to try to force their control on him.

If you do the exercise correctly, your puppy should want to stay so close to your side that you'll hardly be able to shake him! This leads to gratifying dog/owner bonding. And frequent successful practice like this will make your dog a great companion on leash for the rest of his life, as well as shaping him to want to stay near you if he's ever off leash. (See #6 Heeling Without a Leash" in Activities for additional instructions.)

c. Start walking your puppy on the leash:

While your puppy learns to comfortably heel with you off leash, you should also start accustoming him to being hooked on a leash for short periods. The first time you use the leash, casually and confidently hook it onto the pup's collar or harness while offering him a little treat to chew on. Allow the pup to drag the leash around under your careful supervision, just so he learns to treat it as an everyday item and it doesn't overexcite him.

The first place to use the leash is in the house. Call your pup to you as you lightly hold the leash. Then practice the "#11 Umbilical Cord" technique where you keep the leash looped around your wrist or connected to a belt loop as you walk around leading the way. (Find full instructions for this technique, which can also help with housetraining and teething problems, described in Part 3, Activities)

You can walk your puppy around the house for as long as you want- even all day. Or try multiple short sessions each day. Your pup will come to feel perfectly natural walking at your side, watching you as you complete your daily tasks and matching his pace to yours. Your puppy will graduate to walking delightedly beside you as an adult and you will avoid many of the boredom-caused behavior problems many of your neighbors may suffer with their dogs. Instead, your dog will be a joy to live with and a joy to walk.

d. <u>Where is it safe to walk your pup?</u>

Because of undeveloped immunity, until your pup is done with his vaccinations, it's safest to walk him in your own clean backyard or another private area, rather than a street or public space where many dogs eliminate. If you do walk your puppy in public places, try to keep him on pavement and other clean areas and be hyper-vigilant about him contacting the feces of other dogs until he's had his final vaccinations and your veterinarian gives the okay. **You should never expose your young puppy to the droppings of other dogs, because doing so might expose him to deadly infection.**

And also avoid exposing your pup to high levels of stress at this age. You've probably heard that you should socialize your puppy, and it's true that socialization before 20 weeks is vitally important. Exposure to varied stimuli, such as the sight of pedestrians and the sound of traffic, helps your puppy build confidence and learn that the world is safe. But exposure to frightening stimuli (like unfriendly dogs) will make him feel unsafe and make his future behavior unpredictable. So choose a moderate course of action. It's nice to walk your young puppy a little on leash in public areas, but choose a safe and relatively calm and uncrowded location. (See Part 4, Socializing Your Pup, for full details on how to socialize your pup to new people and dogs for optimal results.)

Young pups do not need a great deal of exercise and too much physical strain can hurt them. It is *older* pups and young adult dogs- *not* young pups- that need lots of vigorous exercise. If your pup is young he should *not* be walking miles at a time, especially if he's a heat-sensitive or giant breed or if he has any health problems. Walking just a block or so at a time (ideally in shade or in moderate weather) is all a really young puppy needs. You can always take him on several more short walks during the day and this will benefit him more than one marathon-style session.

e. <u>How to teach your pup to follow you without wanting to pull ahead:</u>

If you learn the theory of heeling correctly while your pup is young, this will guarantee a lifetime of success. In contrast, trying to physically overpower a dog that already pulls will guarantee just the opposite. On your first walks when your pup's 8, 10 or 12 weeks old he's

not likely to wander far or pull on the leash hard enough to injure himself because, at this age, natural instinct makes him want to stay right by you. So, if you simply start walking, making it look fun and exciting, most young pups will tend to follow you without hesitation.

Your pup's level of cooperation depends on your confidence. But don't confuse leadership with dominance no matter what some other dog people might advise. You *never* need to use harsh physical corrections to get a puppy to do exactly what you want. And, ironically, **because of dog psychology and the laws of physics, hard leash jerking or holding the leash too tight will only make a pup pull forward more.**

Positive reinforcement works better because each time your developing puppy cooperates with you by his own choice; it shapes his self concept as a dog that wants to please you. The impact of shaping your pup's personality like this a lot stronger than training him to fear harsh corrections. Your pup will grow into an adult dog that will never think of pulling. Instead he'll recognize himself as an animal that always walks happily right at Mommy's and Daddy's side- even if he doesn't remember how and when he learned.

If, on his first walk, your pup looks like he's going to try to pull you, distract him first. Lure him with treats, sounds or by running backwards to utilize his natural instincts. (A harness may also be gentler for some young puppies than a buckle collar for walking exercises, but never pull too hard on your young puppy, even if he's wearing a harness, since injury is possible.)

At his young age, there's no need for your puppy to learn the command "heel" yet. Your pup will simply learn to walk with you softly on the leash and, if all goes well, this will become ingrained in him as a natural almost reflexive behavior for the rest of his life.

The most powerful thing an owner can do to make their adult dog to always heel well is to practice teaching their puppy to pay attention to them on walks and to match his pace to theirs. And making many unexpected turns and stops while walking is the best way to teach him.

f. How to make your pup match his pace to yours while walking:

1.) If your pup stops paying attention to you while walking, or if he starts to move ahead of you, quickly change direction and he'll follow.

2.) Increase your pace if your pup stubbornly slows, and slow your pace, or stop entirely, if he walks too fast. You can also teach your pup the "Look" command (where the dog is rewarded for looking into his owner's eyes) and use it to make him focus on you at times as you walk. (See 6. "Training Look" in this chapter for a full instructions.)

3.) If your pup starts getting ahead of you or starts pulling on the leash try:

a. making sudden right (wide) or left (tight) turns

b. stopping and refusing to move until the pup returns to your side

c. projecting calm confident body language and walking assertively as though you are setting the pace rather than constantly "checking" the dog's cues for how he wants to walk

These are all effective ways to get your pup to focus on you, accept your lead and walk without pulling. Just be careful when making sudden turns or stops that you don't trip over the leash or the pup, especially with small breeds. But always walk forward as smoothly and confidently as possible and don't keep glancing back at the dog worried about his reactions. Just walk straight wherever you want to go and your dog will follow.

g. <u>**Your young puppy should respond beautifully to walking with you on a loose leash. You should also teach your pup to heel, right up by your side, dog-show style:**</u>

You should train your pup to "heel" even if you think you'll never need the command. When your dog's older, you'll want him perfectly controlled in the face of distractions and teaching him to "heel" when he's tiny will help immeasurably and possibly improve your entire future together. Just exercising your dog in the yard when he's free is not a substitute for the dog-owner bonding and exposure to real-world stimuli provided by daily leashed walks. The only time owners should skip leashed walks is in extreme winter or summer weather. But even on hot days short leashed walks of 10 or 15 minutes are usually comfortable in the evening or early morning when it's cooler.

Sometimes puppy owners feel reluctant to leave their property for reasons like an unsafe neighborhood, or aggressive unleashed dogs wandering the street. A call to police or code enforcement might help. Another solution, until conditions improve, is to load your puppy up and drive him to someplace you both enjoy for his walks- like a safe and pleasant park, a waterfront promenade or downtown shopping district.

Although it takes a little more time, effort and planning than just walking in your neighborhood, **occasionally walking your pup in other venues can improve your entire quality of life.** Walks become exciting, you and your pup can see new scenery and meet nice people and their pets and you can walk in shade rather than hot sun. For example, imagine treating yourself to a latte at dog-friendly café while your pup happily people-watches rather than running the gauntlet at 5:30 in your subdivision when every nasty dog usually tries to lunge at you. Walking in different venues embodies the quintessential joy of having a dog and allows you to expand your horizons with your dog even if you can't afford a five-star hotel with a dog and owner package.

Unless walks or runs will be your dog's primary exercise, **consistency is more important than intensity or how far you travel. Ideally, you should walk your dog on a regular basis several times a day, even if those walks last for just a few minutes.**

Another good idea is to take your pup in your car and combine your pup's walking with other errands. On Tuesday you and your husband can hold hands and walk your pup by the river, while checking out the architecture of the lovely historic homes and discussing dreams for your next remodel. On Wednesday you can walk your pup and bond with your teenage daughter while window-shopping in your dog-friendly arts district. On Thursday your teenaged son and your pup can volunteer to walk with the pretty teenage girl who just came to live in the neighborhood and her new pup. And on Friday your husband might want to decompress after work by taking your pup to the beach for the first time and photographing him playing in the surf with the sunset as a background. And on Saturday you can combine your pup's exercise with a family reunion at the park.

All of these activities integrate the puppy with the family's life, making his care and his daily exercise a joy rather than a repetitive chore it could become if all you do is circle the same block time and time again for walks without ever mixing it up. Even if ninety percent of your pup's walks take place in your neighborhood, adding a special outing every few weeks can make owners and pups more excited about walks.

Ideally your pup should learn to be part of the family and match his pace happily to the regular, everyday, things you like to do. Powerwalking for long distances or for long periods of time is not really necessary unless this is the only way that your pup gets exercise. And highly intense or very long exercise sessions can actually be too much for small puppies, giant-breed pups or heat-intolerant breeds unless your veterinarian clears it.

Once you realize that a walk is most beneficial when it's stress-free and fun, rather than sweaty and painful, your family may be more motivated to walk your pup every day. Seven short walks, one each day of the week, are healthier for a pup than one marathon session on a Saturday. And **each different walk as your pup grows up can become a precious memory for later.**

Any time you have really limited time or options, you can still get some of the important benefits of a leashed walk by clipping on your pup's leash and walking him around the boundaries of your property. This helps dog and owner bond and will also make your pup less likely to want to leave his "territory".

Finding time to walk a pup can be difficult with today's hectic schedules. But most people find it even harder when their pup grows to 90 pounds and becomes intractable, and walking becomes painful and fear-inducing. But these pet parents could have easily prevented the problem by walking the pup for 10 minutes every day when he was 10 weeks old and weighed 10 pounds. Some families own a pup but don't walk him for months or never walk him at all. A good number of people walk an adult dog less than once a month- or even less than once a year. And these people often have the worst problems with their dogs.

Canines are intelligent and athletic animals that need movement and stimulation in their lives. Pups that are consistently deprived of walks often develop behavior problems ranging from counter surfing to barking to knocking people down and they're more likely to lunge at other dogs or people aggressively when they do go out.

All of this points to why it's so important to start leash walking your new puppy as soon as you can accustom him to leash and collar.

2. Training "Sit"

Why it's important: "Sit" is usually considered the "foundation" command that makes dogs open to learning other commands, so owners may want to train this command first. "Sit" is by far the easiest command, it immediately calms and quiets dogs in many situations and it's incompatible with uncontrolled behavior like jumping on people. Note: Some pups jump around constantly and have difficulty focusing enough to learn "Sit" so you may wish to teach the "Look" command (described later in this section) first.

Difficultly level: Extremely easy to train- by far the easiest command. If you don't see any progress within the first 20 minutes, you may be making mistakes that will carry over to all other work with your pup, so go back and review "Troubleshooting" in Section A.

Instructions for teaching "Sit":
Detailed instructions for teaching your pup to sit by either "capturing" or "luring" follow later in this chapter (along with instructions for physical positioning which is not our preferred method.)

But, before you try any of methods, there is a chance your pup already knows the command! (In fact, Emma likes to joke that all dogs are born knowing "sit".) **To test whether your pup already knows the "sit" command:**

Have some treats ready and get your pup's full attention. Then, as he looks up at you, give him an intent stare and command "sit" as though he already knows what to do. Continue to stare at him and give him a few moments to sit. If he does, immediately mark the behavior by saying "good sit" and reward him with a treat and some praise and petting. Then practice the "sit" command enough times that you are sure the pup knows it perfectly and performs even without a treat being offered.

Although a certain number of pups (usually older pups) may have picked up this particular command somewhere without their owners realizing, usually pups *don't* know any commands until you teach them. So don't get judgmental or mad at your little puppy if he doesn't happen to be "born" knowing the command "sit". And don't let your children think this way. If your puppy doesn't seem to recognize the command, you'll have to teach it. And teaching most pups to sit is extremely easy.

<u>Alternative methods for training the "sit":</u>

There are three ways to teach the "sit". The first, and most preferred, way is by "luring" with treats (or a different reward like a toy). **The next method is by "capturing"- waiting for the pup to perform the desired behavior once on his own and then immediately rewarding. And the final method** (which is not preferred) **is by physically positioning:**

1. Training "sit" by the "luring" method:

If you wish to train the "sit" with the "luring" method, which is the most popular method amongst trainers today, hold a treat (or a favorite small toy) and have your pup face you. Concentrate your mind power and stare at him. If he's leashed, you can lift his leash straight up a bit to help position him (don't leave slack, but don't pull too hard or "hang" the pup) and, with a fluid motion, take a step closer to the pup (but don't step on him or knee him) so your body language tends to make him sit back.

Simultaneously, lure the pup with the treat in your hand, lifting it just above his head so he will lift his head and sit back as he sniffs at it and stretches for it. Wait for the pup to sit and give him the treat the moment he does. Practice this movement a few times. Once the pup learns the movement and gets fluent in sitting to get the treat, start saying "sit" each time he moves into the sitting position. Do this a few times.

Next say "sit" first and lift the treat to lure him in the same way. If he sits, enthusiastically say, "Good sit" the second he does it and instantaneously reward him with the treat.

After your pup has sat for you on command a few times, command him to "sit" but don't lure him with the treat anymore. The second he sits on your command, enthusiastically say "Good sit" and give him the treat. Now practice repeated times without luring, giving your pup a treat and praise on each successful completion.

Eventually you should start rewarding with treats for only the quickest compliance, only offering treats every 2nd, 3rd or 5th attempt. Make each training session very short for puppies, but practice frequently many times a day. Increase distractions and surprise your pup by giving him the command in real-life situations. The command will be much more difficult for your pup to obey outside, but take time to practice because compliance with obedience commands outdoors is vitally important. Once your pup masters the command on leash, you should also practice off leash, from near you and from a distance.

And also teach your pup to sit at various times during neighborhood walks. For example, for safety, it's a good idea to have him stop and sit before you cross streets. Also command him to sit if he ever starts getting ahead of you. This stops his forward momentum and can easily teach your pup not to pull you. And get in the habit of commanding your pup to sit before you will throw the ball to him for Fetch. This keeps excitement manageable and keeps control where it should be- with you.

Sometimes offer your pup food treats as a reward when he sits on command; and other times reward with just praise or petting. And at the end of a successful obedience practice you may wish to play with your pup for a few moments as a nice reward for both of you. (See "#34 Get Excited; Then Calm Down" in Activities.)

You may wish to watch a few good DVD's with demonstrations of teaching the "Sit" and other commands. Sometimes video can characterize specific moves better than words, but it's not always necessary. In most cases if you follow all the theoretical suggestions in this Part, act patient and nice and present positive and confident energy, you should be able to train your pup the "sit" with good reliability in much less time than it takes to read this section. Training should be fun and (as long as your pup doesn't start out with serious issues like aggression) if you follow the suggestions in this book and remember to make commands an everyday part of life, you can expect long-term obedience, even in challenging situations.

If you have problems luring your pup to sit and are feeling frustrated, you can consult Troubleshooting in section A. But first try the alternate method of "capturing" described below. This method is usually foolproof even if you cannot get your pup to initially sit on command.

2. Training "sit" by the "capturing" method:

If you wish to train your pup to sit by what is called "capturing" the behavior, just wait until your pup sits on his own and, the exact second he does, say "sit" and give him a treat. The idea is that he will connect the behavior he just performed with the reward and he'll want to do it again. Try "capturing" a few sits and immediately rewarding your pup with treats and praise.

Now, say the command "Sit". If your pup sits on your command say "good sit" and reward him with a treat. If he doesn't, walk him around a few steps to clear his head and then try "capturing" once again. Wait for the pup to sit on his own and, the second he does, say "sit" and reward him.

Now try commanding "sit" again. Your pup should now be able to figure out what you want. If he does not, keep repeating the cycle until he understands what behavior you want, and consistently sits when you command it.

At first reward with treats every single time the pup "sits" on your command. Then start phasing out treats so he only gets them part of the time (perhaps every third repetition) or only on his quickest compliance.

Next increase difficulty by increasing distractions, letting the pup off-leash (in safe area), practicing outdoors, switching handlers and/or practicing off property. (See Section A, "1. Training around distractions" in this Part for more details.)

Practice at spontaneous times throughout the day, or whenever you need your pup to sit, rather than attempting long and impractical obedience sessions. **Start giving the "sit" command in challenging real-life situations like when guests visit.** Many obedience instructors fail to explain to their students how the commands your pup learns during formal classes are useful in everyday situations, but this is the whole point of training. On an average day, you dog may not need any formal obedience sessions, yet you can command him to "sit" hundreds of times. **This ingrains the command deeply in his mind so that obedience becomes a reflex. And life becomes easier when your pup willingly sits whenever you don't want him jumping around.**

Training "Sit" should only take a few minutes:

Most pups love sitting for you all the time once they get the hang of it. But if your pup refuses to concentrate and/or keeps jumping around when you first try to teach him try walking and/or jogging him around a few times and then coming back to training position. You can also get his attention by calling his name or making little "kissing" noises. Some handlers first teach their pups to focus using the "Look" command, also described in this chapter so you can start in whichever order feels more natural. If you still can't get your pup to concentrate long enough to lure him into a proper "sit", you can always teach the command using the "capturing" method described earlier.

Many training resources fail to tell pet parents that initially teaching most basic obedience commands should only take minutes. Be nice, loosen up, act 100% confident and remember that you and your pup are working toward the same goals. **And you may be able to teach "sit" on the very first try.**

3. Training "sit" by physical positioning (not a preferred method):

In our opinion, there are rarely reasons compelling enough to use physical positioning, rather than rewards, when initially introducing new commands like "sit". Between the "luring" and "capturing" techniques, you should be able to initially teach your pup how to sit.

Many old-school trainers and obedience classes today still use physical placement, rather than rewards, to train new commands, although this method is starting to go out of favor as positive reinforcement training gains popularity. Since we're "eclectic" trainers who treat each case uniquely, we occasionally physically position dogs on rare occasions where it's warranted for specific therapeutic purposes. But in the vast majority of cases we try to have pups experience sitting on their own.

One reason you might consider physically positioning a dog while training is if he already knows a command, but refuses to obey it. **A well-known caveat of training is to never repeat a command if your dog doesn't obey the first time, otherwise he might learn to hesitate to obey vital (even lifesaving) commands in future.**

Physical positioning *is* obviously one way to enforce your commands once you give them, although it's rarely the best way. We'll describe several more positive ways to back up a command if your pup ever doesn't obey. However, if you still choose to physically position, when the pup fails to obey, you must use extreme care because if you push down too hard, or push down in the wrong place, you could injure your pup.

If you do choose to physically position a pup so he sits, the safest and simplest method is the "scoop" method:

Bend over, "scoop" your pup's entire rump (and tail, and most of his weight) into your open palm and gently "tuck" it under him so he's sitting. This is comfortable for most pups, although it can be more difficult with very large pups or handlers who have trouble bending, so you should plan accordingly.

Safety Note:
Even though "scooping" a pup into a sit is much safer than just pushing on the pup's back, we still urge pet parents to use the alternatives below rather than physical methods. The reason you would probably try to physically position your pup is if he disobeyed you once you were sure he already knew a command. But if you attempt to physically position a pup and he strongly resists, you now have an even worse problem. The pup may start flopping around on his leash like a panicked marlin, you may not be able to regain control and he'll lose trust in you by the instant. Physically placing a dog into a "sit" or a "down" also puts your face close to the dog's mouth at a moment when you're applying pressure and trying to make him do something he doesn't want. And this could be a bite risk, especially for children. Never let children train pups using physical placement. Instead, we urge families to try the "wait the dog out" method or the "walk around in a circle" method described below if your pup ever disobeys "sit" or other commands.

And, because other methods of physically placing a puppy could be so potentially harmful, if you try the "scoop" method of placement and it doesn't work, you should either try the non-physical methods below or consult a local trainer who is expert in gentle training and dog physiology.

Safer ways to enforce the "sit" if your pup won't obey:
Never repeat a command a second time if your dog doesn't obey it the first time, and never beg or plead, which is a common mistake. Instead, try:
a.) the "wait the dog out" method:
Wait the puppy out and he may come around and do the command in a few moments. This gives you the "last word" and ingrains the obedience even deeper in the pup's mind. This is Emma's favorite technique, and it's surprisingly effective.
Or you can try:
b.) the "walk around in a circle" method:
This is a safe and effective method so you never have to repeat a command and let your pup get the "last word". It is also the best method when children are training. If you ever give your pup a command and he won't listen, simply take him for a little walk around in a circle, either on or off leash. This breaks the chain of thought and distracts him, so defiance

won't be uppermost in his mind. Then just give the command again. If he doesn't obey this time, walk around again and then try commanding again. Or give a different command to get a success and then go back to the command you're trying to train.

Is it safe for children to teach the sit and other commands?

The degree to which children should train dogs depends on the maturity and physical discretion of the particular child and pup. We once let a mature two and a half year-old train indoor obedience with a sweet Standard Poodle pup that was larger than she was. But we've told also other some parents that their twelve year olds weren't yet ready to teach certain commands.

One general rule we believe in is that children should only teach "good" commands. Attempting any command or correction that puts a child and dog in a conflict of dominance or leadership is too risky. (For example, your young children should not have to remove a reluctant dog from your couch.) Some dog trainers instruct children to use forceful commands and to physically correct dogs, but we never take chances like this. "Sit" is a "good" command and you can easily teach it to normal non-aggressive pups without a struggle as long as you don't try physical positioning. So we usually allow children of all ages to teach the command using the "luring" or "capturing" methods while adults supervise.

For safety, don't allow children to attempt the "positioning" method of training any command, especially with larger pups. Parents should also carefully observe whether their child can safely control treats during training. Some pups try to jump at children to "steal" treats, and some younger children are still developing their coordination, so it's hard for them to keep treats hidden. A hungry pup can even knock a young child off their feet! If you notice your young child having problems holding treats while keeping the pup back effectively, you should step in. You can still allow the child to give the command, but you should hold onto the treats, encouraging the pup to act calmer.

This caution refers only to pups that are overexcited or pushy. If your pup ever shows the slightest sign of true aggression around food, treats or toys (such as growling or showing teeth) as opposed to just jumping or slobbering greedily, you can no longer risk children using treats or food with this dog until you first get the advice of a high-level animal behaviorist.

Hint: Rather than having to bend again and again to introduce new commands to small pups or toy breeds, you can sit on a low surface like a chaise lounge, an ottoman, a step or even on the floor. Don't sit on the floor if your pup is large and has a habit of trampling people. And being in a low position with any potentially aggressive dog is dangerous. But you should not train aggressive pups at all without high-level professional help. And, while you can start training commands when sitting, once your pup learns, you should also practice standing at your full height.

3. Training (Lie) "Down"

Why it's important: The "down" command tends to make your dog submissive, respectful and non-aggressive; it prevents dominant behavior and eases thoughts of aggression between dogs. Although it is not a solution in itself, willingly lying down in a relaxed fashion is a peaceable move that tends to be incompatible with aggression and troublemaking. (Note: Don't confuse your pup. The formal "down" command used in standard obedience is *not* the same command as "off", which is the command you should always use if you want him to get down off furniture, or stop jumping on a person…)

Difficulty level: Surprisingly difficult to get the physical mechanics right and to get some dogs to willingly lie down. This is the hardest of the basic commands to train. It is at least 5X's harder to train than "sit" and could be much harder with some dogs.

Instructions for teaching "Down": As opposed to training "sit", training the "down" command (in which a dog lies down on the floor) is not always easy. Frequently a dog or pup will initially resist lying down on command because he has problems trusting humans, or because he has some unresolved dominance issues. But, if an owner succeeds at getting the pup to *willingly* lie down enough times on command when he is young, this can produce a lasting personality change. As an adult the dog will act more peaceable, more willing to calm himself before leaping into action without your permission and more respectful of you, his owner.

Another reason the "down" command can be challenging is that the body mechanics of teaching it can be difficult and sometimes dogs won't lie down if they are in pain or physically uncomfortable. For these reasons it's best to avoid teaching the "down" by physically positioning your dog- he could get resistant and a power struggle between you could eventually cause him to bite. And it's often tricky for owners to position "slippery" young puppies properly without hurting them.

It is, however, possible to teach, or reinforce the "down" when a dog doesn't obey the first time by physically positioning the dog. (Our backs ache when we think about it, and we rarely do it, but it *is* possible). To physically place your pup in a "down", first have him sit. Then position yourself at his side on one knee and slip one forearm under both his front paws, while simultaneously slightly lifting, lowering and sliding him forward until he drops into a lying down position. Keep your other arm curved around his rump and shoulder blades so he does not slip or crawl back or try to "duck" away. When your dog is down, you can lay your hand down *gently* on the "saddle" area of his shoulder blades for a moment so he does not immediately pop back up.

We really don't advocate physically position for first training the "down", but the instructions above are safer than pushing down on your pup in ways that might really hurt him. If you feel you must use the physical method of placement, keep your face safely averted from your pup's teeth and never push too hard. Instead, we strongly recommend teaching with the "luring" and "capturing" methods described below.

Training the "down" by "luring":

Training the "down" by "luring" is a little trickier than luring for the "sit" and some pups and their owners may struggle a bit. If the session goes nowhere after 10-20 minutes, give your pup another command he can easily master like "sit" or "look", get a few positive results, end on a high note and then try again later. Be patient. Teaching "down" is *not* impossible, it doesn't require a professional trainer and it's highly important, so gently persevere. Teaching "down" is easy with some dogs. But those dogs that refuse to lie down on your voice command are the ones that need to the most. If you can't get your pup to obey this command when he's young, it will guarantee defiance and behavior problems like pulling on leash and acting bad around other dogs when he grows up.

Before teaching your pup "down" by luring, you must first have him sit, otherwise luring is practically impossible. So consult the instructions in this Chapter for training "sit" if your pup doesn't know this command.

Obedience instructors always demonstrate standing up in group rings to train the "down" command. We're guessing they get a lot of backaches and other body aches because teaching "down" for the first time isn't easy, and it is even harder when you have to repeatedly bend or get down on one knee. As easier alternative at home when you first train "down" is to sit on the edge of a low piece of furniture, or even on the floor, with your pup facing you either on leash or off leash. (But if your pup is a possible bite risk, NEVER attempt to train him from a low position before seeking professional help.)

To teach your pup "down" by luring, first give the "sit" command to indicate that it's time to pay attention. And, to get the body mechanics of luring right, your pup will have to be sitting before you start.

Once your pup is sitting, you will now "lure" him into a lying down position using a treat. **You must make your movements exactly right to work with the pup's body mechanics.** First, get the pup's attention on the treat close up in front of his face. Almost smoosh the treat in towards him (his eyes should almost cross) but don't let him back out of the "sit". If the pup gets up you must have him sit again before proceeding.

Next, with the treat in front of your pup's face and his eyes and nose fixed on it, start moving the treat down to his chest so that he tucks his head with his nose bending for it. This "scrunches" the pup back on himself so his weight is still on his rump as he sits, but the pressure of his front paws on the floor seems to lighten up a little (you may even observe him lift one paw delicately).

Keep your movements fluid and deliberate and don't stop. Move the treat all the way down to the floor close in to the pup's body, in such a way that he does not stand back up. Now, with the treat almost touching the floor, and your pup's nose pointed down towards it between his legs, still in the same fluid and deliberate movement, slide the treat forward along the floor towards you. Your pup's nose should go with the treat as though it is glued to it. Now, as his face goes forward a little bit to follow the treat, he will flop forward (seeming to crawl) with one paw and then the next. And then he is "down".

Don't allow him to pop back up! Keep the treat in close by the ground and let him eat it while you praise him. Only give the treat if he gets into position successfully.

Then allow him to move around a bit and then put him in a "sit" again. Now practice luring him into a down position again. You will simply use the treat to lure the pup into the "down" position the first few times, until he gets accustomed to the movement.

Once he does, and you both get the body mechanics right, start saying the word "down" the second he lies down, simultaneous with giving him the treat. Practice this way a few times.

Now command "down" first and then lure him. When he gets it right say, "good down!" and smile, praise or pet him lightly (but not too wildly). And practice this way a few times.

Next, you will still let your pup see you have the treat, but stop using it to lure. Some people tuck the treat away and lure with their hands and this tends to work, but it could set a bad precedent. Instead, you can simply hide the treat and then just give the voice command "down" and wait. If your pup doesn't lie down immediately, you can walk him around in a little circle and start again, or physically position him (not our favorite method) or go back to luring him with the treat. If he still can't get it after quite a few attempts, you still want to end the session on a high note. So give him a command for "sit", "look" or any trick that he's good at, allow him to perform it successfully, give him a treat and praise and then end the session and try teaching the "down" again later.

Once your pup is weaned off following the treat to get in position and he will consistently lie down just on your voice command, you should stand up straight and give the command from this position, without ever having to bend to his level. **Many owners hang up at this phase and they forever have to bend or touch the ground to lure their dog to go down. Unfortunately, this is a dog that still lacks trust and healthy submission, so you must get past this point.** Sometimes training your dog to lie down on your voice command without the pointing, crouching, bending, luring only takes being patient and waiting him out.

At other times you may have difficulty getting over this hump and/or you might just not be coordinated enough to get the luring motion right without your pup bouncing back up so many times it threatens to drive you crazy. That is why "capturing" (waiting to first reward until the animal does it on his own) is a lifesaver with the "down".

Training "down" by capturing:

If you cannot comfortably teach your dog to lie down in any other way, simply wait it out. Most pups lie down frequently (although it may not seem like it!) To "capture" a down, the second your difficult-to-teach pup lies down, immediately light up with joy and say, "down; good down!" as you instantaneously shove a highly tasty treat right into his little lips. Your pup may be surprised, but he won't complain. Now lure him into position with another treat as described above, while saying, "Down".

If it doesn't work, walk around with him, shake it off and wait for him to lie down on his own once again. Then immediately give him intense praise and a yummy treat the moment he lies down. When teaching the "down" by capturing (as opposed to luring) you don't have to wait for your pup to sit first. Simply repeat as necessary, rewarding the pup and saying "good down" every time he lies down on his own until he starts to associate the voice command with lying down and then he starts to lie down on command for treats.

Once your pup is performing the "down" reliably, follow the same instructions for the "sit'. Reduce treats to an intermittent schedule and increase environmental distractions. **Practicing the "down" command around other nice dogs when your dog is a young puppy is especially important, because lying down together on an owner's command tends to make dogs more peaceable together.**

And don't forget to use the "down" command many times per day in real-life situations because this will make your puppy much more controllable in his future. Also, occasionally rest your hand softly on your pup's back to keep him in the "down" for a few minutes if possible. Don't press down hard or fight with the pup however. Your energy, more than the light pressure of your hand, should keep your puppy wanting to lie beside you. And this will make him a calmer and more law abiding canine citizen in future.

If all techniques fail and you're at your wit's end because your pup keeps leaping around wildly, giving him some vigorous exercise to burn off energy can make him more amenable to lying down. A trick like this can sometimes break the ice and make this otherwise hard-to-teach command much easier.

Hint: Another method that often works to train "down" for the first time is "luring" off the edge of a step. Have your pup sit on a landing so all his body weight rests there, but his face can hang over. The step enables you to put the treat so low in front of him (even lower than his paws) that he must lean down to get it. This technique often helps with body mechanics, especially with the small breeds.

4. Training "Stay"

Why it's important:
This standard show obedience command teaches your pup the priceless concept of what it feels like to willingly hold his body in one place and not move until his owner tells him to. For some pups that seem to bounce off walls, just experiencing themselves in this unfamiliar calm and relaxed state can completely alter their personality for better mental health. And a dog that will "stay" until you release him from the command is less likely to run away or to take liberties like frightening your guests. Some owners crave so badly for their hyperactive pup to stay still for just a second that when they see him do it, they feel like they are in the presence of magic.

Difficulty level: Relatively easy in most situations.

Instructions for teaching "Stay":

First, make this command easy on yourself by making sure that your puppy has no pressing reason *not* to stay still- no hunger, thirst or intense urge to potty. Take your pup outside first and let him empty bowels and bladder and burn off some energy with a walk or a play session. Then fill your pockets with some non-allergenic training treats, bring the pup inside or to wherever you want to train him, get his attention with a command like "Look" and then practice some of the obedience commands he already knows to "warm up" and let him know that it is now time for his learning session for the day.

You can teach your pup to "stay" from either a sitting or lying down position. You'll usually have more success with your pup lying down but some dogs do better when sitting.

Once the pup has willingly put himself in either a "sit" or a "down" position at your command, stand in front of him facing him, *center your mind*, look him straight in the eye, outstretch your arm and lift one open palm in front of him, fingers pointed up in the commonly recognized pantomime symbol for "stay". It should look as though, with your open palm, you are creating a flat surface to push the pup back, or hold him off with. Rather than using any physical power to make your pup stay, you will use your tone of voice and the power of your mind.

It is essential that you focus completely and believe 100% that just through the energy of your mind you will be able to keep your pup staying for as long as you want him to. (This is the trick to how Emma & Ray teach the command, and it's why we almost never lose dogs from a "stay", even the very first time.)

As your pup notices you holding out your hand in the universal "stay" ("stay back") gesture, and as your mind reaches its peak of concentration, now command your pup, only one once "Stay…."

There's a special way you must give the "stay" command and, if your pup hops up to follow you, the most likely reason is that you did not use the proper tone (or body language). Think of a "stay" command as just the opposite of a "come" command. When you call your pup to come, you want to use a quick high excited voice that will stimulate your pup to come towards you. In contrast, when you say "Stay", you want to make your pup so sleepy and sluggish that he feels hypnotized. You also want him to feel that you've had an effect on his body - perhaps by encasing it in cement- so he couldn't move from his sitting or lying position no matter how much he wanted to.

The voice you should use for the "Stay" command is slow, low and confident and when you do it correctly, it should take you a few seconds longer to utter this command than any other. If you lose focus, so will your pup.

Say "stay" only once. If you repeat it multiple times, it may overexcite your pup so he'll mistakenly come running. And don't confuse your pup by saying his name right before saying "stay" because he might think you want him to come running.

To teach the "stay" command, you must believe you can hold your pup back from moving with only your voice, even if nothing has ever made him stay still before. Say "stay" and, once your puppy locks his attention on you, gazing at you with obvious interest combined with bodily lethargy and eyelids already starting to droop, smoothly take a step or two back, leaving him sitting or lying where he is. Move back slowly- otherwise you risk sparking the pup's natural chase instinct. And be careful, so you don't trip as you keep your eyes and your focus locked on your pup.

Take no more than 2, 3 or 4 small steps back when you first start teaching, to make the exercise easy and to get some immediate success that your pup can later build on. And stack the deck for success. For your pup to quickly learn the meaning of the new "stay" command, at first you should return to him, praise and reward after even the smallest amount of time he remains "staying", even if it's just seconds. (Remaining in the "stay" for 3 seconds can actually feel like progress for certain hyperactive pups whose owners have never witnessed them stay still at all.)

Decide how and when to release your pup based on what he seems ready for. On your very first practice session, we don't recommend talking to the pup, smiling at him or even intently staring into his eyes because these actions might confuse him and make him think you want him to break the "stay". But it's a myth that you can't look at or talk to your dog at all while he's in a "stay". If you speak in a slow, steady, hypnotic and quiet tone you should be able to verbally praise him as he remains "staying". Even though you speak, your pup should still know to remain "staying' as you've commanded until you formally release him. After the pup learns the meaning of "stay", he should also be able to remain in position even if you talk quietly and calmly to someone else in the room.

On his first few practices, it's easiest to keep the pup right out in front of you. But as the pup gets better at staying, you can start walking around him in a semi-circle to make staying more challenging.

On your first session, you only need to wait several beats while the pup remains in the "stay" and then you can release him with one of two techniques- you can either call him to you or you can go to him and then release him.

If you ever observe Emma & Ray teaching the "stay", you'll notice that, although we stick to all other instructions consistently, we favor two different ways of releasing dogs from "stays". Both these methods have merit; and it's best to alternate both while training.

Two options for releasing your pup from a "Stay":

1. Returning to your pup to release him from the "Stay":

One method to release a dog from a "stay" is to return to him, pet him and excitedly say "okay" or whatever word you've assigned to release him. You can also make a gesture like tapping on your leg eagerly to get him moving along with you. Or, if he's on leash you can return to him, praise him and then just walk him forward with you.

2. Calling your pup to release him from a "Stay":

The alternate method to release a dog from a "stay" is to call his name, followed by "okay, come" whenever you feel he has stayed long enough.

We recommend that pet parents alternate both the "returning" and "calling" methods to release their pups from "stays" to keep things interesting and challenging.

Slowly increase how difficult it is for your pup to "stay" by increasing the time, leaving the room, going outside, adding distractions or practicing with other dogs:

Whenever your puppy gets good at a command, you should always reach for more. So each time you practice the stay, you can subtly change one element to make the command more challenging. But don't add more than one new challenge at one time. At each practice session, increase either duration, distractions or distance just to the point that your puppy can succeed and end the session on a high note. Then, tomorrow, you can make the task just a tiny bit harder. This makes training more interesting for dog and owners, and it builds a dog that will obey obedience commands even in the most challenging real-life situations.

a. Increasing the length of the "Stay":

This is the simplest way to increase the challenge, especially if your pup is young, because young pups tend to have a naturally short attention span. You should appreciate if a really tiny puppy (8-12 weeks) can remain in a stay for even a few minutes. So don't expect too much. But, especially at 16 weeks and above, the longer your pup can comfortably remain in a "stay" the better, because it builds self-control and an overall more serene and cerebral personality.

Some adult dogs can remain in a "stay" for as long as ½ hour at a time (think of the dogs you used to see waiting for their owners, untied, outside grocery stores). And, in the show ring, a whole line of dogs must wait for 10 minutes without moving from their "stays" even while all the owners leave the ring and go out of sight and hundreds of spectators and their dogs stare at the lineup. Any 6 month puppy that you practice with for a while should be able to comfortably hold his stay for at least 10 minutes, even if you go out of the room. Just build up in small increments and never force the pup to do more than what he's comfortable with.

b. Vanishing from sight:

Another way to increase the challenge of the "stay", as mentioned above, is to vanish from sight. Don't go far. Hide just around a doorway, or someplace you can peek at your puppy. While he "stays" he is allowed to move around a little and stretch, yawn or lick his paws. But he should still be in the same exact spot you left him when you return. Make this easier by only practicing for very short amounts of time at first.

c. Practicing the "Stay" outdoors:

Practicing outdoors with your pup increases the challenge of the "stay" tremendously, because the pup may feel overwhelmed and overexcited by all the outdoor stimuli- smells, sights and sounds that his owners may not even be able to detect. But having your pup master this challenge is important, because you'll always want to be able to control him outdoors. No matter how well your pup has been doing with his "stays" inside, expect it to suddenly be harder to achieve even minutes of staying still outdoors. But keep practicing, and soon your pup will have no problem "staying" when you ask him to outdoors.

d. Adding distractions:

This can be fun to practice, and you can enlist your kids' help. While one handler puts the pup in his usual "stay" their helper can act as a distractor, making silly faces and sounds or jogging around the perimeter of the room. As with other challenges, first start with something easy, like just having a family member walk into the room and cross between you and the dog. Eventually, as your pup's focus and ability to remain in the "stay" for longer periods increases, you can think up tougher challenges. **Your distractor could jog around the perimeter of the room or they could walk or jog another dog past your pup while he remains in a "stay"**. Combining distractions like this with an outdoor setting makes the challenge even harder.

Hint: Practicing "stay" with another dog: Having your pup practice his "Stay" in a down position with another dog lying down beside him is very important exercise that builds future peace and tranquility between the two dogs. If you own two dogs, or if you host play dates (as described in Part 4) you should frequently practice this exercise.

5. Training "Come" or Recall

Why this is important: The recall is perhaps the most important command for your pup to learn, and you should start teaching it from the first moment he arrives at your home. The goal is for your pup to obey 100% perfectly, coming to you immediately and happily every single time you call him no matter the distractions. Any less obedience to this command could someday cost your dog his life.

Difficulty level: Moderately- highly difficult for some families. The younger your pup is when you start, the easier it is to train.

Instructions for teaching "Come":

If you want to trust your dog to remain glued to your side off-leash and always come back to you, no matter the distractions, you must lay the right groundwork. Many factors including breeding and early husbandry can influence whether your pup can be trusted not to run away as an adult. But if you fail to teach your pup to "come" to you properly in his early weeks, or give him any reason not to like to coming to people, it can make him not want to come to you consistently when he's older. All family members should be consistent, and never make mistakes when calling the pup.

How consistently your pup comes when you call him is also a barometer of the health of communication and respect between dog and owner. It's surprising how quickly other important aspects of the dog/owner relationship fall into place when owners start laying groundwork for a successful recall. When you put in a lot of effort and get the "come" command right, you will likely start to see many other major behavior problems vanish as well.

1. Practice the recall in short sessions throughout the day:

Practice calling your pup to you hundreds of times a day and give him positive feedback each time he obeys. A pup can burn out if you try to teach the recall in overly long formal practice sessions and this will defeat the purpose of the command. Instead, call your pup to you spontaneously during the day and reward him with a food treat, a toy or a pleasurable activity like going out for a walk. But most often, the reward should be your praise and attention.

2. The number of repetitions determines how deeply the recall response becomes ingrained in your pup's personality, so allow enough time to practice:

If your pup spends too much time isolated from human contact- such as many pups that are excessively crated- he'll never get enough repetitions to make the reflex to come humans a critical aspect of his personality. But, **as long as your family spends enough time interacting with your pup, you can easily give him many successful repetitions.**

3. To make your pup want to come to you more, change when you give him attention:

Never give "free" attention when your pup comes to you and acts pushy (even though he may seem cute). If a dog gets "free" attention whenever he wants it, then he won't crave the attention as much when he is called and he may choose not to listen to you. Make a habit of ignoring the pup whenever he acts pushy. Instead, pointedly call him at times when *you* want him, and then give him lots of loving attention when he obeys. Overall, this change in response won't mean that your pup gets any less love, attention, interaction, praise or petting. The only difference is that the pup will learn not to constantly annoy and stress you, but instead to perk up and come quickly when you call.

4. Your pup should never experience ignoring your command to "come":

He must learn, in his deepest identity, that when his owner calls, he immediately comes, and nothing else is possible. Every single time a pup experiences himself refusing to come to a human when he's young, it breaks down his reflexive obedience response. This unfortunately also includes anything that happened at your pup's breeder or former homes.

There are several effective ways (and one potentially damaging way that's still popular with some trainers) to make sure your pup never fails to come to you every time you call:

a. How to train the recall on-leash to reinforce the command:

Leash your pup and have a helper hold your pup lightly. Then step back and call the pup's name in an upbeat voice, followed by "Come!" You can tap your leg, make little kissing sounds, bend low and/or jog backward. All of these things get your pup excited and make him instinctively want to follow. Have a treat ready, but don't show it unless you need to.

If the pup ignores you or acts distracted, and all your excited antics and showing him the treat don't work, gently reel him in towards you with the leash to get him moving. Most pups won't need to be reeled in if you stay close and then act very excited and upbeat as you call. But each time you practice calling him, your pup should find himself by you, whether he got there on his own or with a little gentle encouragement from the leash.

Once your pup reaches you, the very first thing you should do is to lightly grab onto his collar for just a second. (This teaches your pup it's okay to let you take his collar, so he won't "dance" away from you or play games in real situations when he's loose). After you make this contact with his collar, praise and/or pet the pup lavishly and reward him with an especially tasty treat. **Next hold the pup, toss the end of the leash to the helper and have your helper call him.** When he gets to her, she should touch his collar and then reward him with praise and a treat.

Next, repeat the process a few times, alternating who calls the pup and who holds him. Always end the session on a happy, successful note. This exercise can also work with multiple people arranged in a triangle or a circle (see "#40 Learn to Come to Everyone" in Part 3, Activities).

After your pup succeeds on a short six-foot leash, practice on a full-width long lead of approximately thirty feet (not an extend-a-lead, which can be dangerous). You can even hook several long leads together, or use a clothesline with hooks attached to both ends, so that your pup is now coming to you from 60 or 90 feet away.

b. Never utter the specific word "come" unless you can make sure your pup follows through; use alternate ways of calling him when you are not sure of his response:

At first, keep a line attached to your pup whenever you use the specific word "come" to call him. And only remove the line once he's already successful come to you hundreds of times on-leash with no failures.

Indoors, when your pup is off-leash, you should still call him to you many times a day, but don't use the specific word "come" until he's already performed hundreds of perfect repetitions on-leash. Before your pup learns the specific "come" command, when you call him for practical reasons, simply use his name, a kissing or clicking sound, words like, "baby, baby, baby", "here, puppy", clapping your hands together or any way you can call him without using the specific term "come". Only use the specific word "come" when you are ready to follow through by using the line or when you've practiced enough that you are sure your pup won't fail.

Ideally, the command "come" should become a magic word, so that if your pup ever hears the word uttered once, he won't debate; he'll simply rush to you immediately.

c. **Aversive methods of training the recall to avoid:**

The alternative way to train the recall is something that we, and many pet parents, consider cruel, yet it is still the accepted method among many dog trainers (and what your pup might experience if you send him away for advanced obedience training at certain facilities). These trainers want owners to put an electronic shock collar (euphemistically called an e-collar) on your pup, let him get a distance away from you, then start zapping with the painful shock, call him and only stop electrocuting him when he turns to come to you! If the trainer is ethical, they will wait until after 6 months to use the shock collar to prevent physical damage to the pup.

But we, and most pet parents we know, think that hurting a dog with shock is always cruel, at any age. Six months is also too late to start training a recall. Little pups should start practicing happily coming to people hundreds of times a day from the time they are 8 weeks (or even earlier if you are the breeder).

In the past many dog trainers have historically used shock collar methods with apparent success, including with some high profile working dogs. But, unfortunately, shock collar training can backfire in many ways and it frequently brings out fear and aggression in susceptible dogs. In other cases, dogs that have been shocked learn to be savvy and they only mind the handler when they know the collar is working and the handler is holding the remote. Often this creates problems for the average suburban family.

We personally feel more secure training our pups to come to us in the same way we'd teach children- not using fear or aversive methods- but teaching youngsters that listening to Mommy and Daddy is always in their best interest.

Other trainers don't use shock collars, but they use other aversive methods, like throwing a choke collar or a balled up sock at the pup if he doesn't turn back and come to them when they call. The trainer tries to throw the item so the dog only associates the negative stimulus with his actions rather than with people in general. But timing this can be quite difficult and it doesn't always get results. And while we understand the rationale behind methods like throwing the balled up sock, these methods are tough to execute correctly without alienating the dog. We find that our methods, based in everyday practice and 100% consistency, make much more sense. These methods work with a pup's psychology and instinctive nature to make him *want* to come to you.

5. Practicing the recall off-leash:

Once several days or weeks pass, and your pup comes to you hundreds of times successfully from a long distance on the leash, start practicing without a leash in a safe enclosed area, like a fenced yard. Reduce the distance between you and your pup so that you're quite close together like when you first started training the on-leash recall. Take your pup's leash off and have a helper hold him or put him in a "stay". Then call him, using his name followed by the command, "Come!"

Offer a really great food reward, like pieces of hamburger, chicken or cheese that your pup can smell from a distance (if he's not allergic). **It's essential that, if you use the word "come", then your pup must always come.** And, since you'll only be training with gentle methods (unlike the cruel methods described later in this chapter) it's essential that you act very compelling to make him want to come to you. When you start practicing you should only be a few feet apart. You should act eager and excited and offer either extra special treats or irresistible toys like squeaky toys if your pup prefers these.

If your pup comes to you obediently, reward him as described above and continue practicing off lead, gradually increasing your distances apart. But, if he fails to come twice in a row, clip the lead back on and continue practicing on the leash again until his recall gets stronger. Then try off-leash again. Keep alternating if necessary until your pup successfully comes to you off leash every time.

All owners should also practice the off-leash recall indoors frequently each day with their young puppies, especially if they don't have a fenced yard. **Also practice the recall occasionally when your dog matures.** This is not hard, since people call their dogs all the time. Just make sure the dog always comes obediently the first time you call. **If he starts to get a little lax, go back and repeat the techniques in this chapter.**

Refusal to come is often the first indicator that serious problems such as aggression could soon show up, especially if the pup just came into his full sexual maturity and temperament at a year or 18 months. But going back to basics and getting the dog coming to you reliably again can often remind him to respect you and head off future behavior problems without any need for conflict.

Where to practice off-leash exercises:

For safety, practice all off-lead exercises in enclosed areas, like fenced yards, pastures or ballfields. Your pup could be killed if he's left free in an unfenced area, and it could also violate the law.

But even if you never intend to have your dog free in public places, every dog must learn a perfect off-leash recall, so that he'll always come back to you in any situation that might come up. And every owner should be able to control their dog 100% by voice, even if the dog gets out the door or breaks his leash- to prevent the tragedies that can occur if a dog is not perfectly off-leash trained. Under normal circumstances, you do *not* need a professional trainer to help you with this training. You can do it yourself if you are careful and consistent.

The ideal place to practice off-leash recalls and obedience is a large fenced property or somewhere like a ballfield, where your pup will be safely enclosed, yet feel free. Practice with your pup in the largest contained area available. If you can't find an area like this, then use the longest lead, rope or clothesline you can find to simulate a feeling of freedom- just make sure the pup does not entangle his, or your, legs.

Also try practicing recalls and other obedience on the long line in areas like public parks or town squares where the pup is exposed to a large number of people, dogs, bicyclists, cars, buses and everyday distractions. The long line will give control of the pup in an emergency but meanwhile the pup learns to control himself perfectly.

You may wish to practice your recall in an enclosed dog park, thinking this would be the ideal space and also include distractions. While it is a matter of personal choice, we discourage dog park visits because of certain irresponsible owners who bring diseased or aggressive dogs. You might get lucky and your pup could have some great times at a dog park. On the other hand, a single attack, bullying experience or exposure to disease might damage your pup for life. If you do go, seek out the emptiest, cleanest and safest at off-hours, and ask your vet if your pup's immunity is sufficient.

6. Practicing the recall around distractions:

When you are sure your pup will come to you 100% successfully off-leash without distractions, go back to on-lead and start increasing distractions like guests, children playing or other dogs. Start with a mild distraction that is located quite far away from you (perhaps a dog in a neighbor's yard). When your pup demonstrates multiple successes coming to you with the distraction present, take off the lead and practice calling him while he is exposed to the same mild distraction. Next, try a stronger distraction when he is on the lead. Then practice calling him around the stronger distraction when he is off-lead.

7. In order to make kind methods of teaching the recall work, you must stay 100% consistent. And your pup must never experience anything negative after you call him:

a. Never yell at your pup meanly when you call him to "come". Always use the word in an eager, positive tone. Don't ever beg or plead, because this sends an inconsistent message. You should use a calmly assertive tone, just as you would with a child for an important command. **But if you ever sound like a Nazi while calling your pup, you may have ruined your pup for life.** (This is also why you never want to expose him to any dog trainer who sounds at all aggressive, impatient or threatening.)

b. Never call "come" and then grab your puppy and hurt or scare him.

This may sound like something most owners would never do, yet many people do exactly this when they notice their pup had a bowel or bladder accident. They call "come" and then they correct him quite intensely for the accident, scruffing him and hurrying him outside, yelling at him, or even rubbing his nose in the waste. This pup may have forgotten when he had the accident several hours before, but he'll never forget what happened when he responded to your "come" command- and he might be frightened about coming when you call him in future.

c. Even if your pup runs away from you, if he *does* eventually come back, you must act nice, or at least civil. If you punish your pup when he comes back, he may learn to fear coming to you.

Sometimes kids get frustrated and impatient and raise their voices while calling "come" and simultaneously trying to catch the puppy. And adults can get too "handsy", bellowing "come" and wildly trying to catch a feisty little small breed that tries to escape them under every piece of furniture. This can be a potentially traumatic experience for the dog.

Even petting and play, often by children, can be too rough and wild and this can make a sensitive pup act flinchy and not to want to come to people. Pups that came from previous abuse, such as puppy mill survivors (like most pups purchased from pet shops and over the Internet) are especially nervous about being grabbed and manhandled. Yet if you back off and use an upbeat tone and really appealing rewards it can "magically" start making your pup come when you call.

Never use the word "come" if you need to do something to your pup that he doesn't enjoy (for example, claw clipping). Instead, calmly and silently lift him up and/or clip on his leash. Only associate the word "come" with good things. And don't forget to withhold your attention when he pushes on you so he'll have to come when you call. Even though this is the command many families struggle with the most, it can soon become your favorite command to practice.

Hint: For distance, teach your pup to come to a sound like a whistle. First blow the whistle and hand the pup a treat each time you do it to "heat it up". Then blow the whistle from increasing distances and reward your pup when he comes.

6. Training "Look"

Why it's important: When your dog looks in your eyes at your command, it can focus him and prevent him from overreacting to outside stimuli.

Teaching your pup to "Look", or gaze into your eyes and concentrate on you completely, may be the first command a pup should learn, even before "sit". Focusing on you keeps the pup from running after every distraction. This makes it easier for him to care for you, anticipate your needs and follow your instructions. This increases bonding and makes owners feel infinitely more empowered.

Many owners complain about pups that won't listen to them, focus on them or pay attention to them. Unfortunately, owners and their dogs caught in this cycle of frustration can sometimes spend years without really connecting. But the "Look" command (sometimes also referred to as "Watch Me" or "Look at Me") **can provide the first connection between owner and puppy, and the first indication the pup is paying attention and is ready to work with other commands.**

Learning to look to their owners on command is tremendously helpful for every puppy, including those that are shy, hyperactive or those that overreact when they see outside stimuli like other dogs. The "Look" command centers and soothes problem dogs of every size and age and you can use it regardless of any physical limitations on the part of owner or dog.

You can practice "Look" any place, any time and as frequently as you like in everyday situations with your pup. The more you and your family practice "Look" with your young puppy, the better. This is truly an all purpose command with no downside, and sometimes it's the best command to initially get the attention of a dog that won't focus or won't keep his body still.

For owners, such as first–time owners, who have doubts about their capability to work with their dog, succeeding at this tremendously easy, yet incredibly meaningful, command will immediately build confidence and rebuild their faith in dogdom. When done properly, a dog practicing "Look" resembles a show dog staring up at his handler. And, when you teach your antsy little puppy to "Look", he may surprise you with how attentive he suddenly becomes, making clear that he just craves to work for you.

Difficulty Level: Medium to highly difficult to train; but more difficulty is a sign you absolutely need this command to control your pup's behavior. This is not a good command for young kids to teach.

Instructions for training your pup to "Look" at you on command:

When your pup is relatively calm bring him in front of you, on or off leash, as you stand facing him. Most people first tell their pup to sit, but he can also stand or lie down. You will be teaching your pup to look into your eyes on command to receive a reward. **After enough practice, your pup will learn to focus on you on command whenever you want him to, even if a herd of bison rushes by the two of you on the street!**

Just like with the "Sit" command, you can train "Look" by "capturing" the action. When training this way, you keep the treat (or toy) hidden and the second that your pup's eyes flicker and meet yours, you say "Look!" and instantaneously give the pup the treat (or other reward) immediately, along with a smile and praise. Next, command "Look", and the second the pup's eyes go to yours, reward him.

Capturing is an interesting way of training the "Look" command, and we like it for the challenge. But most people prefer not to wait for their pup's eyes to do what they need. Instead, they use **the "luring" method. To do this you hold a treat in your right hand, along with a gesture of holding up a pointed index finger in front of your face with that hand, to lure the pup to look at you until he learns the command.** The official hand signal for the "Look" command is similar to the universal gesture for "Shhh". The difference is that you hold your index finger up over your nose to draw attention to your eyes, and you don't actually touch your face.

The first few times you train "Look", you can start by holding the treat relatively close to the pup's nose and then smoothly move your hand, with the treat in it, up by your face, while making the "shhh-type" gesture with the index finger. This first focus your pup's attention on the treat, and then draw his attention up by your eyes as you move it.

Make sure to keep your face a safe distance from the pup (so that he doesn't lunge for the treat and try to help himself, meanwhile bumping or accidentally toothing your face). Most pups won't try this, because they will be so mesmerized by your new strange behavior. But they may be confused and start jumping around. (So be careful and never let kids teach the command until you are sure of your pup's behavior. And very young children are not usually able to coordinate the treat and the positioning safely.) **Continue standing erect and stay calm and focused until your pup focuses on your face and the treat in front of it. The second he does, instantaneously say "Good look!" and immediately reward him with the treat.**

Timing of your treats/rewards is important for teaching every new command, but teaching the "Look" is one command that depends 100% upon this timing. If you do not get the timing 100% perfect, your poor pup will be 100% confused. The Look" is the most subtle of the commands to teach. Sometimes a very young pup may just flop over because his attention span wears out as you try. But don't let this frustrate you. **All you need to do is to make the clear connection in your pup's mind that one tiny little action- putting his eyes on you- gets a reward.**

Unfortunately, about 75% of owners have just as serious problems understanding the "Look" command as their dogs. Some owners, including many adults, never understand it. Since we cannot demonstrate in person, the next best thing to explain how the command looks and functions is to compare it to when a handler holds up a treat to focus a show dog in a "stack" pose while the judge looks the dog over. If you look carefully, you may even notice a show handler holding the dog treat between their teeth! If you've never seen a dog show, you could do some research online or at your local library or talk to a friend who has shown dogs. Don't bother trying to train the "Look" until you understand exactly what your pup's complete focus on your eyes should look like.

Reward your pup the very second his eyes meet yours on your command. Unfortunately quick moving pups look away just as quickly as they do everything else. But you *must* get the timing of this absolutely right. If you lag, and your puppy glances at you but then quickly looks away and *then* you reward him, you are rewarding the exact wrong behavior. Your pup will think he got rewarded for looking away. To prevent this cardinal sin from happening, if you miss when the pup looks at you and don't give praise and a treat quickly enough, just do nothing. Keep a pleasant attitude and cheerfully try again. This time, be ready to get a treat into the pup's mouth the second he looks at you.

Soon your pup will get good at looking at you to get his rewards. Some dogs are amazingly good and will stare happily into your eyes until you and the dog both feel a little drunk. But make practice sessions with this command very short to keep your pup's interest. When your pup starts performing perfectly, make things more difficult. First, stop putting the treat anywhere near him to lure him. Don't let him see the treat. Just make the gesture by your face with your hand. Then, when he looks at your eyes, reward with the treat that you have been hiding in your other hand. Practice at this level for a while.

Now trick your puppy to go to the next level. Hold out some treats visibly in your left hand while making the "Look" gesture with your right and saying "Look". Most pups will first get a little distracted and frustrated by the treats you are waving around. But then they will eventually glance back to your eyes. **The second the pup's eyes flicker to you, say "Good Look!" while immediately rewarding**. Practicing at this level is a precursor to practicing with him out on the street.

Once you've got your pup looking at you every time on command inside the house no matter what you do to distract him, start phasing treats out, so he only gets them on the best performances or every 2nd, 3rd, 4th or 5th time. Get him accustomed at this level.

Now you can either: 1) move outside or 2) start introducing other family members as handlers. Either change will act as a greater distraction. You and your family should practice "Look" at greater levels of difficulty as frequently as you can with your puppy. Start working outdoors in public places where he will see many strong unexpected distractions like other dogs.

Never make sessions long for this command. From one to five repetitions in a formal session is sufficient, but you can alternate "Look" with other commands, and you can easily practice spontaneously a hundred times a day in real-life situations.

Remember, the ultimate purpose of the "Look" command is to get your dog to focus on you and focus away from distractions anytime you ask, including on walks. The command can distract your dog from living things ranging from kids on bikes, to dogs on walks, to squirrels and chipmunks running under his nose.

But note that the "Look" command in itself is not enough to stop a truly vicious or extremely reactive dog that might hurt people or animals. Consult a qualified trainer or animal behaviorist if suspect your pup might actually injure a person or animal.

The "Look" command is powerful, but not bulletproof:

If you want your dog to focus on you so he won't go after a distraction, you *must* **get his attention** *before* **he "locks and loads" on the distraction in a stiff, alert hunting posture with his ears up and forward. If you delay too long and your dog gets into this posture, you'll have problems getting his attention when you ask him to "look".** At best, you'll look silly. Or at worst, you will be violently dragged off your feet if your 200 lb. St. Bernard sees that squirrel *before* you get his attention with the "Look" command.

Frequent practice sessions where you control the distractions when your pup is young are your best defense. Stage scenarios with distractions you have arranged, such as friends walking by with their dogs. This way you will be sure that your pup always responds to "look" with 100% obedience before you start practicing in real-world situations. After this you can practice with increasingly challenging real distractions and success will tend to build on success.

Teaching the "Look" command when your pup is young will shape him into a dog that will look to you before he gets into real-life trouble. The stronger your control of your dog with this command, the less you'll have to fight his instincts, even in the most challenging situations.

Alternate methods for teaching the "Look" if you are having problems:

1) Reverse the order of commands:
You can teach your pup the "Sit" command first (see #2 in this chapter). Sometimes teaching sit first gets past those pups that remain mysteriously jumpy about "Look". You can even train all the basic commands first and then go back and try teaching "Look".

2) Allow your puppy to let off some steam by moving around
Try some exercise or play to let off steam before the training session. If your pup seems jumpy, leash him and walk him by your side in a few broad circles. Or take him out to empty his bowels or bladder and get a little air. You can even teach "Look" for the first time outdoors or while walking.

3) Try other positions:
Most trainers first teach the "Look" from a sitting position, but you can also mix it up and teach "Look" from a lying or standing position.

Some toy breeds get frightened if they must immediately leave their couch arm or pillow. So you can accomplish your first training of the "Look" there, and then move it down to the ground if possible. Owners with tiny toy breeds who have problems walking or bending can sometimes teach the "Look" command while their dog sits in their lap. This may not be absolutely ideal for perfect behavior, but it works better than giving up obedience entirely if there is no alternative.

4) Try a different reward:
Not all dogs love food treats. So, if your pup doesn't respond to treats immediately, try using a squeaky toy, or other favorite toy, to first train him to "Look".

Troubleshooting if your pup still has problems:

Teaching your pup to "Look" is tremendously easy where there's already a great dog/owner bond. And failure is often a litmus test of whether the handler's behavior is effective with their dog.

In nature, when dogs stare directly at each other it can indicate dominance and disrespect. But a proper execution of the "Look" command is different from a "hard stare". When your dog "looks" on command he should be alert, focused and clearly express that he's watching you for your next instruction. His expression should have a certain energy, freshness and feeling of cooperation about it. And, even though it may feel slightly intimidating for the pup to look into the eyes of his human leader, he should never feel terrified to look when his owner asks him to.

If puppies or dogs are scared of people, they won't look at them:

We work in particular with fearful dogs, some of whom have turned the corner into neurosis or aggression. Sometimes two spouses try obedience commands and the dog will show problems looking into the eyes of the spouse who uses noticeably more intimidating body language and tone of voice. These dogs often have a previous history of a dog trainer intimidating them through harsh voice or roughly yanking on their collars and choking them when they were young. And the spouse the dog won't look at is usually the one who brought the pup to the obedience class and learned the same hard training style. This is because pups often shut down completely and stop listening if they've been frightened.

Of course, if you go to the other end of the spectrum and weakly plead with your pup to look at you, he may realize your heart's not in it, and he'll decline to look at you because he doesn't believe it's important or relevant. So the right way to give the "Look" command is with full confidence and belief that your pup will pay attention, combined with kindness and encouragement.

Children may be too young to teach "Look":

Another time teaching "Look" may not go perfectly is with children who are really too young to train it effectively. Young children often have problems with frustration, lack of understanding or lack of timing. A child who raises his voice petulantly, yelling "Look, look, look!" while making hitting motions at the pup, or who swings around with the treat flying in circles can't get the desired result. And this may just have to do with maturity.

But adults who have problems teaching the "Look" command may have much more serious issues. Even if your pup comes to you from a puppy mill or background of abuse and is afraid looking in human's eyes in general, his new Mom and Dad are usually the best ones to teach him to trust and get him past this highly significant problem.

Once all family members (other than extremely young children) have the pup looking in your eyes on command, you are on the way to success with anything else you ask of the dog in his lifetime. But, until you get it right, you must take the temperature of the dog/owner relationship in your home.

Safety Note: Older kids can practice this overall positive command with nice, non-aggressive pups, ideally small pups. Yet younger kids often lack the timing and coordination to control treats properly without confusion. Even worse, a child could accidentally make a pup jump right at his face with the pup's mouth open trying to get the treat! So, if you want your kids to teach the "Look" command, you should supervise them carefully. Never allow your child to train this command if you have any doubt how the dog and child will work together, especially if the puppy is large and/or jumps a lot. And if you have any suspicion that your pup is maliciously food aggressive (really angry and possessive, not just hungry and drooly) or that he might deliberately snap at your children for any reason, you should protect them from future contact with him until you can get the advice of a qualified animal behaviorist.

Danger: Dominant and possibly aggressive dogs may refuse to look at people:

If you followed all the instructions perfectly and patiently, and you're certain your pup doesn't fear your gestures, verbal tone or intentions, it may be time to question whether the pup has potential serious dominance or aggression issues.

You may have a serious problem if, in addition to refusing to look attentively and happily into your eyes, your pup also: won't react with even a flicker of attention when you call him; won't take food from your hand although he takes it from other spots; pushes past you in doorways; pushes people over or tries to push them off furniture; pulls on leash extremely hard without looking back and sometimes seriously hurts people; knocks children over or runs into kids and never looks into their eyes; just wants to be with other dogs or acts crazy or aggressive with other dogs and shows possessiveness or aggression for objects or spaces by growling or snapping at dogs or people.

Since a dominant dog can perceive humans staring at him as a challenge, if your dog shows a number of the warning signs above, you don't want to stare into his eyes too long. This could lead a potentially aggressive dog to bite. Perhaps because of careless breeding and abusive husbandry in puppy mills these days, a significant number of puppies come to their new homes showing real aggression. If your pup shows possession aggression or a number of the other dominant behaviors above, you may wish to seek the advice of a qualified animal behaviorist before you attempting to teach "Look" or other commands again. They can assess the reason for the pup's behavior and determine if you need their professional help or if you can safely continue teaching obedience on your own.

7. Training "Drop It" & "Leave It"

Important for: The essential "Drop It" command can save your pup's life because he will willingly drop dangerous items at your command; and the "Leave It" command, which keeps your dog from lunging at every forbidden item or passing animal, can save your sanity. "Drop It" is also the basis for training many other skills, ranging from "Fetch" to assisting owners by picking up objects they cannot bend for.

Difficulty level: Moderately to quite difficult. Training "Leave it" requires more finesse than "Drop It". Always train "Drop It" first.

Instructions for training "Drop It":

The cue "Drop It" is a command we feel all owners should teach their puppies. One day this command may save your pup's life by getting him to drop something poisonous before he swallows it. It can also spare your fingers, since you won't physically have to pull dangerous items out of his mouth. Have you ever given an adult dog a bone and then had him refuse to give it back to you? This possessive behavior is dangerous; and owners should be able to take any item out of their dog's mouth at any time. One day the item your pup refuses to drop may be something that could kill him- a chicken bone, a fishhook or a poisonous snake!

Please don't listen to trainers who tell you to take items by force; because this is not the best way to get something out of a dog's mouth. Some dogs may learn to fear you if you use force or intimidation to take things away from them. A dog like this may learn to run from you every time he has something he thinks you may want to take. He may not want to come to you at all and this will undermine the bond between you.

Some dogs have food or possession aggression, and these tendencies can even be present in puppies (although the problems usually show up after sexual maturity). A dog like this needs careful rehabilitation so he'll learn to drop possessions at your command. But suddenly using force against a dog with this problem can be dangerous. And, if you use excessive force or intimidation, this could cause "redirected aggression". Your dog may no longer give *you* problems when you try to take items out of his mouth, but he may suddenly turn on other dogs or other less dominant people- particularly kids.)

Puppies are known to constantly put items in their mouths. Some of these items may be of value to owners. Other items represent a danger to the pup. So owners may instinctively grab for items to try to pull them away from their pup unless they know a better way. But teaching "Drop It" as an alternative is so much easier.

Practice teaching your puppy the command "Drop it" by giving him a fun item that he likes but that does not have an extremely high value to him. After he takes this item and begins chewing on it, show him a particularly yummy treat or item that you know he desires more. As the dog drops the first item to get the more valuable item, tell him "Drop it". Let him eat the treat, praise him, and then give the first item back again. (This way your pup will learn that dropping an item at your command is always a win-win scenario for him, because by giving you what he already has, he can get something better and may even get the first item back.)

Practice multiple times, when he's holding an item you give him. Then test the puppy by spontaneously telling him to "Drop It" at various times around the house, when you see he has an item in his mouth. Each time he willingly drops it for you, say "good!" and immediately reward him with a treat, or another more valuable item. When your puppy gets more and more predictable with the "Drop it," command, you can move on to practice with items the dog holds in higher value.

Practice frequently, and carry some high-value treats with you on walks so that you can start practicing in real-life situations. But do not offer a treat every time. You want the payoff to be unpredictable. You will only offer a treat every so often and eventually your dog will no longer need treats to obey the "drop it" command. Most puppies are very happy to drop items for the reward of their owners' praise and approval. And seeing their pup's delight at dropping potentially dangerous things whenever they tell him to will give caring puppy parents much more confidence and peace of mind when it comes to taking him into real world situations as an adult.

Of course, there is only one thing better than having your pup willingly drop bad items when he's already grabbed them- and this is for him to be willing to ignore those items completely at your command.

Once you have successfully taught your dog the "Drop It" command, you can now teach him "Leave It", the command that should make it so that you can stop him before he goes for things. "Leave It" is a command that makes your dog take his focus away from any item, or animal, that he wants to chase, go after or take in his mouth. For example, if you forgot you left dark chocolate candies (which can be poisonous to dogs) on the coffee table until your pup came in from his grooming appointment and ran straight for them, you could call out "Leave It" in an emphatic voice and he would stop before he ate any. The same would be true if the item on the ground was even more dangerous- broken glass, antifreeze or a coral snake.

Both "Drop It" and "Leave It" are delightfully rewarding commands to teach young pups. But they are obviously highly serious, and no less than 100% compliance is acceptable, because it only takes one bite of something poisonous for your pup to die.

Instructions for Training "Leave It":

Another important way you can use the "Leave It" command is to keep your pup from chasing moving creatures. Some pups and dogs (especially hunting, sporting, terrier, herding and some working dogs) have extremely high "prey drive" or an extremely high instinct to chase after (and possibly hunt down) moving things. You probably know if your pup is like this if he goes crazy chasing after balls you throw or if he is fascinated chasing bugs or lizards in your yard. You may know the familiar "lock and load" posture- a scarily intent level of focus similar to when a pointer "points" at game"). If your pup gets into this posture he looks like he is about ready to spring on something- which could be a ball rolling on the floor, a squirrel streaking across the yard or even your neighbors' beautiful white toy poodle, fresh from the groomers. Whether your pup intends to kill and eat the living thing he is "locked" on, or whether he just intends to pull the leash out of your hands and jump on the animal, making lots of trouble, is something you never want to find out. You may notice that when a dog is already "locked and loaded" it is almost impossible to regain his focus back to you, even if you offer treats. That is why it is important to give your pup "Leave It" command as soon as you can when you first notice him start to focus on an item, or living thing, in an improper fashion.

It's essential to practice extensively until you get the "Leave It" command perfect before there's an emergency. Because, in an emergency, "Leave It" may be your very last line of defense before something physical, even possibly deadly, happens to your pup.

To teach the command, start with a similar set up to the "Drop It" in which you deploy an item that your pup will find attractive, with the intent of getting him to focus away from it and focus on you. The "Leave It" teaches the pup to willingly and happily control his own impulses and desires because his owner wants him to, teaching him to turn away from an item he would usually grab. There are some variations of your set-up depending on which trainer you ask. Ideally, the name of the game is to make your pup make a choice and decide not to take the item he is looking at. The second he makes this choice, you give him either a higher value toy or treat.

Some owners may ask what to do if their pup does *not* choose to turn from the item and, instead, goes for it and eats it. Obviously, you can't let the pup get item because this will teach him that he can take something even when you're telling him not to.

Some trainers teach the command by leaving a treat, a small toy or rawhide on the floor with their hand or foot ready to cover the item in case the pup lunges at it. Then they say "Leave It" and wait. The second the pup breaks his focus on the item and looks away, they say "Good leave it" and reward him with a chance to play with an even better toy, or a bite of a much better treat. Then they repeat the sequence until the pup learns to pull his focus away on command.

The object is not to "lure" the pup with the better treat or toy. In fact, you should keep the reward semi-hidden until the pup removes his focus from the item you want him to. You want the pup to understand that he's not being lured away with the better item. Instead, he's following your command to "Leave" the first item. And only when he's willing to do that will he get his owner's reward and praise.

In another variation, rather than trying to cover the "test" item with hand or foot, you can keep your pup leashed. This way, he's close enough that he can choose to focus or unfocus his attention, but he can't physically grab. Personally, we think this is preferable to having to lunge for the item quicker than your pup does. Either way is an option for puppy owners. Or you can try our personal favorite method. Don't do anything in particular to control the pup or the item physically. Just use a careful choice of item and your own compelling energy to stop the pup without any physical intervention. To do it this way, which can be more challenging at first, choose your test item carefully. It should be something that appeals to the pup, but only very weakly. Put your pup in a "Sit" or a "Down" and then place the item somewhat high up and at a distance a bit more than arm's length, so there's not much chance of the pup actually getting it. Say "Leave It".

Now, watch him with absolute concentration to notice the slightest flicker of his eyes away from the "test" item. Now, timing perfectly, reward him. Do this enough times that he makes the connection between sacrificing his focus on the item and getting an intense reward and amazing love and praise from his beloved owner. Next, move the "test" item a little closer, practice some more. Upon more success, switch the test item out for something a little more appealing. Then practice some more. Upon more success, move it closer…

However you teach "Leave It", make sure you have 100% success under controlled experiments in the home before taking the command outside where you will be testing with real stimuli, like the garden sprinklers, falling leaves, another puppy from the household running by. Only when he's doing well with non-dangerous stimuli will your pup be ready to be tested around more intense distractions like a squirrel running past or your neighbor's pet iguana strolling under his nose.

We stress that you should practice these commands with your young puppy as much as you need to every day to make him perfect. If you have to practice 10, 20 or 50 times a day, it's still worth it. Always be firm and confident when teaching this command, however always be nice. Don't say "Leave It" or "Drop It" and then lash out at martial arts speed for his mouth and wrestle him like a rag doll if he makes a mistake. You must find the perfect balance so that your pup respects you, yet wants to obey you because he knows you as his Mom or Dad and source of all love and resources, not a tyrant to be feared. Even if your pup generally does great with his "Leave It" command, but one day, when you are out on a walk, he makes a mistake and takes something dangerous in his mouth stay calm. Assertively command "Drop It". Since he already knows this command, most likely he will obey.

If, for some reason he does not, you can smoothly cup his muzzle while sliding the item out and away. This works better than "wrestling" or yanking which can cause panic, aggression and, if he's a big pup or dog, the item getting swallowed anyway because you cannot outpower a dog's jaws. Nothing you can do physically can work better for the purpose than the "Leave It" or "Drop It" but, if you've ever been unnecessarily mean or rough when pulling items out of his mouth, it will take longer to practice in the positive fashion to win back his trust. If your dog is still a puppy, however, he will have surprising "bounce back" and, with frequent repetitions with the proper timing and attitude on your part, you may be surprised how willingly your little "vacuum cleaner" or "cat chaser" will abandon desired items at your command.

Hint: Giving the "Leave It" and "Drop It" commands is perhaps the only time in teaching obedience when it's okay for a handler to use a loud tone of voice. In another words, **when you say "Leave It!" or "Drop It!" you should say it with an exclamation point.** Say it like you mean it, and like your pup's compliance is the only thing that matters in the world. Because the truth is, these commands are meant to keep your pup from either hurting a living thing or consuming something deadly. As an example, Emma gives all commands to dogs in a surprisingly levelheaded, quiet and ladylike way, no more intense than everyday conversation. She never raises her voice, with humans or dogs or even when joking around, so sometimes it's easy not to even notice that she's commanding a dog rather than just bonding with it. Because both authors train so gently and easily, owners often relax, lose track of time and become highly tranquil during sessions. But we've seen owners suddenly wake up when Emma gives the "Leave It!" command. Don't be mean, but don't allow a pup to view these commands as optional. If done correctly, your pup will remember you love him even when you are insistent about "Leave It" and "Drop It". Dogs are working animals. Your pup will realize that it's truly important that he drop things when you tell him to and comply happily. And this could save his life.

8. Training "Go to Your Place"

Why this is important: Essential & easy command that teaches pups to go where you want them, rather than underfoot. Versatile and extremely helpful for every household and every dog, with no downside.

Difficulty Level: Moderately difficult, but also enjoyable to train

Instructions:

This is a versatile command that teaches your puppy to go to any set place in your home whenever you ask him to, so he won't interfere with the activities of family and guests. Ideally, the pup will also get into the habit of going to his place on his own when needed. For the "place" you can choose any place you think your dog will be comfortable, but not be underfoot. For example, your dog might like a certain corner of the room near the fireplace or the back door. Or you can teach him that his designated "place" is a particular rug, dog bed or towel and this way you can move the item to any place you need to in any room, or even when you are traveling.

Your puppy will learn that he always has a comfortable place to retreat to for a while, and you can avoid some household chaos.

Begin teaching your pup, "Go to your place" by pointing at the "place" you desire and giving him a treat as soon as he walks to and stands on the spot. You might have to start with the pup on a leash so you can show him exactly where you want him to go, or you can throw treats onto the spot (for example a rug or dog bed) to lure him. But always be positive and gentle. Never drag the pup or force him to go to his "place", because you always want him to associate going to the place with good things. Once your puppy gets the idea that you want him to go to the particular place, you can now teach him to go to the place from increasing distances. Next you'll start phasing out treats, only offering food treats for the best performances- when he goes to the place the quickest or remains there calmly the longest.

At first you should teach only one spot, so you don't confuse your pup. Later you may want to try teaching the pup spots with different names. (For example, "Go to your bed," "Go to your red rug".) If you feel this is too complex for the pup at his age, just teach him to go to a surface like a particular towel, and move it to any new location when you want him to go there. A lot of people make good use of this command for when their dogs try to jump up on guests or bark at the windows. But don't ever use the instruction as a punishment. **Keep the command fun for your dog and let him think of his "place" simply as a place he can relax and get his thoughts together, near but not right on top of the chaos of overstimulating family activities.** You may find that your dog actually learns to *like* going to his place, and he may often go there on his own at all the right moments!

Hint: You want your pup to learn not just to go to his place, but to remain there for a while. To accomplish this:

1.) While your pup is in his "place" back away as though he's in a "stay", but don't use the formal "stay" command. Your energy should be enough to keep him in the place. When you first teach him to stay there, even if he only remains a few moments, return to him while he's still lying down and relaxed and reward him with treats and praise. Do this until he gets the idea that remaining in the "place" and relaxing there for a while will always be rewarding for him. Later on, stay at a distance for longer periods but return to the pup periodically to give him the occasional warm glance, kind word like "good baby" or occasional treat. **But don't get mad, punish or scold your pup in any way if he leaves the place. You always want the pup to associate going there with free decision making and good things.**

2.) Also, ensure that your pup's "place", such as his dog bed placed in a cozy corner, is truly a retreat where he can go to get away from stress and decompress. For this reason, explain to your kids that, no matter how much they love giving the pup attention, his place is off limits to them whenever he's resting there. Teach them not to run up to the dog bed, etc. when the pup goes there to rest or to escape a busy party. The "place" needs to be your pup's own little Zen-like space where he voluntary retreats to calm down and reset his energy level.

Chapter 6:

Introducing Your Pup to New Stimuli & Different Surfaces

Section A: Why & How to Introduce Your Pup to New Stimuli & Different Surfaces

If you want your pup to develop into a well-balanced adult dog that won't overreact to every new situation in the outside world, it's essential to introduce him to various different surfaces and items- like the 100 everyday items on the list in the second half of this chapter- when he's young.

Introducing your pup to new items in a positive fashion prevents fears, builds mental stability and increases your pup's trust in you. It also engages the pup's senses and builds balance and coordination at the time when canine muscles and nerves are undergoing critical development. Pushing your wobbly little pup to develop physically like this will make him stronger, more coordinated and athletic and less vulnerable to injuries.

Meeting new challenges also builds character and courage, and the best time to start is when your dog is as young as possible. As a puppy, your dog possesses an open and inquisitive mind. When you introduce him to new things in positive fashion early, he'll accept those same things properly and without stress if he encounters them in the "real world" in later life.

As trainers specializing in the treatment of dogs with severe emotional problems, **we often see adult dogs that are terrified of surfaces including: grass, trees, stairs, water, tiled floors, sand, decking, stone, surfaces that tip, moving cars, brushes and combs and raised surfaces like grooming tables.** We must then work with the owners to carefully undo these fears through painstaking desensitization combined with other therapies, and **it's regrettable since some of the fears could have been easily prevented if the owners had just taken the time to introduce their puppy to these stimuli when he was young.**

The benefit of introducing your puppy to different surfaces also extends to other new stimuli for all his senses, ranging as far as your imagination. You should introduce him to sounds, smells and textures in different lighting conditions. For example; teach him to boldly walk through billowing sheets on a clothesline; crawl through a nylon tunnel (the type used for canine agility or at a kids' playground) or mince through crinkly newspapers or wrapping papers on your living room floor. Your family members are only limited by your imagination and the stimuli your pup needs to learn in your particular locale. (For example, it's more important to introduce a Florida puppy to water than to snow.)

Introducing your puppy to novel items is easy to do, even in an apartment or on the road and it's fun and interesting for the whole family. Whenever you find yourself with only a few minutes you can do something productive for your dog by introducing him to a new surface or a novel item.

Even if you can't transport your pup to many outside venues (for example if you're elderly or don't own a car) you can still create many novel experiences and textures in your home. There are literally thousands of different new stimuli your pup will find enjoyable, interesting and pertinent.

Just make sure your puppy stays safe and never gets terrified when trying a new surface or this experience will defeat the purpose of empowering your dog! For example, if you want your puppy to confidently step on a wobbly surface, you must make sure that he doesn't slip and hurt himself. And, when you first introduce him to water, start with the top step of your family pool rather than chilly ocean waves. Pups also go through "fear periods" at certain phases in their emotional development. At these times a puppy will naturally act more timid, so you shouldn't push him too hard and stress him. Take your cues from your puppy and present leadership combined with caring to urge him past hesitation and timidity and help him conquer new things.

It's okay to urge your pup past hesitation and worries, because this will help him learn to trust you in future situations. But don't attempt to push a pup (or dog of any age) past flat-out panic or terror. If your pup seems overly fearful, don't give up the day's work entirely, but stop the new activity. Calmly direct your puppy back to a less challenging activity that you already know he can master confidently, end with a positive attempt and then revisit the tougher surface or stimulus on another day or even a little later in his development.

If a problem with a particular item or stimuli persists beyond your reasonable efforts or resembles a phobia, or if your pup acts snappy or aggressive when encountering new items, you may need professional advice or help from a high level behaviorist. But be cautious of any trainer whose methods might intimidate the dog more.

An adult should always introduce the pup to new things first or supervise children carefully if they attempt it, just in case the puppy gets overly afraid or tries to snap or bite. Usually introducing a pup to new surfaces and stimuli is extremely easy and enjoyable and it's one of the best ways to spend time with a puppy.

Safety Note: Unfortunately certain rescue or shelter dogs may have violent triggers from previous abuse that new owners may not know about, so be especially careful about introducing new stimuli with these dogs. Proceed carefully and don't push a dog that stiffens or seems like he might bite to do something he doesn't want to do. It's always a good idea to enlist the help of a high-level behavioral expert with scientific background to ease the transition for any rescue dog whose background you're uncertain of.

<u>Section B: List of 100 Different Surfaces & Novel Items To Introduce Your Puppy To</u>

If you ever feel at a loss for something to do with your puppy, you can introduce him to one of the 100 novel stimuli listed below:

1. Leash & Collar

2. Slick Floors

3. Strange Sounds made by people (hissing, blowing, clicking)

4. Different scents to follow and indentify

5. Stairs

6. Being turned on his back while resting & while playing, if no health conditions prohibit.

(Use extreme caution with short-snouted dogs who may have difficulty breathing turned

upside down, and with temperamental dogs that might bite. Never hold a pup on his back as punishment.)

    7. Nail Clippers

    8. Baths

    9. Enclosed spaces

    10. Riding in the car

    11. Wide open spaces

    12. Darkness

    13. Rain

    14. Snow (with caution)

    15. Bright sun (with caution)

    16. Moving leaves/fronds overhead

    17. Dried leaves underfoot

    18. Underbrush (caution for snakes, ticks, etc.)

    19. Wobbly surfaces (don't let pup fall)

    20. Shallow water (like a kiddie pool, puddle or marsh- but be cautious of drowning, chemicals and bacteria/protozoa)

    21. Natural bodies of water like ponds & lakes (walking in shallows with caution, or just looking at water)

    22. Wind

    23. Grass

    24. Treed areas

    25. Crinkly wrapping paper underfoot

    26. Mystery boxes in middle of room

    27. Large hat or open umbrella in middle of room

    28. Sandbox

    29. Vacuum cleaner

    30. Moving flashlight

    31. Person wearing hat

32. Balloons

33. Soap bubbles drifting in the air

34. Ramp (for ex., to climb into car)

35. Standing on picnic table (caution)

36. Tolerate lifting by owner

37. Sheets flapping on clothesline

38. Passing through streamers

39. Owner hiding

40. Toys that make noise (caution for ingesting small parts)

41. Contrast of different smells (natural only; no harsh perfume or chemicals)

42. Contrast of different sounds (not too loud)

43. Sound of thunder

44. Animal sounds

45. Television (only to desensitize; don't force your pup to tolerate TV all day with no escape)

46. Watching/listening to turning wheels

47. Water sprinkled on pup (should be fun)

48. Tolerate brief moment under cloth as game rather than stress

49. Owners wearing different costumes

50. Tolerate brief time of witnessing owner with cloth over head

51. Balls of different sizes rolling all over the floor

52. Ice cubes or frozen treats (caution)

53. Small, occasional snacks of safe vegetables and fruit

54. Lifejacket

55. Harness

56. Backpack

57. Practical dog clothing

58. Being in water. Some older puppies can learn to swim; but never push an overly fearful pup; let him mature and gently try to teach him again when he's older and/or hire a professional to help

59. Being briefly rubbed or covered with towels

60. Roll over, lie down and stay lying down for humans on command without fear or aggression

61. Staying behind baby gates without fear or overexcitation

62. Brief separations from owners

63. Balance walking up on a log (carefully supervise- don't let pup fall)

64. Walk a narrow line

65. Walk through cones or weave poles with owner

66. Walk or crawl through tunnel

67. Jump over small hurdles (not too high, don't endanger hips, especially with larger breeds)

68. Challenging game: pup sits on a sheet & calmly remains on it while owner slides it

69. Highly challenging game: Pup wears a harness and then pulls something that's very light, but annoying (like a blanket, or something that makes noise) with confidence. Dog should be coaxed with plentiful rewards & lots of praise. Never use a heavy load!

70. Varied terrain on walks. If safe, alternate between grass, gravel, concrete, earth, etc.

71. Safe moving water, like a trickling stream only a few inches deep (supervise carefully)

72. Walk together up and down hills, around curves, in between trees

73. Show your pup a view from a high vista

74. Show your pup the sea

75. Take your pup boating (with extreme caution & wearing lifevest)

76. Pup should be able to watch humans dancing

77. Pup should be able to watch humans cuddling/kissing

78. Once you're sure your pup won't hurt you, he should occasionally have to interact with his owners in unfamiliar positions- for example, lying on their backs on the floor- and he should behave appropriately (could be dangerous for children; control the dog carefully)

79. Should tolerate being briefly "swaddled" in cloth playfully. (Reward & don't force.)

80. Safe confetti, flower petals or leaves falling around him

81. A branch with leaves being dragged over the ground and being moved over him.

82. Large shadows or objects moving over him

83. The smell of other dogs on bedding

84. Mirrors

85. Objects that flash or reflect light

86. Fans

87. Blowdryer (with care)

88. Hose (gentle spray)

89. Objects that roll or rattle

90. Swirling objects (pinwheels)

91. Ride in baby carriage, kids' wagon or sled

92. Gravel or small stones

93. Teeter Board

94. Slats (as on a pallet)

95. Street grates

96. Ride calmly in handheld carrier/purse for small dogs (briefly only)

97. Stay calmly in a carrier for travel (no extended crating)

98. Mock vet office, including slippery table

99. Strangers in different types of hats and uniforms

100. Allowing handling by a friendly stranger while owner is in sight

The list of 100 items in this chapter doesn't include people or animals. But your pup should also safely and comfortably encounter new people, dogs and other animals in his first months of life. This is what is referred to as puppy "socialization" . Read details on the best ways to introduce your pup to new people and animals in Chapter 10, and use the "List of New People, Places and Things Every Puppy Should Encounter" in Chapter 9.

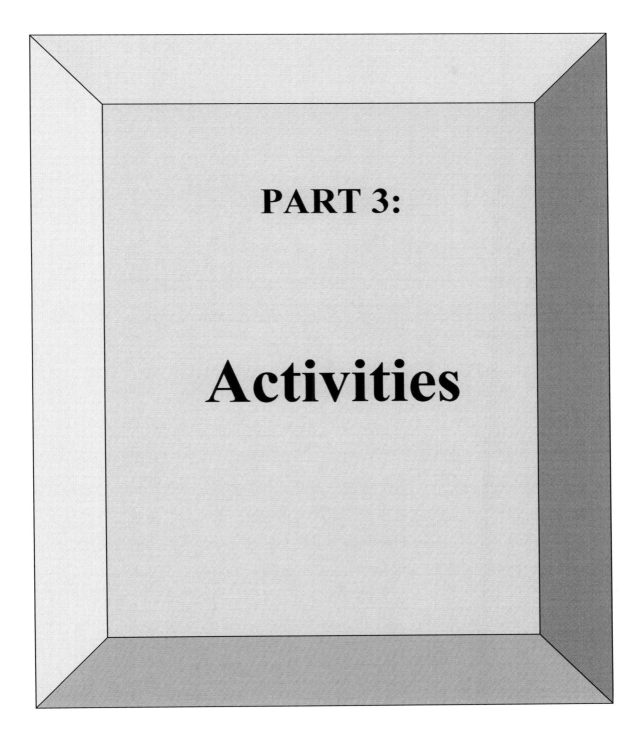

PART 3:

Activities

Chapter 7:

Activities & Games to Make Your Puppy a Better Dog

#1 "Follow My Eyes"

Known for: Unique activity we designed to take dogs to a higher level. Teaches pups to *want* to act considerate!

Helps: Pups bond better with owners and look to their owners before acting; huge implications for lifelong good behavior without stress or struggle

Which pups? Reinforces bond with owners in well behaved pups & can prevent future problems in pups with difficulty focusing

Which owners? All owners gain priceless insight into human/canine communication, even if they've never trained, or owned, dogs before.

Time, Effort & Cost: Minimal. Engages pups anywhere, even if all you have is a minute.

Cautions or risks: Minimal. Almost no downside. Good for older kids; but not for young kids who might feel confused or might get hurt if they try to hold the pup or prevent it from getting the treats.

Instructions:

The activity we call Follow My Eyes will teach you why we call the dog man's best friend. Many people misunderstand the capabilities that dogs have to communicate with humans. When people think of dog communication they think of the dog licking their face, wagging its tail or barking. But most people never think of the millions of little signals a dog is capable of giving. Dogs are capable of a myriad of facial movements, almost like humans. We always tell people that even though dogs aren't people, all you have need to do to read your dog is look at his face and think of what you would think if a human was making that same face.

If you want to learn more about reading dog's emotions through their expressions, check out the book *For the Love of a Dog* by Patricia McConnell. People should know that, for many years, our dogs also been studying how to discern what we are trying to say by reading our faces-especially our eyes. And this game helps your puppy learn the crucial skill of how to read people.

To start this activity, all you need is two paper cups, a handful of soft small treats and a helper; maybe one of your children. First walk a few feet away while your helper holds the puppy. Then get the pup's attention while you put a treat in one of the cups, leaving the other empty. Mix the cups up to confuse the pup about which has the treat; and keep the cups upside down within arms' reach, but clearly separate from each other. Then say your pup's name and wait until he looks at your face. Once your pup looks at your face, start intently staring at the cup that has the treat, in order to signal that this is the correct choice to go to. And now allow your helper to release the pup.

If your pup immediately goes to the cup you looked at, this means that you have a great bond with him. Lift the cup, allow him to enjoy the treat and praise him, showing you love when he looks at you.

If your pup goes to the wrong cup first or just comes over and licks your face, shake your head and speak some mild words of disappointment, such as "silly boy" or say, "no, sorry". Have your helper approach and take the pup away before he gets any treats. The next time you try the exercise with this puppy, wait until the pup looks at your eyes. Just before your helper releases the pup, give the pup a stronger hint than last time by not just looking at the cup that has the treat in it, but turning your head to that side. Try as many repetitions and/or sessions as necessary until your pup realizes that the only way to find out which cup has the reward is by watching his owner's signals.

As soon as your pup gets the correct cup, let him eat the treat and praise him lavishly. After a few correct repetitions your pup will start to learn that, in order to get a treat and praise, he has to look for you to give him a signal. The more skillful he becomes at reading your signals, the smaller and more subtle you can make your cues. This powerful exercise will help entrench the knowledge in your pup for the rest of his life that everything his owner does has a meaning. This knowledge, in turn increases your dog's obedience, his consideration for you and the strength of the bond between you.

Hint: At first, less attentive dogs might need broader signals than just turning your eyes or head to understand, so you can start by pointing at the correct cup with a finger and then transition to the eye signals once your pup starts to catch on. Don't get frustrated if it takes quite a few repetitions for some dogs. Be patient. When you succeed, this exercise can be life-changing.

#2 *"Find Your Way In To Me"*

Known for: If a pup has problems figuring out this task, he definitely needs the practice.
Helps: Improves frustration tolerance & teaches your pup to think before pushing ahead
Which pups? Especially good for very young pups; also any pup (or dog) that tends to act before thinking. Use caution with adult dogs or large pups that jump violently.
Which owners? Adults who can set up & hide behind a barrier. If your pup is small & gentle, this can be okay for kids with adult supervision- but not very young kids
Time, Effort, Cost: Can take some effort and time to set up
Cautions or risks: Don't let the "barrier" fall on the handler, the pup or bystanders, especially children; don't risk large overly boisterous pups knocking into anyone

Instructions:

This activity tests your pup's ability to solve problems and improves his frustration tolerance. It also makes him learn to think before he reacts, and it can make him a better thinker later in life. In this activity, your pup must endure frustration in order to find his way around a simple barrier to get to you and receive a reward.

There are several different ways to construct an appropriate barrier to block your pup for this game. The easiest method is to stack a few rows of cardboard boxes in an "L" shape in the center of the room high enough so that they can momentarily block your pup from getting to you. You could also create a partial "wall" that your pup cannot easily get around out of plywood or similar material.

Next take some treats and stand behind the barrier with your pup on the other side, and then call him to you. The object of this activity is to make your pup figure out how to follow the line of boxes or the wall until he finds the opening. As soon as your pup correctly finds the opening and finds you, immediately praise him and give him a few small treats.

If you use boxes or bins for this activity, your pup might immediately try to jump over the barrier to get to you. If he tries this, let him know this isn't what you want by physically blocking him and/or shaking your head and saying, "uh uh".

When first doing this activity with very young pups, don't make the opening in the barrier too far down the line. You just want your pup to learn to think out the answer to a puzzle presented to him. If you make success too hard to achieve at first, you pup might give up- and this is the last thing you want. You only want your pup to experience frustration to the point where he learns to deal with it positively; you do not want to present so much frustration at first that it overwhelms him. In other words, you want your puppy to learn frustration tolerance, not frustration.

You may be surprised how quickly some very young dogs learn how to solve problems like "Find Your Way In to Me". On the other hand, you may also be surprised that many dogs have problems figuring out this simple task. They may stand at the other side of the barrier barking and showing increased frustration that they can't get to you, rather than just trying to walk around the barrier. Obviously, dogs or pups that experience the most problems figuring out how to master this activity also seem to have the most problems with frustration and these are the ones that need the most practice.

The first few times you practice with your pup, leave the opening in the same spot in the barrier so he can easily understand what you want. As he gets better at finding his way around the barrier rather than giving up or trying to push through it in frustration, you can next change the spot where the opening is. This will increase the challenge and keep the game interesting. As the pup gets even better at finding you behind a barrier, you can erect more "walls". You could even get to a point where you have four sides to your little castle. And, if your pup is small and well-mannered, your children could also have fun playing the game.

Never push your pup too much and always make sure you're both having fun.

Hint: If your pup is especially good at finding people behind barriers, you might just have a future search and rescue dog or police K-9 on your hands. But you'll have plenty of time to make decisions on how you will use your pup's talents. This activity is meant as a fun way to acquaint very young puppies with frustration tolerance in the most basic sense.

#3 *"Yours and Mine (Frustration Tolerance)"*

Known for: Easily teaches sharing- one cornerstone of a gentle well-mannered dog

Helps: When a young pup learns to enjoy this game, it can prevent possessiveness about toys and objects; it also teaches pushy and greedy pups more patience

Which pups? All very young pups; can also be used therapeutically (with caution) for pups who act pushy, greedy or hesitant to give up toys. But never try it with aggressive pups.

Which owners? Careful adult owners with good timing and sensitivity to their puppies only! If they understand the point of the exercise, highly mature children can sometimes practice with young, small gentle puppies with adult supervision.

Time, Effort, Cost: Quite easy & pleasant and can be done spontaneously in free moments, but remember to pay attention. No distractions with this game!

Cautions or risks: This game is designed to make normal pups gentler, and prevent future risks when they're adults. But if your pup already shows any food or possession aggression, no matter how young he is, you cannot play this game and should instead seek professional advice (see Safety Note below). Parents should never allow children to try to take toys away from potentially aggressive puppies, or any dog with an unknown history.

Instructions:

This is a game that's lots of fun to play, but it's vital for teaching your pup that there's nothing wrong with sharing. Playing "Yours and Mine" enhances healthy dog/owner bonding and can help shy or withdrawn pups feel comfortable playing.

This game is very simple and requires no special supplies, other than a safe, non-edible toy that your puppy really likes. (No bones or rawhides!) Most people like to play "Yours and Mine" on the floor, but you can just as easily sit on a low chair or ottoman if you have problems getting down on the floor. (You can also play with your pup on the couch with you, as long as you plan to allow him on furniture in future.)

To play the game, start to move the toy around in front of your puppy until he gets a little excited. Once your puppy acts like he wants the toy, you can let him have it, *but do not let him run off with it* (you could start playing with the pup leashed if you think this will be a problem). When the puppy has the toy in his mouth, say "Yours." Now let him enjoy the toy for a few seconds. After he's played with the toy for a few seconds, say the word "Mine" and gently, yet smoothly and confidently, take the toy away.

If your puppy doesn't want to let go of the toy, *don't* pull on the toy because this will make him pull the other way. And having your dog struggle with you to hold onto possessions is exactly what this game is meant to prevent. Instead, if you cannot smoothly remove the toy, just show the puppy an extremely yummy treat (or tidbit of non-allergenic human food) and he should let go of the toy in order to take the treat. But don't use treats unless you need them, and phase them out as soon as possible.

When you take the toy away from the puppy, do it in a friendly voice, praising your puppy and telling him that he's good. Now you go back to playing with the toy on the floor for a few seconds, acting as though you are enjoying it.

Now, say "Yours" and let the puppy have the toy again. In few seconds, say "Mine" and take the toy back for yourself.

After you practice like this a few times your pup will start to learn that sharing is just one big fun game. Each time that you say "Mine" and take the toy, you'll notice your pup becoming more willing to surrender it. In fact, he will actually start liking to give the toy up. This is because, each time he gives up the toy, he gets to interact and have fun with you. Rather than your pup thinking that you're stealing from him, he'll realize that by giving an object to you he'll not only get your praise and attention, but he can get the object back also.

"Yours and Mine" is an important learning activity for every normal healthy young puppy to practice as soon as possible, because it helps to easily shape a puppy into a more mellow and generous dog. "Yours and Mine" is also meant to be therapeutic so it can help pups that have some minor issues about sharing and shy, tentative or fearful pups that need to learn to trust people more and understand what playtime is all about.

Hint: Playing "Yours and Mine" correctly requires a little subtlety. One trick that makes it easier is not to allow your pup to get too possessive of the toy the first time he holds it. Don't forget and allow him to play with the toy too long before taking it back the first time. If the pup literally only holds the toy for a couple of seconds the first time, this will allow him to surrender it more easily. Then you can allow him to hold and play with the toy for slightly longer periods as he becomes better at the game and more willing to share.

Safety Note: This activity can help mild possession issues like being pushy, impatient or somewhat reluctant to give up a toy. And it often keeps these minor issues from turning into big problems. But it is too late and this game is *not* appropriate if your pup already shows any possession aggression- including snapping, growling, raising hackles or stiffening if a person tries to take a toy away from him. Possession aggression can be extremely dangerous, even in a very young puppy, and especially around children. If your dog or pup of any age ever violently bites a human or ever shows any aggression around toys or other possessions, you should immediately make sure of any children's safety and then contact a high level animal behaviorist for advice before attempting any self help.

Also, don't confuse the game of "Yours and Mine" with the very negative, yet highly popular game of tug-of-war. A person should never get a pup highly worked up when he's holding an item in his mouth and then try to pull the item away from him. Regardless of the fact that tug toys are sold in stores, this popular activity sometimes leads to dominance and bites when pups get older.

#4 "Forcefield (Control Your Pup with Your Psychic Energy)"

Known for: A secret most people don't know about, although popular television trainer Cesar Millan touches on it by often talking about owners' "energy" influencing dogs

Helps: Gets your pup to pay attention to you and makes every command work better

Which pups? Every pup can respond to mental energy. It's easier for those that are emotionally balanced, but sometimes it's a way to get through to dogs with problems

Which owners? Not for everyone, since results aren't guaranteed. Good for open minded owners who want to explore a different dimension communicating with animals.

Time, Effort, Cost: Zero extra to add mental energy to commands you are already doing

Cautions or risks: None, but never try this if you'll get frustrated if you don't observe results immediately. Frustration and doubt has a very negative effect on pups and will outweigh the good of trying the technique.

Instructions:

This activity teaches you to control your puppy by "magic" It's not exactly a game or an obedience exercise, but it can improve every other activity with your dog. It's also the secret behind why some of our highly enlightened home training clients do so much better in the long term than their contemporaries and even better than some dog trainers.

You will notice that in the instructions for teaching your pup most of the standard obedience commands, we first mention that you should "center your mind". This kind of focus and confidence is essential to relating to your puppy and getting him to do what you want without a lot of wasted effort. Have you ever seen a dog owner who says "Sit?" to their puppy as though there was a question mark at the end? And have you noticed how the command doesn't seem to work? It is essential for *you* to believe that your dog will perform the command before your dog believes it.

This kind of mental confidence is completely different from the kind of dominance that some dog trainers' advocate. Some trainers or handlers like to command "Sit!" as though it ends in an exclamation point, so loudly and intimidatingly that the pup cowers and leaks urine and people blocks away cover their ears. Others yank the puppy around by the leash or shove him down roughly with their hands to get him to comply with their orders. But none of this is necessary; and it's not even highly effective. There's no need to "dominate" a puppy to get his respect, and dominance is completely different from true leadership (if you ever take a dog's leash off, you may immediately notice the difference). Confident leadership is the quality that dogs are born to follow. And it's through true confident leadership that we teach pet parents to express their wishes to their dogs.

Using mental energy takes the concept even a bit further, and how much dogs know about us beyond the regular five senses demonstrates how important "energy" is to them. **Dogs can sense what their owners are feeling at all times with complete accuracy** (although improper husbandry, physical abuse or excessive crating during early puppyhood can sometimes interfere with this natural ability to read humans.)

Average, emotionally healthy, pups will be completely tuned to your energy and your true internal beliefs in any situation. This is why you should never train a dog when you feel stressed, scared, burnt out or frustrated. And it's why we always tell our customers to believe their dog can succeed.

A good example of using a mental "forcefield" is the way Ray trains dogs to stay back at the front door, waiting to be invited out by their owner before moving. This one skill can prevent a dog from acting overly dominant towards people in a hundred other ways. And, because it stops door darting, it could someday save your dog's life.

Some dogs act so crazy at the front door that owners are afraid they will tear up the sidewalk tiles and knock the house down as they exit. But Ray likes to demonstrate to owners how to hold dogs of any size back at a door with no physical force, no physical correction and not even the command "stay". What does he do? With really extreme cases, he may keep a leash on the dog to gently hold it back once or twice. But this is rare. Sometimes he blocks door-darters with his body once or twice without using any physical touch. But most often he does not even have to do this. He simply steps out the door, stands in front of the dog, and stares at it, while applying his strong mental energy to keep it still until he instructs it that it is okay to "come". The dog stares back at him, taps into the energy and respects his wishes.

The use of energy like this is why many people call Ray a "dog whisperer", and why he's also able to accomplish seemingly impossible communication with wild animals. As he holds a previously uncontrollable dog back at a door using nothing but mental energy, the dogs' owners usually react with complete stillness and awe- until they find out that he wants them to practice next. Usually most owners act shocked and protest because they don't believe they can stop a wild 100 lb. dog with just their energy. Even Emma, who has trained obedience since childhood, felt a flicker of concern when Ray first asked her to demonstrate this particular exercise to a customer on her own. But it worked because she knew it had to! And it can work for any size or strength adult owner with any size dog. But it only works with total confidence and belief.

Try it yourself. Work with a door that opens to a screened porch or a fenced yard, or keep your pup on a long leash or line just for insurance. Then put your head in the mindset that the pup will stay back until you ask him to walk, and that you can hold him with just your mental energy. Now stand confidently in front of him and "hold him back" with your energy for a moment. If he waits patiently, say "good dog" and then "okay" or whatever command you choose to release him. If you can't get it right at the door to your house, first practice with any interior door in your home. Once you've practiced controlling your pup with mental energy a few times, even for just a few seconds, your confidence will build.

You can also use mental energy to call your dog. This is one of Emma's favorite things to demonstrate when she first meets new dogs that have a history of refusing to come. Start with the dog close to you, stare at him and then "draw him to you" with your mental energy at the same time you call his name. This makes the command a lot more powerful. Try it in a safe location, really focus your mind and see how it works.

If you still can't get your pup to calm down enough to stay back at the door or to come when you apply your energy, there are several even easier ways to train using mental energy. Focused energy can help you train both the "Look" and "Stay" commands described Part 2, Chapter 5, Obedience Training. Select the command you want to practice and read over the instructions if you have not already. In the "Look" command, you want your pup to stare into your eyes, rather than focus on distractions. And the stronger you focus and mentally "pull", the more powerfully your pup will focus on you.

Teaching "Stay" is another great way to feel your mental focus working on your dog. Place your pup in a "stay" lying down, but instead of simply backing off and holding your hand up, also "push" your energy out at him to "freeze" him in place. Most owners can easily feel the difference when they apply mental energy to their pup in this way. **If your pup has a tendency to get up from his "stay" before you tell him to, once you apply your mental energy, he will stay happily rooted to the ground until you ask him to move.**

You will notice if your mind ever starts wandering because this is when your pup will likely get up and break the "stay". This connection is clear enough to make most people believers in training with mental energy.

Hint: Once you're confident enough to believe you can influence your pup with your mind, try it with heeling on leash. Ray tells pet parents that, when they walk their dog, they should stand up straight and project confidence, while imagining walking into the situation where they feel most comfortable and confident in the world. This could be walking into a board meeting if you're a successful executive, walking down to great waves if you're a surfer or walking into a designer clothing sale if you're a fashionista.

Mental confidence is only one component of training your puppy to walk on leash (read full instructions in Part 2, Chapter 5, "Training Heel"). But confidence is sometimes the final piece of the puzzle that makes everything work. Customers who previously feared their dogs wouldn't heel properly suddenly stand up straight, with smiles on their faces and walk forward like kings and queens. And their dogs fall into place, walking calmly and smoothly beside them. It's almost like magic.

#5 *"Hurry to Mom & Dad"*

Known for: This little trick makes a pup want to come to you. (Also see "#40 Learn to Come to Everyone" in this chapter & instructions for training the Recall in Part 2.)

Helps: "Imprints" young pups to return to you, which is vitally important in adult life

Which pups? Best for pups under 16 wks. You can also practice with emotionally balanced pups under 6 months that won't jump or chase too hard. But most of the psychological benefits are lost once the canine personality has fully developed. This game could make older pups too rowdy & and could be dangerous with aggressive dogs/pups.

Which owners? Able-bodied adult (or teen) owners with careful judgment & an able-bodied helper

Time, Effort, Cost: More fun than work, but requires able bodied handler (and helper) who are able to move around quickly

Cautions or risks: Serious risks with children, especially with large breed pups that tend chase too vigorously, and with pups over 6 months. Any pup that chases people aggressively and bites, nips or knocks people down is a serious danger and requires professional help. **No pup should play this game with young/small children.** See the "Hint" for additional cautions.

Instructions:

One of the most important things you can teach your puppy is to love coming to you; and this fun and easy game requires only minutes of your time. The game capitalizes on dogs' natural tendency to follow. This natural instinct helps wolves run together as a pack. And you've probably noticed that young puppies under 16 weeks tend to follow their owners everywhere.

This desire in your young puppy to stay near you is vital to the health of your future relationship. A pup that wants to stay by your side when he's young will be more likely to come to you from a distance when you call as an adult (rather than running away from you, darting out the front door and possibly being killed on the highway). And he'll be more likely to walk properly by your side on leash, rather than ignoring you and pulling so hard that he knocks you to the pavement.

The stronger you can make your pup's desire to follow you when he's young, the better, because each week over 4 months pups grow more curious and motivated to explore the world on their own. But if you can shape your young pup's psyche so he always wants to follow you, he's unlikely to act overly independent as an adult. He will also be less likely to act dominant.

Carefully choose the right time to practice "Hurry to Mom & Dad". So your pup stays excited enough to want to run to you, he shouldn't be tired or sleepy. But he also shouldn't act overly wild or rowdy. Choose times when the pup is in a medium energy state and a curious and alert frame of mind, but avoid his highest excitability. Play for only a few minutes at a time so your pup doesn't burn out and get bored coming to you. But if you keep sessions short, you can play as many times per day as you like. You can play outdoors or indoors, but secure all breakables because you and your pup will both be running.

Start with an able-bodied helper (ideally an adult, teen or physically mature child) holding your pup while you pet him and talk to him. And then, while your helper still holds the pup so he can't follow you, start moving away in a playful upbeat fashion. Jog, scamper, skip, spin around, sing, clap your hands or act silly in any way you like. The idea is to arouse your pup's curiosity and/or chase instinct. Your pup will probably get excited watching you run and will badly want to chase. But since your helper is holding him, he may bark, yap or jump around in frustration because he can't get to you. This is exactly what you want. You want to set a precedent for him to want to run to *you* when he's in an excited state, rather than wanting to run away on his own and get into mischief.

The first time that you play, don't make it too difficult for your pup to reach you. Stay in the room, or don't go very far from your pup if you're outdoors, before allowing your helper to release him. For this particular exercise do not call your pup's name, do not call "come" or use any other verbal cue. The point of this game is to make your pup immediately and excitedly run to you just because he got so excited seeing you run away.

When your pup reaches you, greet him with sincere praise. It's okay to make this a playful moment, because you want the energy to stay high. (Some people may also wish to reward their pup with a treat at this point, but that is optional. We use treats in other recall exercises in this book. But with this particular activity it's ideal to teach your pup to respond just for the joy and fun of reaching you. If you do use treats as a reward for running to you, alternate the treats with praise and only give treats for the times your pup reaches you quickest.

This is one game you don't want to practice too many times in a row, since it can easily lose its edge and this could defeat the purpose. But, if your pup's energy remains high and he seems to be having a great time, you can try one, two or three additional repetitions. Or, you and your helper can change off and get in a few repetitions with each of you. Once the game is done, do something else with the pup that he enjoys, like a nice walk, a game of Frisbee, a play session with his favorite toy or a relaxing massage if he seems tired. This additional time for fun and bonding will reinforce his belief that coming to you is always a good thing.

Leave off on a good note for the first day. The next day, or as your pup gets faster at reaching you, you can practice again and increase the challenge by moving farther away from your pup before your helper lets him go. This time you can hide behind a wall if you are indoors, or duck behind a shrub or run to the far side of the yard if you are outdoors. Now see if the pup will still run to you from you from the greater distance. Practice at this level until he gets really good, increasing the distance, and the challenge, a little each day.

A few days or weeks later you can make the game even more difficult by starting to introduce a few minor distractions. Start by having extra family members or pets present. Next practice around a guest who'd ordinarily distract your pup. But always work from success- and always stop while your pup is still reacting perfectly. Don't get too ambitious. And never push the difficulty to the point that you fail, because this could introduce to your pup the notion that, at times, he does *not* want to come to you.

If you notice your pup start to lag and drag he's probably getting tired or bored. If your pup's slow seeking you out, you can avoid a negative outcome, where the pup wanders away instead of running to you, by scampering around even more energetically. You can also casually get closer to him as you dance around enticingly or crouch down on the floor (which tends to attract dogs). But never let the pup fear that you're going to try to grab him by the collar and pull him to you. And never let him see frustration. You must stay in a good mood and get the puppy to come to you one more time on his own so you can retire the game for the evening on a high note.

If all your silliness or crouching on the floor still doesn't get the pup to come to you, now would be the time to break out that especially yummy treat or piece of human food that you've been holding in a baggie in your pocket just in case. Wait patiently until his nose leads him to you and the reward. And once he comes, praise him. And next time you practice start out at a much less challenging level that you know he'll easily achieve.

Hint: Should pups chase kids? Right now your kids may love to have your puppy chase them all the time- they may be making him chase them right this minute as you try to read! But unfortunately, when young kids invite an overexcited pup to chase them, it could someday lead to injury when the pup gets bigger. **No dog or pup should ever learn to chase after small children, and kids should never play chase games with dogs.** In many households children invite a pup to chase them, and next the pup starts "herding" by nipping at their heels. If this is the case, you can teach your children to freeze if the pup starts to chase them so that they become boring to him.

Other pups with high prey drive chase violently every time they see children run and they deliberately knock children down and/or bite them. In these serious cases (which go beyond "herding") the parents must remove their children from contact with the dog until they can get help from an animal behaviorist with advanced qualifications.

For adults: The idea behind this game is to teach *very young* pups to respect you and never feel complete unless they're following you. But some pups with existing issues chase even adults inappropriately. If a large pup older than 6 months chases you so roughly that he makes you feel truly uneasy, he just might be chasing you like prey! If your pup gets inappropriate like this, stop this game immediately, and never do anything to get him worked up again. Instead, teach him to come to you with more control, using techniques like "#11 Umbilical Cord" described in this chapter) or heeling beside you off lead (see "Training Heel" in Part 2, Chapter 5). If this doesn't make him treat you more gently, consult a behaviorist for help.

#6 *"Heeling Without a Leash"*

Known for: An activity very few pet parents think of, but it works almost magically to teach your pup to follow you

Helps: Unmatchable for making your dog always want to stay by your side and never pull on leash

Which pups? Almost every pup. Since this activity doesn't involve forcing your pup, he'll naturally learn to follow your leadership, with no chance of conflict. The only exception is if a large pup deliberately tries to trip you or "tackle" you when he's off-leash. If you feel that your dog will injure you and you cannot manage the behavior on your own, seek professional help.

Which owners? Owners of any fitness level who are able move around at all with the pup walking beside them, indoors or out. Can work if you use a wheelchair or walker if your pup is well behaved and you proceed carefully. And small children can practice *with gentle, non-aggressive pups with adult supervision.*

Time, Effort, Cost: Minimal.

Cautions or risks: Low. This is usually easier and safer than walking a pup on a leash if you practice in an enclosed area, and if your pup doesn't jump at you violently when off- leash. Adults should supervise very small children so pups don't try to jump for treats.

Instructions:

Look for additional detailed instructions on how to teach your puppy to walk beside you off leash in "Training Heel" in Part 2, Chapter 5. Teaching a pup to heel beside a handler off leash is often the first step we use in teaching the pup to heel nicely on leash.

In general, this activity capitalizes on your pup's wonderful inborn tendency to want to follow his family, so you should project positivity while practicing. Start with your pup off leash and call him to you. Then lure him along beside you as though he were heeling, by holding a treat in your cupped hand at your left side just out of his reach. You can give a small bite of treat occasionally, alternating with verbal praise, as your pup walks nicely beside you. Some pups don't even need a treat, and will just heel beside you, as if you are holding an invisible leash, just for the pleasure of moving together.

Walk everywhere in your house this way. Start with just a few steps and then reward the pup if he walked by you appropriately. Then keep building on success and try for greater distances and longer intervals each time you practice. When your pup gets really good indoors, next take practice outdoors to a safe enclosed area for a much tougher challenge. And next switch off to let other family members. Even young kids can safely practice this with adult supervision.

Practice heeling off leash frequently in short intervals in safely enclosed areas, many times a day and every day of your dog's life. A pup that does this activity well also respects his owner and wants to stay near, so you can never practice too much. Heeling off leash together is always good. It's a positive activity kids can do with pups with no need for power struggles. And **the activity always promotes love and bonding between people and pups.**

Hint: Some adults may perceive they'll look silly or get bored "walking" their pup without a leash inside the home. But you can make the exercise more challenging by working outdoors and walking with your pup around obstacles like trees, cones or weave poles.

#7 "Follow the Flashlight"

Known for: Our child-safe version of a "classic" game that lets your pup get a little crazy and burn off energy
Helps: Quickly drains frustrated puppy energy in small areas indoors or out
Which pups? Pups with excess energy and high prey drive. Even shy pups love it.
Which owners? Helps tired owners, busy families and owners with physical limitations quickly give their pup some exercise and stimulation
Time, Effort, Cost: Minimal
Cautions or risks: Highly serious risk of injury, especially to children, unless you follow instructions exactly and only use a flashlight. NEVER use a laser pointer around a pup and never

let kids use one, even if friends or other dog trainers do it. Laser pointers, used incorrectly, can seriously injure children and dogs. Also- remove breakables from the play area; and stop playing if your pup acts overexcited or obsessive.

Instructions:

First, start with a bored, inquisitive highly excited pup of any age that has been waiting for something to do all day. (Think of our buddy, the beseeching 9-month old Chocolate Lab that happily posed for the cover of our book *The Cure for Useless Dog Syndrome*, or the adorably alert little boxer on the spine of this book. We know she is cuddly, but she also acts like a little firecracker the moment she stretches and fully wakes from her naps!)

If your family owns a pup like this and it's that hectic time just before dinner when you're trying to do ten things at once and your kids are begging for something to do with the puppy, all you have to do is find a small flashlight or a larger flashlight with some opaque tape over it to make the beam smaller.

Now you can head on out to the patio with kids and pup, or dim some lights in the family room or playroom, just dim enough to see the flashlight beam well, but not dim enough for anyone to trip.

Now call your pup and then do the honors yourself, or allow one of the children to do it. Switch on the flashlight and swirl the light beam in moving patterns on the floor or even on the low part of the walls. Don't move the beam too fast. Catch your pup's attention with the beam of light to get him to chase it, always moving it away just before he can "catch" it. 95% percent of healthy puppies will first cock their head and then the chase will be on. They will gleefully chase and pounce on the light in adorable ways that will make the whole family start to immediately laugh and smile. Pups love this game. Some pups are highly prey-driven and they will immediately go wild chasing the light. Even the shy ones that usually don't get excited about anything are usually interested in this. And the game seems to have a similar ability to mesmerize kids- and even parents.

Make sure to participate for a while as your kids practice with the pup, just to make sure everything is going nicely with no rough play on the part of either kids or puppy. Generally, most kids understand how to play this game appropriately. We recommend that parents always supervise all young children when they are with dogs or puppies. But older kids or preteens can safely play this game to keep a gentle pup occupied while adults take care of some multitasking in the same general area.

This is such an engaging game that often the adults don't feel like going back to their chores right away. Everybody seems to just relax and have fun together. Imagine setting the patio table on an early summer evening, sipping a cool Diet Coke and smiling as you listen to the sizzle of your husband flipping steaks on the grill and your kids laughing as they play with the puppy. If you live alone, as evening falls, imagine relaxing on a comfortable chaise on your rooftop terrace with a glass of white wine, and manipulating the flashlight so your pup chases it around while you laugh and allow a week of workday cares to fade away...

You can do this activity spontaneously, indoors or outdoors for 5 minutes at a time whenever your pup needs to burn off some energy. Just don't play around breakables.

Overall, Follow the Flashlight is one of the easiest, cheapest and least demanding games to immediately get your pup romping. But unfortunately many people are told to play with their dog with the moving light from a laser pointer. You may also know that laser pointers can be terribly dangerous, especially if misused by children. So don't endanger your children or your pup. Always play with a flashlight and never bring a laser pointer into your home.

Some dogs with especially high prey drive may become obsessive about chasing moving light, and this is no longer healthy. (See additional information on compulsive behaviors in the Hint below.) If your pup gets a glazed look in the eyes, or almost scares you with the intensity of his frozen stare on the last spot the light was seen- or if he leaps on you trying to force you to get out the flashlight, it's time to retire this game. Compulsive reactions like this are different from a highly engaged puppy having fun. If your pup ever starts acting excessive or insistent with this game, it is cruel to persist, and there's a fine line between giving a pup endless joy and laughing at him because he feels unable to stop.

Hint: Don't let your pup become obsessed. This will not happen with most normal dogs, but some dogs suffer from a condition where they become inordinately fixed on stimuli like dancing lights. This behavior may have a neurologic or genetic basis, and may combine with other stereotypic behaviors (like tail chasing) or compulsions (like always barking at, or carrying, a certain object). Many of the disturbed dogs in the population we help with have such compulsions. If you notice your dog becoming so fixated on following moving lights or shadows that you are afraid he may hurt himself or people, or if he can no longer focus on other essential activities, you will want to stop all games like Follow the Flashlight forever. Sometimes redirecting the pup with other games, tricks or obedience commands that don't allow for unhealthy focus is enough to break the cycle of compulsions. But if the pup's problem doesn't respond to these interventions and is serious enough to interfere with normal life, you may need to seek the professional help of an applied animal behaviorist.

#8 *"Ring a Bell"*

Known for: Owners say, "I wish *my* pup could do this"; it's hard to believe a pup could make it this easy to let you know he wants to go out!

Helps: Helps housetraining & builds communication skills between pup & owner and can be the basis for learning many assistance skills

Which pups? Clever pups only; try it with yours, but don't expect all pups to master this

Which owners? Patient, involved owners committed to teaching their pup amazing accomplishments

Time, Effort, Cost: Quite challenging, you need much finesse & patience.

Cautions or risks: The only problem would be if you act impatient & mad & scare a poor pup that just can't learn this

Instructions:

Teaching your dog to ring a bell can be handy for many purposes. Learning this skill occupies your pup's mind and enhances dog/owner communication. The skill required to ring a bell is also the foundation for many other important tasks including assisting physically disabled owners. But the main reason most pet parents are highly motivated to teach this skill to a young pup is so that he can tell you when he has to go outside while being housetrained. It can be infinitely helpful for a pup to give a clear signal like ringing a bell every time he has to go outside, rather than having an accident because you missed subtle cues like his sniffing the floor or pacing in circles.

To start, you can choose whichever type of bell works best in your home. If you are training the pup to ring a bell solely for housebreaking purposes, many people like to use an inexpensive string of bells (like Christmas bells). You could also purchase a desk bell (like the ones on hotel check-in desks) in an office supply store, online suppliers or some online dog catalogs.

If you are training your pup to ring for purposes other than housetraining, you'll want to use a desk bell or similar bell so you can place it on the floor in various locations. But, if you start with one type of bell and your puppy seems to have problems with it, sometimes all you need to do is to change to the other type for better progress.

If you are teaching your pup to ring a bell to let you know whenever he needs to relieve his bowels or bladder, first bring the bell over to the door that you customarily use to take him on walks. Set the bell on the floor beside the door if it's a desk bell, or hang it from the door handle if it's a strand. Now bring your puppy to you and say the words, "Ring the bell". At the same time ring the bell yourself. Do this three or four times as your pup watches you.

Next get your pup's attention with his name, say "Ring the bell" and wait to see what he does. A good number of puppies will imitate you and try to make the bell ring with their nose or paw right away. If your pup does this, immediately reward him by praising him, opening the door and taking him out to relieve himself.

If, rather than imitating you and ringing the bell, your puppy just stares at you in confusion, give it a few more minutes, wait and see what happens. If this doesn't help, next try pointing to the bell and repeating the command. At this point many puppies will follow your finger and hit the bell by accident, making it ring. The second this happens, praise your pup and immediately walk him outside.

Each time your puppy prepares to go outside for a walk, first command, "Ring the bell". If you're consistent with this and never let the pup outdoors without the bell first ringing, most pups will learn to ring the bell in order to get you to open the door whenever they feel a need to empty bowels or bladder.

However, if your pup still seems reluctant to touch the bell, you can use a trick we like. Start by standing at the door with your puppy when you know he's impatient to go outside. Than ring the bell yourself while saying, "Ring the bell", then immediately step out the door with the puppy so he can relieve himself. In this way, he will learn to associate the reward of easing his bodily needs with the sound of the bell. Practice this a few times before you again ask the pup to "Ring the bell" on his own.

Many pups will finally master the process at this point. But if yours still acts confused, every family member should continue to ring the bell every single time before the pup goes out. Eventually he may make the connection and start ringing on his own.

If you're using a bell for housetraining never leave the bell by the door when you're away or busy, because you don't want your puppy to ring the bell and get no response. If this happens too often he may give up and stop ringing the bell.

If you want an even more foolproof method of teaching your pup to ring a bell whenever you tell him to, or if you're training for purposes other than housetraining, you'll want to use a method called the "touch" method. This method works for a desk bell, and you can also use it to teach a dog to tap or push on different items to help an owner. Many positive reinforcement trainers currently use this highly effective method to teach dogs varied tasks like turning on lights or appliances in the home, ringing doorbells and opening automatic doors for people with disabilities.

To teach the command "*touch*" start with a handful of treats and a small piece of colored tape that you put on the tip of your finger. Put the tape on your finger and ask your puppy to touch the piece of tape by saying "touch". Then praise him immediately and/or offer a food reward the second he touches the tape with his nose. Practice a few times, each time moving your finger a little farther away from the pup. If you push too far too fast, it could confuse your puppy. And, if this happens, you'll have to go back and start again so he can have success.

Once your pup becomes good at touching the tape on your finger, you can now place the tape on the floor and see if the puppy will touch it on command. If he's a fast learner he should have no problem mastering this. But if your pup needs a little help to learn to touch the tape, rather than still trying to touch your finger, you can practice a few times with part of the tape on your finger and part on the floor. Move more and more tape off your finger and onto floor until the pup learns to seek out and touch the tape when it's on the floor and you point to it and command "touch".

When he succeeds at this, next practice telling him "touch" when you place the tape on different objects and pointing to them- his bell or any other object. The second he touches the item you've pointed to, immediately praise and/or reward him.

Eventually you can teach your pup to touch various objects on command without the tape. This skill then becomes the basis for teaching your dog many entertaining and/or highly useful commands- the possibilities are almost unlimited. (Some dogs have actually learned to call 911 using special telephones, although you'd need to consult an expert assistance dog trainer to help you to teach this extraordinary lifesaving skill.)

If you are training your pup to ring a bell to go outside using the "touch" method, you should put the tape on his bell by the door and command your pup, "touch" so that he rings the bell as he touches the tape. Now praise him profusely and immediately take him outside to relieve himself.

Hint: No matter how hard you try, many pups seem unable to physically learn how to ring a bell. But there are other ways pups can actively signal you when they have to go outside. If your pup doesn't tend to give false alarms, you can rely an old standby and take him out whenever he runs to the door and barks to get your attention or brings you his leash to indicate he has to go out. You could even bring your pup's doorbell into the bedroom with you at nighttime and teach him to ring it if he needs a late-night bathroom break. Ringing a bell works beautifully with a good number of pups. But perhaps in the near future, technology and training techniques will further automate the odious process of housetraining, making it more comfortable for pups and their owners.

#9 *"The Finger Pointing Game"*

Known for: A favorite and unbelievably easy game we recommend to deeply shape a pup's psychology & build respect for his owners
Helps: Teaches a pup that his owner knows better & wants to help, so he'll always look to you first before reacting inappropriately
Which pups? All pups (& dogs) should practice this. It's especially important for impulsive pups.
Which owners? All owners should practice to truly understand communication with dogs
Time, Effort, Cost: Minimal & lots of fun
Cautions or risks: None

Instructions:

This is an activity that shows how well you and your dog work together to achieve an objective. During the game, your pup will bond with you as he looks to you to solve a problem he can't solve on his own. **Looking to an owner for guidance is an important skill for a dog to be an optimal companion.** And dogs are, by nature, very good at this. (In contrast, wolves raised in captivity will try to solve problems on their own rather than looking to the humans that raised them for help.)

To play The Finger Pointing Game with your pup you'll need a few tasty treats and three airtight opaque jars or similar containers (such as small lidded plastic boxes) which appear identical to your pup, but which have identifying markers for you. Most folks have suitable jars or containers around the house, so there's no need to buy anything to have a great time with your puppy and increase his intelligence at the same time.

To teach your pup to work better as a team with you, first show the pup a treat in your hand. Then put the pup in a "stay" as you walk over to the three jars. Let your pup watch you put a treat in one of the jars, and seal all of the jars. (You can teach your pup the "stay" command before starting the game. See Part 2 for directions. If your pup hasn't mastered the "stay" command yet, you can ask a second person to hold him so he doesn't just come running and try to grab the treat before you get it into a jar.) Once the treat is safely sealed in one of the jars, hide all three jars behind a piece of furniture or behind your back and shift them around so your pup won't know which holds the treat.

Now bring the three jars back into view and invite your pup to approach.

He'll likely start sniffing for the treat. But, since the jars are sealed airtight, he won't be able to smell anything.

Now offer him help by placing your pointed index finger on top of the jar that you know holds the treat. As soon as your pup gives up trying to use his nose to find the treat and instead approaches the jar you are pointing at, you should immediately praise him, open the jar and reward him with the treat that was sealed inside.

For the next round, bring your pup back to the spot where he started, show him another treat and ask him again to "stay". Return to the jars, show him that you're putting the treat inside one and then conceal them and mix them up to confuse the pup where the treat is. **Release him from the "stay" (or have your helper do it) and this time, immediately place your finger on the jar that hides the treat and see if the pup goes to it. If he does, it shows he's learning how to take your direction, so you should immediately praise him, open the jar and reward him with the treat that was inside.** If he doesn't immediately go to the jar your finger is on, just wait and say nothing until he goes to the right one. When he does, immediately praise him, open the jar and reward him with the hidden treat.

If your puppy doesn't immediately approach the jar you have your finger on, you will have to practice a few more times until he starts getting it right. **Once your pup figures out that he should first wait for you to indicate a jar before he chooses one, you can now move to the next step in the activity.**

Again, put the pup in a "stay", hide the treat in one of the jars and mix the jars up. But **this time, sit back a few inches and, rather than touching the correct jar with your finger, point to it from at few inches away. When your pup figures out you are pointing to the correct jar and approaches it, immediately praise him.** Then open the jar and reward him with the treat.

As you and your pup get more advanced, you can move farther away from the jars and he will learn to look to you to help him make his choices. This will teach your pup to trust you to make good choices for him in other situations. It will increase his respect for you, keep him from making impulsive choices and enhance your overall lifetime bond.

Hint: Since the point of playing this game is to teach your pup to trust you, you should never play it in such a way to make the pup learn *not* to trust you. Never deliberately point to the wrong jar and then laugh at your dog when he goes to it. Playing games at your pup's expense like this can make him feel unsure whether he can trust you, and if this happens too many times it can undermine the kind of bond everyone wants with their dog.

#10 "The Gate Test Game"

Known for: Test of a dog's intelligence; actually teaches dogs to use tools

Helps: Builds intelligence, self-control, communication & frustration tolerance

Which pups? All; increases lifetime potential of even "flighty" pups by making them think. Also used to test the problem-solving skills of wolves.

Which owners? Any owner, handler, trainer or shelter staff person will gain insight into dogs' mind & potential and will love & respect them more

Time, Effort, Cost: Minimal; takes a few minutes to set up and may take several practice sessions, but it's a priceless learning experience

Cautions, risks: Negligible. Makes pups more centered & trustworthy. Good game for adults & older kids if your pup is nice with no food aggression. But don't allow young kids to play games involving food & frustration with any dog.

Instructions:

What could something called The Gate Test Game do for a puppy? When people first hear the name of the game, they might think it doesn't sound like much fun for anyone. But what makes this game so special is what you do once your pup is behind the gate. **This game will test your pup's intelligence, or IQ, to let you know where he stands. Practicing can also make your pup a better problem solver, because he'll learn how to use tools to get food when he can't otherwise reach it.**

To play the game you'll need: a baby gate that fits securely across one of your doorways, a piece of thin rope a few feet long and a shallow plate or pan with a small handle or an opening in the rim where you can connect the rope. Or use a shallow plate or pan like a disposable aluminum pie pan and punch a hole to thread the rope through. (If your dog or pup is very small, use a thinner rope and very small plate or pan, such as a tart tin.)

For your set-up, securely affix one end of the rope through the hole in the plate, leaving a few feet of rope that your pup can pull on from the other side of the gate. Set up your baby gate across a doorway with the bottom of the gate a few inches off the floor, high enough that your pan can slip under it, but not high enough that your pup can easily get his muzzle or paws through. With small pups, keep the gate quite close to the floor. With tiny teacup pups less than 2 lbs, you'll want to keep the gate extremely close to the floor, so you may wish to improvise a slightly different set up.

If you don't have a baby gate around, you can use another item like a screen to serve the same purpose. The item you use to block your dog must be clear enough to allow the pup to see and smell the food, but strong enough to hold him back from getting it until he figures out the key to the game. For safety, make sure the item you use to block your doorway won't allow your pup's head or paws to become caught, and affix it steadily so it can't fall on the dog during the game.

Once you have your gate in place, grab a handful of treats or food you know your puppy loves and put some onto the plate or pan. Call your pup over to one side of the gate with you, command him to "Sit" (see instructions in Part 2, Chapter 5) and, when he does, reward him with a treat or a couple pieces of food off the plate so that he understands he will be working for rewards that are on that plate. Next, slip the plate under the gate to the far side where the pup can't get it, but leave the hanging rope on the pup's side near him.

Now release the pup from the "sit" and observe what he does to try to get the plate with the treats. Just wait to see what your pup does, but don't let him jump the gate. If you have one of those rare pups that sees the food but just sits there looking at it, you can encourage by saying "Get the rope," in a happy voice. At first, your pup will probably run directly to the gate and sniff the food from afar. Then he will either bark, scratch or try to stick his paws under the gate to try to reach the plate.

As your pup finally realizes that he can't reach the food plate, he'll start considering other ways to get the food. How he reacts will give you insight into his temperament and frustration tolerance. If your pup becomes angrier with each failure, or if he just walks away when he can't get what he wants, this may indicate a dominant temperament and a pup that reacts more like a wolf than a dog. Even wolves raised in captivity won't look to humans for help when they're frustrated in this game. But it's dogs' nature to look to humans for help to solve problems like this. **If your pup looks to you for help when first confronted with this game, it indicates a good dog/human emotional bond.**

If your pup immediately grabs the rope and uses it to pull the food under the gate where he can eat it, this indicates very high intelligence and problem solving skills.

Not all pups will figure out how to get the food this quickly. You can reassure your pup as he tries, but encourage him to keep playing because you want to find out his full potential. How quickly he can figure out- on his own- to pull on the rope that extends to his side and drag the plate under is a measure of his intelligence, so try not to give any hints with this particular game. You can act upbeat and encourage your pup to "pull the rope", but do not indicate the rope by pointing at it or touching it at this time.

Even if your pup doesn't seem like he can figure out how to grab the rope, you can train him to touch the rope by shaping, a method of training that rewards other behaviors that lead up to the final behavior.

To proceed with shaping, if your pup touches the rope at all, even by accident, praise and encourage this. Eventually, most pups will figure out that pulling on the rope will get the plate of food to come closer to the gate. Once your pup figures this out and grabs the rope, immediately say the word "rope" or "get the rope", along with more verbal praise, and let him pull the plate all the way under the gate so he can eat his reward.

This will be a good skill to teach your puppy if you'd ever like him to be able to help a person with a physical disability. By teaching your dog the command "Rope" you can teach him to pull on anything you attach a rope to when you command him. This could include dresser drawers, the television remote or even the refrigerator door.

Hint: Don't hold it against your puppy if he simply never finds the brain power to pull on the rope to get the food no matter how many times you try this exercise. Most of the games and activities in this book work best when you practice with your pup as early as possible, starting at 8 weeks. But this activity is a notable exception. Some pups will mature into more brain power as they approach 6 months, especially if you practice other intelligence enhancing activities described in this book. But if you've allowed time and tried the Gate Test Game multiple times and you're certain your poor pup will never figure it out on his own, you can start giving him hints. You can wiggle or pull on the rope. Or shape your pup's actions by giving him small treats to reward accomplishments like touching the rope with his mouth, since these steps will eventually lead to the final desired behavior. You can even pull the plate through several times on your own to show your pup how it's done.

#11 "Umbilical Cord"

Best known for: Legendary for building your dogs' lifetime allegiance if you're willing to be connected to him for a few days
Helps: Teaches pups to like walking beside you. Shapes personality and can often prevent pulling & running away for life
Which pups? Helps all pups become trustworthy and never run off or pull on lead. Also therapeutic for pups that refuse to come.
Which owners? Those who can devote a few days concentrated effort for major long-term payoff.
Time, Effort & Cost: Intensive time & effort for several days
Cautions or risks: Risk of falling or injuring the pup if you trip on the lead or if the puppy winds it around chairs or table legs. Unsuitable for young children or anyone with problems with vision, balance, standing or walking, Unsuitable for frail or teacup pups and large, strong or clinically hyperactive pups.

Instructions:

This is a good activity to practice when you first get your new puppy, especially if he chews on possessions or eliminates in the house, because it gives a fundamental sense of the natural leadership relationship between dogs and man and teaches the pup to feel natural following your lead. And this can prevent many future behavior problems.

First get the pup used to a harness and lead (see instructions for "Training Heel" in Part 2, Chapter 5). Next put the puppy on the lead and either hold the lead or secure it to your belt loop. Now simply walk around your house naturally and praise the pup when he walks with you. Go ahead and do all your normal daily activities in your home, with confidence that the pup will smoothly follow you wherever you go. You do not have to call him. As long as you move gently, and don't drag the pup off his feet or hurt him in any way, you should move around and stop and start without warning, so the pup gets used to following your every cue. (Imagine how this will help on outdoor walks.)

Alternate moving around and sitting down, as you usually do during the day. If you need to check email, go ahead and sit at the computer and your pup should lie down patiently beside you; if you stop at the window to check the view, he should stop also and, if you settle in to watch some television, he should lie beside you and take a little nap. You do not have to change your movements or daily activities to accommodate the puppy linked to you (except for when he genuinely indicates the need to relieve himself outside). The object is not to pull the puppy around, but rather to glide along smoothly with the two of you connected. Your pup almost becomes a part of you, and you both learn each others' rhythms.

If your pup tries to walk ahead of you, immediately stop, so he will realize that pulling on a leash, or pulling on his owner, will never get him what he wants. As soon as he gets the message and stops trying to pull, proceed walking.

Following an owner around the house like this is quite easy for an emotionally healthy young puppy, because dogs are genetically programmed to want to follow their "pack leader". As long as you move carefully and never yank, being linked to you by an "Umbilical Cord" can also feel quite comforting and comfortable for a dog. Practicing helps socialize your puppy and it allows him freedom in the house while keeping him out of trouble. It also makes him feel natural sticking close to his owner's side.

Later on you should practice this same game without a lead (see #6 "Heeling Without a Lead" in this Chapter). Or you can alternate between the two exercises. Most pups will follow you easily and naturally, but if your pup gets distracted, you can hold a treat by your leg to encourage him to move along with you.

Practice Umbilical Cord inside, outside, with distractions and with different family members and practice it frequently.

A benefit of the Umbilical Technique is that it also teaches your puppy how to go on neighborhood walks with you comfortably and without pulling. All you have to do is add the word "heel". If you've had dogs that pulled on leash in the past, you may be surprised how quickly and easily your new pup will adjust to leash walking after you've practiced the Umbilical Technique indoors. The exercise quickly eliminates fighting with your dog, and your pup quickly learns to enjoy following their owners around the house!

Hint: In the real world many harried and time-crunched owners seem to have trouble pulling off this highly ambitious technique for any length of time, even though it's known to be so effective. Other pet parents get frustrated and cranky because with a puppy hooked to them, so they completely abandon the effort. However the umbilical technique is so incredibly transforming that sometimes even a few hours practice can completely turn around an intractable pup that never wanted to be near his owners. So any amount you practice the technique will likely help to some degree- even while you're relaxing outside or watching TV.

#12 *"Find Hidden Rewards"*

Best known for: Simple scenting game alleviates boredom
Helps: The nose is vital for dog's understanding of the world and natural well-being, but families often forget to include nose games for their developing pup
Which pups? Good for almost all pups, except aggressive pups or problem chewers
Which owners? Okay for everyone, but supervise kids so pups don't act pushy
Time, Effort, Cost: One of the cheapest & easiest standbys
Cautions or risks: Variable. Great for about 75% of pups- but no aggressive pups or pups who bully people on furniture. If you worry your pup might learn to search the furniture when you're away, only play outside

Instructions:

This basic game that can be used with most young pups is flexible and entertaining. And it integrates all your pup's senses- particularly a dog's most powerful sense- the vital sense of smell. This sense is vital for your dog's balanced functioning in the world. "Find the Hidden Reward" teaches your pup to use his nose, his eyes and his mind to look for things, as well as being a fun bonding experience for pup and owner.

Start the game by practicing a few obedience commands your pup already knows (like "sit", "down" or "look") and reward him with a treat or two to warm him up and let him know he's about to learn something new. Next, sit down on the floor in front of your pup, wave a treat in front of him so he sees and smells it and then place it on the floor behind your back where it's out of sight. Now say "Find the treat!"

Most puppies will first try to search your hands, so show your pup they are empty. Then give him some verbal encouragement the moment he starts sniffing around looking for the treat. Cheer him on and give him guidance with hints like "Yes" or "No" or "You're getting colder; now warmer..." The moment your little puppy finds the treat behind you, praise him enthusiastically and say, "Good find the treat!"

Once your puppy has successfully sniffed out the treat a few times behind your back, the next step is to get him to remain in a "stay" so you can back up and hide the treat farther away from him. Hide the treat behind something like a piece of furniture, a door or doorframe. Then return to your puppy, release him from the "stay" and ask him to "Find the Treat". At first "hide" the hidden rewards out in the open so that it isn't too hard for your pup to find them. As he gets better at the game, you can make the places you hide the rewards more complex. For example, you can even have your dog stay in one room and then ask him to sniff out a treat you have hidden in another room. (And, for more related ideas, see #13 "Nosework", below in this chapter.)

Because of the mental concentration involved, you'll notice that a simple fun game like "Find Hidden Rewards" can burn off a lot of frustrated energy for even some large, high-energy breed pups. And this sometimes turns a corner for owners who have problems controlling their pups.

One of the most useful activities dogs can perform for their owners is retrieving lost items (or, of course, finding lost people- which can be lifesaving). Teaching "Find the Hidden Reward" can help with this. It can also teach a young pup basic skills he'd need for future search and rescue or bomb/drug detection work. If you think you'd like your pup to someday do this kind of task, you should stop using edible treats as the object you ask your pup to find. Substitute a non-food item like a toy and go through the same steps teaching the game, commanding, "Find" rather than "Find the Treat". Now, each time the pup finds a hidden item, you can reward him.

Real detection dogs are also trained not to disturb an item once they find it, but to bark while "pointing" or looking in the direction of the hidden object while waiting for their handlers to come and take appropriate action. You can shape this same kind of behavior at home by teaching your pup that he will get a reward from you if he sits in front of the hidden object and gives a few barks to get your attention. You can teach your pup to bark to announce he has found an item by practicing covering the item with a cup or bowl that he cannot remove. Once he barks, uncover the item and reward him.

Now, teach him that, after he barks, he must also sit to get his reward. This will teach him the habit of sitting in front of the hidden item once he has found it and barking for you. To reward your pup once he has accomplished this, you can offer him an edible treat, a ball to fetch or verbal praise and petting.

Hint: Once your very young pup has mastered "Find the Hidden Reward" at the basic level, you can now try increasingly complex variations described below in #13 "Nosework" just for fun or if you want your pup to do any kind of scent work later in life.

#13 *"Nosework"*

Known for: Nosework adds a new avenue of stimulating sensory input for your pup and provides real tasks to devote his creative energy to. "Owning" the natural power of his nose opens up vast new worlds to your pup and makes him feel useful rather than bored

Helps: Nose work helps every pup become happier and better, because the incredibly sensitive canine nose is vital for a dog to understand the world & realize his highest potential. Practicing nose work with your pup also relieves boredom, making a more balanced dog that's happy to work with owners in other areas.

Which pups? Every dog. Reintroducing scent work can heal emotional imbalances & stop bad behavior.

Which owners? All owners, including most kids, that want to know their canine better.

Time, Effort, Cost: Low cost. The tasks below range from very easy to others that require a lot of planning, patience & time to work with your dog.

Cautions or risks: Quite safe for even for pups that act wild or have behavior issues. But don't play nose games with aggressive pups that act violent around food or possessions. And even if your dog gets amazingly good at sniffing people out, never rely solely on him to save a person's life, unless he's been professionally tested & trained for this work.

Instructions:

Do you know the secret power of your puppy's cute little nose? Canine noses are many, many times more powerful than ours. In fact, if you were lost, your pup could easily smell you from a mile away, and he could sort the trail of your footsteps out from all the others in a crowded shopping mall. Yet most owners never practice any type of nosework with their dogs or pups- even simple games. And this is a shame because **scent or nose work, added to a pup's regular exercise, can be a powerful way to alleviate the boredom of a "latchkey" pup** after he's waited for you all day. It focuses him on positive tasks rather than on mischief and destruction. **Many behaviorists also suggest that incorporating the use of the senses into your dog's daily repertoire can also make him happier and more emotionally balanced overall.**

To do true justice to the subject of scent work, we would have to devote an entire book to the subject. And, if you want to learn more, there are many good books on scent work available for sale or through local libraries. Here we will just hint at some different possibilities to get your young pup's nose involved in activities and games, and then you and your family can get creative and come up with more.

Sample activities to hone your puppy's nose power:

a. Find a treat hidden in one of multiple boxes

This game helps your puppy think things out, which will make him smarter when he's older. And the habit of thinking things out, rather than immediately reacting, will also help prevent him from developing fears and problem behaviors. Your puppy will use dexterity in this game and he'll also use his nose, refining his sense of smell.

Start with three or more identical cardboard boxes. Show the puppy a treat and then put the treat in one of the boxes with the lid open. Mix the boxes up, put them back in the middle of the floor together and then just sit back and let the pup's natural instincts take over. He'll start sniffing around each of the boxes and he'll easily find the treat. As soon as he finds it, allow him to eat it while offering lots of praise and encouragement.

Next make it harder by closing the boxes, so the pup has to find a way into the box before he can get to the treat. You can also increase the challenge and make your dog have to think more by putting the boxes in different rooms around the house.

Or use several upended identical plastic boxes or bins if you worry about your pup chewing on cardboard.

Use the command "Go Find" when you release the pup to look for the treats.

b. Teach your pup to find a treat hidden in your home or yard by scent:

You can have your puppy find a treat a hidden treat or toy by scent either outside or inside your house. Make it as easy or difficult as his age and his nose abilities allow. Read full instructions in "#12 Find Hidden Rewards" above in this chapter.

Adult dogs and older pups can usually be trusted to search for treats in the home, and to understand when game time is over. But we suggest you keep this game for the yard if you have any fear that a (younger) pup might try to search your furniture when you're away, looking for treats. If you play in the yard, make finding the treats more difficult for the pup by having a helper block the pup from seeing what's going on, and hide the treats behind or on top of items like lawn ornaments. Or place an item like an empty flowerpot or a large banana leaf partially over the treat to hide it.

Whether you play inside or out, your pup should use only scent, not sight, to find the treats in this exercise. To make it easier for your pup at first, choose treats that have a somewhat strong scent. You can next progress to hiding other scented items that are not food, as described below. Use the command "Go Find" to indicate that you want your pup to sniff out the treat.

c. Have your pup sniff a scent in your hand and then have him find it somewhere you've hidden it

In the obedience ring, your dog would sniff out the scent of your hands on a dumbbell. But to make it easier for you and your little puppy when starting, you should use a strong scent your pup would find appealing and saturate a small cloth, like a thin washcloth or small handkerchief with the scent. Bring the cloth up by your pup's face and encourage him to sniff it (most pups will do this out of natural inquisitiveness; some will also try to grab the cloth, but don't let them). As soon as the pup has taken a good sniff, put the pup in a "stay" and walk a short distance away (or have a helper hold the pup) and place the scented cloth somewhere very easy to find- like on the floor in plain sight. Release your pup and eagerly tell him "Go Find". You can verbally encourage him and even point to the cloth. The second he sniffs at it, immediately tell him "Good Find" and immediately offer him a treat as a reward.

Next practice in exactly the same fashion, but hide the cloth somewhere further away or out of sight. But don't make it too difficult to find yet. Practice until you feel your pup is really getting the hang of the exercise. (This could take only hours. More likely it might take multiple practices over several days or even weeks.)

Once he is comfortable finding the initial scent, you now make it even more challenging by starting over with a new and novel scent. Practice with as many scents as you like.

You can scent the "rag" with any scent that is safe and non-toxic for dogs. If you happen to be a hunter who has trained retrievers, you will know that you can buy commercial "bird scent" just for this purpose. If you think you'll ever want your dog to retrieve game, obviously this would be the perfect product to use. But if you don't want your pup going after any animal scent, you can also use any harmless natural flavoring like vanilla (don't use too much and don't let the pup eat it) or smoke flavoring. You could also rub some juice left over from boiling hot dogs or fish or rub some strong smelling cheese over the cloth to guarantee the pup will search for it the first few times, but if you use extremely smelly items, do not bring them in the house where they would permanently scent your furniture or the floor. Some chewy dog treats are also moist and have a strong scent, so these could work. You just want the scent to be something novel (a scent that is not already found in your house or yard) and somewhat appealing.

As your pup gets better at the task, you can start using more subtle scents, like the vanilla, that hold no natural appeal for him. This is a fun game in itself, and it's always fascinating for dogs and their owners. But you will also probably want to try the next activity- trailing a scent- if you ever want your dog to be able to track a human's movements or find a lost human.

d. Trail a scent for your pup to follow

Now that your pup is able to sniff out a particular scent in the air, he can now become proficient at following a strong scent that you trail. To do this, leash your pup and first start with a strongly scented rag (or similar item), as described above. Now place the pup in a "stay" or have a helper hold him and slide your scented rag along the ground to the spot where you will hide it. You can tie the soaked rag on a string and drag it, making sure it keeps good contact with the ground. This exercise works best outdoors where you have some room. (You could also do it on a floor that you could clean afterwards, but never do it on carpet.)

Drag the scented item far enough away that the pup will have to follow the trail to find it and hide it just out of sight. Then return to your pup and bring him to the start of the trail with a leash. Encourage him to sniff and lead him along the trail as you best remember it. You could also "mark" your route ahead of time by painting the grass or laying down a thin string, or any tactic that your pup won't register but that will help you remember exactly where you put the trail.

Follow where your pup leads you with his nose, but also try to guide him if he needs it. And give him some verbal hints or discouragement based on how "hot" or "cold" he is. Ideally, the pup will take you right to the scented item and he'll start sniffing at it. When this happens, immediately praise him, saying, "Good Find" and give him some great treats to eat.

Eventually you will want your dog to be able to distinguish the scents of individual people. So, once your pup becomes good at finding other scents, introduce an item that has the strong scent of a person he has never met and allow him to find this. You could start by putting the item in plain view, a short distance away from you when you say, "Go Find". Next, trail the scent of the human after allowing your pup to sniff it, but only hide the scented fabric a short distance away. Wear plastic gloves when you touch the item, so your pup doesn't get confused and think you are interested in him finding your scent. When your pup succeeds at trailing the scent of the human, try the next step.

e. Have your pup sniff a human's scent and then find the human

To make this extremely challenging task easy for your pup at first, start with an item scented by a person who's not usually in your home, but ideally someone the pup has met in the past and likes. Or you can practice in a remote location like a park as long as the assistant can hide.

Only touch the scented item of clothing with plastic gloves. You MUST keep the pup on leash at this time and NEVER practice this activity with a guard-dog pup or any pup that you suspect might act aggressive to an uninvited guest in the home or yard or any hidden human. If you are sure your pup won't hurt a surprise visitor, arrange for the human to be hiding somewhere (either in your home or in the neutral location) while you hold the pup.

Allow your pup to get a deep sniff of the person's item of clothing. Once he does now say, "Go Find" and allow him to lead you on the leash. Don't release the leash. If your pup has accomplished all the preceding scent work correctly, he will now run directly to the hidden person. The second he does, immediately say, "Good Find!" and give him some great treats. If he's still having problems, you could drag the scented item on the next practice, allowing the scent to reach right up to the hidden person. If this doesn't work either, you could allow the person to reveal themselves. Let the pup sniff the item and then let him go straight to the person standing right there. Praise him by saying "Good Find" and reward, and then try again with the person hidden.

f. Once your pup is good at finding a guest's scent, it is time to try with the scents of particular family members.

This can be much more confusing, and you may have to start with the family members in sight. In this case, if your pup already knows family members by name (as in the activity called "#15 Identify Family Members" described in detail later in this chapter) you can have your pup sniff the family member's piece of clothing. Then command, "Go Find" and add the family member's name. But only give the verbal command if the pup has trouble following just the scent at first. Ultimately you don't want to have to refer to verbal information, and the dog should learn to find people just by scent.

g. Have your pup follow a human's footsteps

Now that your pup can find a person at some distance just by scent, it's time to try him with just the scent of the person on their footsteps. When your pup cannot see, have the particular person walk a relatively far distance from the spot where you are standing with the pup to a spot where they are hidden out of sight (inside a vehicle with windows up and air conditioning running or inside a shed or just inside a commonly unused entrance to the home would be ideal.)

Now let your pup take a good sniff of their item and tuck the item back in your pocket. Keep your pup leashed, tell him "Go Find" and encourage him as he sniffs along the path, until he gets to where the person is hiding. The person now reveals his or herself and you immediately praise your dog by saying "Good Find" and giving lots of love along with lots of yummy treats or the chance to play a favorite game like Fetch.

Scent work is not easy. If you and your family members get your pup under a year in age to the point where he can find a person as described above, this is a magnificent achievement, and you may wish to do even more as described below in the "Hint". But even if your pup can't find the person and only accomplishes one or two of the activities described above successfully, this is still a great way to bond together as you channel his energy and activate his nose. And this kind of practice makes for a great everyday companion for life!

Hint: Scent work is a serious part of work like search and rescue. It's part of many sporting activities and competitions including advanced obedience. If you think there may be scent work in your pup's future, training is fascinating. Start investigating at your library and online. Research the AKC (American Kennel Club) and other local clubs to find various competitions involving scenting and tracking. And you may be pleasantly surprised to find activities, competitions and obedience clubs to suit your dog in your area.

#14 *"Which Hand?"*

Known for: Great basic game to teach mental focus

Helps with: Increases mental focus, teaches pup to think before acting and this simple game is sometimes the first real two-way communication between a pup and owners

Which pups? Every pup can learn to play it in seconds, but never play with food-aggressive pups or dogs

Which owners? Anyone can do it, but not recommended for unsupervised small children since it involves teasing a puppy with treats

Time, Effort, Cost: Absolutely minimal

Cautions or risks: Generally safe unless you allow a small child to play with a (large) food aggressive pup or pup that jumps violently, which could cause serious injury.

Instructions:

This game makes a dog think, and this is always good for a puppy! The more your dog is made to think when he's a puppy, the smarter he'll be when he's grown up. And who doesn't want the smartest dog on the block? You can probably tell from the name of the game what this very easy and basic game is about. The owner shows their pup a treat and then puts it behind their back. You make a show of moving the treat from hand to hand behind your back, and then you hold your closed hands out in front of the puppy and ask him, "Which hand?"

At first your puppy may use his nose to find out which hand the treat is in. Let the puppy pick a hand. If it is the right one, praise him and give him the treat. If the hand he chooses isn't right, just say something like, "Oh, oh, wrong hand. Try again.**"**

After a little time you can make it harder for your puppy and not let him use his nose as much. If he tries to use his nose just laugh and say, "Oh, stop your cheating." If he looks at you and stops using his nose, then leave your hand out to continue play. If he keeps using his nose, just put your hands behind your back and stop playing for awhile.

You will know that your pup is playing using his mind when you notice him trying to predict patterns; for example, if you put the treat in the alternate hand after each trial, you'll notice him always looking in the alternate hand. This is a good sign of an intelligent dog.

As soon as your pup masters one pattern, change to another. You can also make the game more challenging by having two people play. Which Hand is a fun and easy game for all but small children to play with nice gentle pups. (Just make sure the pup isn't big or pushy enough to overpower the child to try to get the treats. And no game is safe with pups that show aggression or food aggression- these pups first require professional assessment and you may need a behaviorist to help your family with their training.)

Hint: "Which Hand?" could be the first official "game" you ever play with your pup. Often, families ask us what we mean by "working with a dog's mind" and, rather than answering in words, it's easy to demonstrate what we mean with this simple, 2-second game. And we've never yet seen a dog of any age (8 weeks-15 years)- even some with serious challenges- who failed to enjoy it.

#15 "Identify Family Members"

Best known for: Vital building block for making your dog more useful & a joy to observe
Helps: All pups become the caring & helpful dogs they should be
Which pups? Every dog should recognize his family members by name & be willing & able to find them. This skill may also completely turn around a pup's bad behavior.
Which owners: Especially important exercise for families to do together; shows families how their dogs can & should be helpful
Time, Effort, Cost: Training ranges from easy to fairly involved depending on the pup
Cautions, risks: None. A dog with this skill has the first building block for saving a life, so it's negligent for parents to fail teach their pup the kids' names & how to find them

Instructions:

In "Identify Family Members" you teach your dog to recognize the different names of your family members and how to go to a family member when you ask him. If your dog learns as a puppy, he'll then be able to confidently perform this helpful, and even lifesaving, skill as an adult.

Teach this activity with two or more people. One person holds the dog while the other person walks a short distance away. The person holding the dog now commands, "Find Mommy" (or that person's name) while the second person whistles, makes noise or taps on their leg to get the puppy to come to them the first few times. When the puppy reaches the person, they reward him with petting, praise and/or treats.

Once your pup reliably goes to the person on cue, start increasing the distance between the two people until he can find the person anywhere in house. You can even teach your dog to give one bark when he gets to the named person or to gently take the person's hand to lead the person back to you when you say, "Bring Mommy".

> **Hint:** Don't just stop at teaching this once. Practice frequently with real-world situations like telling him "Go see Mom, she's ready to take you for a walk" "go to Adrienne; she wants to play with you" or "go upstairs and check on Benjamin". Start at first with easy requests like telling the pup to go to your child across a yard. By the time he matures, you can make more complex requests- almost like talking to another human.

#16 *"Interactive Toys"*

Known for: many people still don't know about this great option with no downside
Helps: inhibits boredom & separation anxiety when you leave your pup; also keeps pups from constantly bothering people
Which pups? Pups that must stay alone for long periods, also redirects hyperactive pups
Which owners? Owners with problems keeping pups occupied when they go away
Time, Effort, Cost: $6-$30 for one; most homes buy more
Cautions or risks: Significant risk of ingestion & injury with the wrong toy. Supervise carefully & only leave a pup with the toughest toys

Instructions:

Puppies are highly intelligent and, when they're young, they're also in a period of intense development, so they need plentiful stimuli for their bodies and minds when you're away. Boredom, and lack of something productive to do, can also cause a pup to get into mischief, such as jumping on furniture or chewing on possessions. And, in a worst-case scenario, a pup could develop a disorder known as separation anxiety. Symptoms can include excessive barking or crying, soiling in the house or damaging furniture or fixtures. Dogs with extreme separation anxiety can even hurt themselves whenever their owners leave. True separation anxiety can be serious and may require the advice or help of a behaviorist. But mild cases can sometimes be treated by bringing more positive stimuli into a dog's life. And, by giving your pup adequate stimuli whenever he's alone, you could prevent separation anxiety from developing.

One of the best ways to keep your pup occupied and prevent frustration is to offer him "interactive toys". These are toys designed to provide more stimuli than common toys and make dogs think.

Many interactive toys are specially designed to dispense a reward when your pup manipulates the toy correctly. These toys provide mental stimulation in addition to the pleasure of chewing. The reward could be a sound, another toy inside or, most commonly, a food treat. Interactive toys come in all levels of difficultly, all sizes, shapes and prices and they are available online, at most local and chain pet stores and through pet catalogs. Some are shaped like rubber balls that your dog can roll or throw around, and the reward falls out through a hole. Others feature flashing lights, glow in the dark, funny sounds or even a recorded voice. (While most types are safe with supervision, not all types may be safe to leave a puppy with alone.)

The more intelligent your puppy, the more complex interactive toys he will enjoy. And these toys are not just good for leaving dogs alone, but also for dog-owner playtime. One example are complex, new interactive dog puzzles packaged in large flat boxes. (These are available at pet stores like Pet Supermarket and online). While you and your pup spend time together, you can cheer him on to figure out a puzzle. Or you can offer him an interactive toy loaded with goodies as a reward- for example, after he completes a successful obedience session.

You can also set an interactive toy down for a rambunctious puppy whenever you want some quiet time. Offer your hyperactive pup a Kong toy or similar toy filled with treats or filling and you won't have to give him constant attention. Offer the toy and watch your pup immediately stop flinging around the house, lie down calmly and begin licking it. **This first moment of calmness may be enough to break a hyperactive cycle and set the stage for further therapy and training.** The toy can serve a similar function to the use of mood altering medication in humans with emotional disorders. And it's an easy way to give owners a short break!

Interactive toys are also a smart choice for puppy teething, because they occupy puppies much longer than non-interactive toys. Some are also made specifically for chewing. But be careful to select a toy that will stand up to your puppy chewing harder than you might expect. If your pup's a very tough chewer, use the adult version of the toy and/or one of a larger size or tougher material.

Perhaps the best known interactive toy is the highly popular rubber "Kong". The classic rubber Kong comes in sizes ranging from tiny to extra large. It's cone-shaped, with an empty cavity in the middle, which you can stuff with a special paste, dry treats and/or a (non-allergenic) filling of your choosing. Depending on how tightly you stuff the Kong with treats, your pup may work at it diligently for minutes or even hours.

Some Kongs are made particularly for puppy teething, and some come in stick shape. And the company has recently introduced new models with different configurations to increase challenge. You can buy many other brands of interactive toys that work on similar principle- keeping your dog busy working for his treats while you're away or occupied. For the purpose of this section, we will refer to them all as Kongs.

Kongs are quite popular and we know of many dogs that have good success with them, although we usually recommend other interactive toys in addition. We like the fact that the stronger level Kongs are made of an especially tough material that's safe to leave most puppies alone with for long periods. (In one rare instance we heard of a dog swallowing pieces of a Kong, requiring surgery.) And owners must always use extreme care when they leave their pups alone with any toy. If your pup is teething, we suggest erring on the safe side by choosing a model of Kong designed for older pups and tougher chewers.

Often dogs lose interest in an interactive toy as soon as all the treats are gone. So some owners freeze a filled Kong to make it last longer. Others try "Kong Time", a unit that sits on a surface like a countertop and dispenses multiple Kongs over a period of time. And every day companies are introducing new and interesting interactive toys.

Some interactive toys we often recommend include the Busy Buddy, "Tug-a-Jug" and Buster Cube. These are designed to occupy smarter dogs that quickly get bored with other games and toys. The hard plastic Buster Cube has a maze inside, and your pup must manipulate the toy to get dry treats out. With the Tug-a-Jug, your pup has to pull a rope on one end to get the treats out of a bottle-shaped toy. These toys stimulate and sharpen a puppy's mind and, while he's working for his treats; he won't get bored, and your furniture will stay undamaged.

Hint: To make your interactive toys work best to distract your dog when you leave home, keep certain toys that you never offer him at other times. This way he has something special to look forward to when you leave home.

#17 *"Explore a Tunnel"*

Best known for: This is part of formal agility competition, but it can be better at home...

Helps: Builds pups' courage & trust of owners, along with coordination

Which pups? Good for occupying & exercising high energy terriers & small breeds. Also helps shy or low energy pups perk up and build confidence

Which owners? Easy & fun for most owners, including kids. Requires a bit of flexibility to either bend or get down on floor

Time, Effort, Cost: Low. Owner usually has to encourage the pup to go through. Official dog agility tunnels can cost $50 or up, but you can spend less than $10 if your dog is small & you substitute a "cat" or "kids'" tunnel from a department store.

Cautions or risks: Minimal. Have your pup walk, rather than crawl through a tunnel if he has back or joint problems

Instructions:

Walking or crawling through a tunnel is good exercise, stimulates a pup's senses, develops coordination and aids his emotional development. And owners/ handlers can easily play with their pups with a tunnel anytime they have a few minutes. The skill of getting through an enclosed tunnel can teach your pup not to fear strange objects and situations and to always trust you later in life. And of course, you should teach your pup the skill if you someday plan to enter him in agility competitions.

If you've never seen a tunnel, you can find pictures online or in your library when you research "agility competition". Once you've seen what they look like, purchase a tunnel or tube that's wide enough for your puppy to run through so he won't get stuck. Consider getting a size large enough for the pup to grow into and make sure your selection can't collapse on your pup while he's in it. Plan to use your tunnel indoors, outdoors or both.

Tunnels are available specifically designed for dog agility competition. Beginner's agility kits are available in pet catalogs and in some pet stores that carry agility equipment (you should call to make sure). Or you can buy an inexpensive tunnel made for children or for cats at some department or grocery stores if the size is right for your dog.

To teach your puppy to enter the tunnel the first time, start with a shortened tube. Have a helper hold the puppy at one end of the tube while you kneel at the other end. Call your pup to you, offering a treat as your helper simultaneously releases him. As your pup steps into the tunnel, encourage and entice him. When he gets to you, offer praise and treats and then repeat the process with your pup running through the tunnel in the other direction to get to your helper.

If you want to make the tunnel crawl more challenging, you can make the circumference smaller so the dog has to crawl through the tube. The additional challenge of crawling through the tunnel may appeal more to breeds that were used in the past for hunting game in tunnels underground. Dachshunds will naturally love the tunnel game; so will many terrier breeds and some herding dogs. (But don't force a pup to crawl through if he has any physical problems. Dogs that have problems crawling can still run through a wider tunnel.)

Start with a short tube before you make the tube longer. And, while you should attempt to coax timid pups to try the tunnel, never force a pup past extreme fear. The worst thing that can happen at the first practice session is if your pup gets stuck and panics, since then he'll feel reluctant to enter the tunnel again.

Once your dog is comfortable, you can expand the length of the tube. To further increase the challenge, make some bends in a long tunnel. Or introduce the "chute" type tunnel used in agility competitions. This tunnel starts rigid, but the far end is a fabric sleeve that the dog has to lift as he crawls through. When first training your puppy to master the "chute" type tunnel, you should hold the far end open so that he can see you.

Hint: Some pups enjoy going through the tunnel so much they'll do it on their own. As long as you know your pup won't chew on the tunnel, you can leave it for him to play in.

#18 *"Play Soccer"*

Best known for: A fun way to burn off excess energy; pups can even play alone
Helps: Physical fitness, coordination, makes dogs playful rather than frustrated & grumpy
Which pups? Every pup with energy to burn
Which owners? Able- bodied adults or older children if you plan to play with your pup; or any owner can teach their pup to play alone
Time, Effort, Cost: Low unless you plan to do some running
Cautions or risks: Not for pups with health problems or some giant breed pups; clear with your vet first. Don't let pups play too long in hot sun or extreme heat

Instructions:

Playing soccer teaches your pup to work with you as a team and builds body/eye coordination- he learns to watch the ball as you kick it around and then he runs with it, pushing it with his nose or his feet as you attempts to grab it. This game is easy to learn for both you and your dog, it comes naturally for people to enjoy kicking a ball around and most puppies love to chase anything that moves.

The only equipment you'll need is an old soccer ball, blown up tight so your dog can't get a good bite on it. Or buy a soccer ball from a pet store that's made of hard plastic meant for dogs, so it can last forever. When you first play this game, just kick the ball around the yard and see if your puppy wants to join in the fun. If he shows interest, gently kick the ball over his way. But don't spoil your pup's first game by kicking the ball so hard it hits him in the face and he falls over and whimpers, or he may never want to go near the ball again!

When you first start there's usually no need to even kick the ball very close to the puppy. If it looks like you're having fun, your puppy will probably come over and chase the ball, trying to get it from you. When he does this, allow him to steal the ball, run around the yard a little and have some fun. Now you can come over and try to steal the ball back from him, play with it awhile and then let him get it again. Some pups eventually learn to push the ball over your way and "invite" you to take it just to continue the fun. Now your kids will have a soccer partner who'll happily knock the ball back and forth with them for hours.

For safety give the pup rest breaks and opportunities to drink. (But don't allow him to drink large amounts of water immediately after exercise as this could cause life-threatening bloat.) And, if your pup is a large or giant breed, you should prevent him from jumping and running around too vigorously until he is fully grown, to prevent future hip problems. Consult your veterinarian for exact guidelines for your particular dog before introducing any vigorous exercise.

Your puppy can also learn to play soccer on his own, happily chasing the soccer ball by himself while you relax in your chaise lounge or finish up an outdoor project. Just don't forget to give your pup companionship and keep an eye on him to keep him out of trouble. And you'll still want to play soccer with your pup on weekends or at family gatherings.

Hint: No substitutions! We suggest a soccer ball for specific reasons to improve dog on dog relations and prevent possession aggression around dogs and people. A soccer ball is just the right size and consistency to teach your pup the right way of thinking, because he can never get his teeth into the ball, but he can hit it and chase it endlessly. This actually shapes your pup's personality to want to chase and play, but to never grab onto an item and become possessive. Soccer type balls are also good for dogs/pups to play with independently, because they don't tend to puncture. If your pup bites at the ball really badly, you can buy a hard plastic ball approximately the same size at pet stores; one is made by Kong.

#19 *"Mock Veterinary Exam"*

Best known for: Essential for health & safety. The younger you practice, the better
Helps: Teaches your pup to be comfortable with vet exams.
Which pups? All normal non-aggressive pups should practice learning human touch is OK so they'll never become fearful or aggressive. Start as young as possible
Which owners: Adult owners good at reading canine body language so they don't hurt the pup or get bitten; no kids
Time, Effort, Cost: Minimal, but stay fully focused for safety
Cautions, risks: Significant bite risk in pups with existing aggression and/or unknown history. But this risk is weighed against the bigger risk of lifetime problems at the vet if you don't practice mock vet exams while the pup is extremely young. Because of the bite risk with pups of unknown temperament (such as those adopted from shelters/rescues), young children should never do mock

vet exams. If you strongly suspect your pup might bite during a mock exam, you may need to practice at first with a muzzle, and/or get help from an animal behaviorist.

Instructions:

"Mock Veterinary Exam" is an activity that can save your puppy's life one day. Have you ever taken a 90 pound dog to the veterinary clinic, only to have him flail around in panic when the veterinarian looks into his mouth or touches his paws? Perhaps your dog even growls at, or nips at the vet. If this happens during a routine physical exam, imagine the risk to your veterinarian and his assistants if your dog is ever injured or has a face full of painful porcupine quills! The veterinarian could get bitten or he may tell you he can't help your dog because your dog gets too upset and bites during exams. Some veterinarians have to handle aggressive dogs by tranquilizing them. But not all vets will do this and, medically, it's a risky way to treat a sick dog.

Instead, make life easier for yourself, your veterinarian and your dog by getting your puppy used to people touching him all over his body when he's young. Most puppies under 16-weeks old naturally want to be near their owners all the time, so before 16 weeks is the best age to start teaching your puppy to stay relaxed with human touch. Practice by "playing doctor" with your pup.

The process is easy. Have you ever watched your vet give your dog a good looking over? He looks into the ears, mouth and eyes and he also runs his hands all over the dog's body to see if he can feel abnormalities like a suspicious lump, weak hips or a bone the pup injured during play. A trained professional can tell a great deal about an animal's health just running their hands along the animal's body.

Just like your veterinarian looks for small inconsistencies that may be the first signs of illness, you can also observe minor problems before they become serious by regularly examining your pup.

When you first teach "Mock Veterinary Exam", *never call your pup to you.* Instead, pick him up and place him on your lap or a secure table or piece of furniture. Or kneel down beside him if he's too large to pick up. Have some special treats to offer if he presents resistance when you try to touch certain spots. (And also give him some treats at the conclusion of a successful "exam").

Now pet your pup on one of his cheeks and then move up to examine his ears. Touch the ears in a smooth gentle way that the puppy likes and speak to him encouragingly. As he calms down more, lift each ear and look in like the vet does. Praise your pup for allowing you to do this.

Next move your hands gently over his body. If your pup flinches when you touch a particular spot, first check the area carefully to make sure that there's no visible injury, swelling or broken skin. (Ear infections are common in young pups that have come from pet stores or unfamiliar breeders- and often the first sign of an ear infection is a pup that flinches away if you attempt to touch his ears or head. Ear infections cause excruciating pain and this pain is a common reason why pups snap when people touch them. If you suspect an ear infection, get your pup veterinary care as soon as possible.)

If you rule out physical injury or illness, it's likely that you've stumbled across one of the common sensitive areas on a dog's body. You can now desensitize your puppy by praising and giving him tiny treats as you gently work your way closer to touching the sensitive area. Practice this when your dog is a puppy and you can avoid common problems with touch when he's an adult.

Some spots you may initially have problems handling are the mouth, ears, tail and feet. It's important not to let these problems persist. Practice until your puppy becomes comfortable with touch in these areas, since continued sensitivity could cause flare-ups when people touch him as an adult. Children often grab dogs' tails and you don't want your pup to ever reflexively turn and bite a child. Your pup must also allow his feet to be handled, so a groomer can clip his nails. And, of course, you want to be able to safely approach your dog's mouth. If your dog lets you open his mouth without a fuss, he'll allow you take away dangerous items that he picks up on the floor. And you can also start brushing his teeth, another healthy necessity.

If you gently touch your puppy all over his body when he's tiny, you probably won't have any problems when he matures; he'll completely enjoy human touch. Unfortunately some owners may buy or adopt their puppies after the pups have already developed an aversion to human handling. This often happens in overcrowded "puppy mills" where the young puppies aren't adequately socialized. If new pet parents suspect their dog came from a puppy mill, it helps to understand the root of the problem and understand that the lack of early socialization *can* often be overcome with patient, positive training.

Never get angry at your puppy for acting fearful when you touch him, and never take it personally. If your pup seems to hate touch, the worst thing you can do is to give up and stop handling him. This will definitely make the problem worse. Even skittish dogs that are fully grown can be helped with careful practice (plus the help of an animal behaviorist, if the problem is serious). But if your pup is still quite young and he acts nippy or skittish- as opposed to showing full-blown aggression- when you touch him in certain areas, correcting the problem at home is simply a matter of patient practice and the right reinforcement.

Note any places on your pup's body where he shows a resistance to being touched. Dogs with less early socialization with humans tend to naturally dislike touch on the paws, the ears, the tail and the mouth. Make sure your pup doesn't have pain or other physical symptoms and that he's resisting touch on certain areas of his body because he's attempting to control the situation. If your pup acts protective of a certain area, *yet he doesn't show any apparent pain or injury there*, hold a highly tasty treat in front of him the next time you approach that area. As he eats the treat, touch him extremely gently on the sensitive spot. Practice repeatedly, never pushing him too far beyond his comfort zone, and your pup will learn to associate people touching him with the pleasant stimulus of receiving treats. Act affectionate and confident and your pup will learn to enjoy his mock veterinary exams.

Hint: Part of what makes a vet visit intimidating for some dogs is the feeling of the cold, high and slippery examination table. Try the Activity "#44 Pup On the Table" in this section to safely accustom your pup to being up high under less stressful conditions.

#20 *"Soft Mouth"*

Best known for: One of the most important things to train pups
Helps: Do this rather than letting your pup grow up to bite you
Which pups: Essential to teach this to every pup so they'll have proper empathy with owners; helps "mouthy" young pups change their personality before it's too late.
Which owners: Every owner should learn the right way to respond in case the puppy ever nips them, and adults should always step in for extremely young kids
Time, Effort, Cost: Minimal & the payoff is priceless because it protects people
Cautions, risks: Low, unless you confuse "nippy" or "mouthy" puppies with truly aggressive pups that are highly dangerous and require immediate professional help. If a pup shows real aggression, rather than playful mouthing, never expect children to deal with it. ANY response from small children, including running, crying, or attempting to "train" an aggressive dog or pup, may lead to serious injury. Kids can practice "soft mouth" with pups that are only playful nippers to teach that their skin is delicate.

Instructions:
Everybody wants a dog that won't nip their hands, their body or their family members when he plays or feels excited. But many methods people try to prevent nipping do more harm than good and often make dogs bite more.

Some people unfortunately think they can break a pup of biting by holding him by the back of the neck and shaking and yelling at him. But this will only make your pup afraid of you, and it won't teach him to use a soft mouth. An even worse response is to punch the pup or shove your fist deep into his mouth when he nips. Despite the fact that it strikes us as terrible, many people do this. But hurting a pup that nips won't make him a gentle dog. Instead, it will make him fear and distrust humans. And it may incite him to bite harder next time or to bite a weaker handler, such as a child.

Pushing roughly at a dog's mouth or sticking your hands in his mouth in any context, including play, will teach him to bite. If someone treated humans this way, we might want to bite, too. If we want our dogs to be gentle, we must show gentleness.

The first step in dealing with a mouthy puppy is to teach him to stop biting you. One easy way to discourage your pup from biting you is the same way the pups' littermates would. If your puppy ever puts his mouth on your skin, immediately "Yipe!" sharply like a puppy in the litter would. Your puppy will most likely stop what he's doing and look up at you with a shocked expression on his face. As soon as he does, praise him and put your hand back in front of him. (If the pup is physically teething, and you think this is why he put his teeth on you, also offer him an appropriate chew toy.)

If your pup tries to nip again, yelp and then walk away from him for a few moments to deprive him of your company. This teaches the pup that, if he bites, you'll leave the room and take your treasured attention away from him. **All family members should act consistent with this and no one should ever give the pup any attention if he bites.** Even swatting at him, squealing or reprimanding him is still a form of attention, which the puppy may crave. But he should never get anything he wants when he is biting at people. **You must teach him that people feel revolted and will momentarily abandon him if he ever uses teeth hard enough to cause pain.** For a dog, especially a young pup, the desire to stay in the company of his pack is vastly powerful motivation. If he knows he can never get a person's love or attention when he mouths or bites, he'll learn never to use his teeth this way in the future.

If stepping away or setting the pup down is not enough and the biting episode continues with the pup acting very pushy, you can give him a short time out in another room to control his behavior. And you can repeat short time-outs if he repeats the unacceptable behavior. If, however, the pup aims for the face, draws blood, bites viciously or chases people down if they try to escape these are signs of serious aggression and you should not attempt self-help without first consulting an expert behaviorist.

After you've shaped your pup's behavior according to the instructions above so that he learns to stop deliberately biting at your hands or other parts of your body, you can proceed to teaching him how use a "soft mouth" and use his mouth on people properly. To practice, hold a treat in your hand with a very small piece showing out the edge of your fingers. If the dog tries to take the treat too fast or too hard, turn your hand so he can't get it. Show the treat again and say the word, "Gentle." Only give the pup the treat when he'll take it gently, and praise him when you give it to him. The point is to teach your pup that he'll be rewarded for using his mouth gently when he interacts with you. Practice this whenever you give your pup a treat. If you need more practice, you can always work with individual pieces of his dry kibble.

You can also teach your pup to always use a soft mouth on your possessions just like retrievers are trained not to damage game. To do this, offer the pup a toy, but only allow him to have it when he attempts to take it softly. (You will know your pup is grabbing too hard if you offer a squeaky toy and he makes it squeak.)

Hint: Teaching pups to kiss and lick trains a better alternative than using teeth on people. See instructions in "#21 Give Kisses" below.

#21 *"Give Kisses"*

Known for: Teaches dogs and pups to kiss hands, rather than nibble on them
Helps: Especially helps young pups that are almost compelled to chew on people, because this completely breaks the cycle of their behavior
Which pups? For compulsive nibblers who don't mean harm, but haven't received proper education from previous owners, mother dog or littermates; good for young pups
Which owners? Most families (especially those with kids) feel more comfortable once they successfully have this game in their arsenal
Time and Effort: Fairly easy; somewhat messy
Cautions or risks: Be careful! This game is only meant for pups with MINOR nipping problems relating to play, overexcitement or teething. It is NOT safe with pups that cause injury, break skin or show other signs of aggression or unfriendliness towards people, especially kids. Such pups require professional assessment/treatment and they should never work around children and food.

Instructions:

"Kisses" is a game that helps dog owners who are having difficulties with a "nipper" or a "mouther". Kisses will teach your pup to always act gentle with human flesh. And kisses feel a lot better than nips. To teach the command, call your puppy to you and spread a little honey or peanut butter on the back of your hand (as long as your dog has no allergies). As your pup starts licking your hand say, "Give kisses," and praise him. Practice a few times.

Then, don't apply anything to the back of your hand. Call your pup to you and just say "Give kisses." When your pup starts licking your hand on cue, immediately offer a treat and lots of praise. Now practice multiple times each day, gradually phasing out treats, so the pup only receives treats occasionally. After this point, if your pup ever looks like he's about to nip, instead command him, "Give kisses".

You can also command him "Give kisses" as a more polite way for your pup to greet guests than jumping on them or nipping them, as long as they don't object to being licked.

Hint: Should your dog ever give kisses on the mouth? The only acceptable answer for our readers is, "no!" We confess that we have personally allowed many dogs to kiss us, starting when we were toddlers. And we felt completely charmed the first time we gave the command and our darling Great Pyrenees imitated her Mom and kissed Emma right on the mouth, smacking her lips just like a Palm Beach socialite. But the truth is, for safety, an owner should never encourage their dog to go right to people's mouths, because many instances of dominance, and many facial bites, can start this way. And not just big dogs create problems- facial attacks are common with toy breeds. Especially if you have children, stay safe and always confine your dog's loving kisses to hands, and not faces.

#22 *"Grooming"*

Known for: Just doing a pleasant comb-out or towel rub daily can be enough to make your pup more manageable, emotionally stable and increase your bond

Helps: Outstanding daily activity that builds dog/owner bond, replaces unhealthy activities, and answers the question, "what should I do with my dog right now?"

Which pups? Therapeutic for tentative pups and those that don't like or trust human touch enough. Also essential for long-haired breeds

Which owners? Every adult should feel comfortable grooming their dog, not for young kids of any age if the pup might snap

Time, Effort, Cost: Could save hundreds or thousands if you decide to do regular grooming at home, rather than hiring someone. It can take some time, which also counts for bonding time

Cautions, risks: Be advised- the purpose of practicing grooming is to make pups comfortable with grooming at a young age so they'll never snap at people. But in some cases it may be too late & pups may bite during grooming. Grooming could also hurt a pup if done wrong, so save it for adults, teens and (supervised) older kids. Be gentle and keep your mind on the task.

Instructions:

Gently brushing or grooming your puppy for a few minutes every single day is one of the best things you can do to create a good temperament in your adult dog.

As home dog trainers specializing in severe canine emotional problems, we often encounter dogs and puppies who won't tolerate their owners' touch! These dogs' reactions range from showing stress and discomfort and shying or jerking away, to growling at, snapping at or even biting whenever their owner tries to touch them! Only some dogs show severe reactions like this, and these reactions can stem from complex problems that require professional assessment. But there *is* a strong correlation between proper handling during a pup's developmental stages and how the dog will react to human touch throughout his life. Unfortunately, once a dog starts resisting activities like grooming, his owners may give in and avoid the activity, creating a vicious cycle.

Sadly, some pups also experience extremely rough handling at professional groomers' and this can lead to serious fears and intolerance of human touch. The groomer may then try tougher interventions like muzzling or drugs without the owner's knowledge and this will lead to even more problems at home. The best solution is to take the pup to a gentle groomer who will attempt true remediation.

Proper grooming is important to dogs' health and well-being and it's also one of the cornerstone activities for developing a healthy dog/owner bond. Not every breed of dog requires the same amount of attention to their coat. Some short-haired breeds don't physically need to be brushed every day, while some of the popular small breeds with lush coats need proper trimming and brushing to avoid illness. But *every* dog requires time to experience his owners' gentle touch every day, and grooming time is the perfect opportunity.

Canines naturally groom each other in the wild as part of their bonding ritual, and puppies should understand that their owner grooms them out of caring. Thus the process should feel good. Start by brushing your puppy with the softest brush you can find- the equivalent of a human baby brush. Or wipe your pup down with a soft towel or a mitt made for shorthaired breeds. If the pup resists at first, you can simply hold him close and wait for him to calm down, or you could hold a treat out for him to nibble on. This is not, however, a time for you to set your pup down, even if he wiggles and tries to get free. He should learn that the grooming process is overall pleasant and nothing to fear; but he should also learn that his owner knows best and that he must tolerate his owner manipulating his body, whenever required.

The best way to create a healthy mindset in your puppy is to start young and practice every day. Make daily brushing a pleasant experience and also introduce your pup to tooth brushing, nail clipping (or touching nails), ear cleaning and bathing at a young age. Family members should alternate brushing the puppy, so that the pup will come to enjoy and respect everyone's touch. And parents can use this time to teach children how to handle dogs with a calm and gentle touch, so that the tiny puppy will fall asleep happily in their arms. Rather than playing too rough with the puppy, children can learn a steadier and calmer manner of interacting through practice.

It's generally not advisable for very young children to groom dogs or pups. **You may want your older children to learn to groom your puppy, but adults should carefully supervise grooming sessions at first, to make sure the children handle the puppy correctly. Parents must also confirm that the puppy reacts appropriately and never attempts to snap.** Unfortunately, a good number of adult dogs and even some puppies that come from unknown backgrounds may not have been adequately socialized prior to coming to their new families. These include pups bred in "puppy mills" (substandard breeding facilities that are known to sell to pet stores and over the Internet) and pups that have suffered abuse. Dogs and pups that are highly sensitive to human touch, including small breeds, may bite severely during grooming, so young children shouldn't be in charge of grooming on their own. Adults should carefully supervise until you are certain of your pup's temperament.

Start as young as possible with your puppy, offer occasional treats and lots of praise and soon grooming will become a highly relaxing daily ritual that feels completely natural to everyone. And even your pup will happily anticipate grooming time!

Hint: Offering a nervous or squirmy pup treats during grooming time can sometimes get him past many hurdles, even if he had bad experiences at his breeder or former home. And while it's not a panacea for fearful or slightly snappy pups, offering treats sometimes helps an owner so they don't have to hire a professional behaviorist. Offer treats each time your pup shows slight resistance. As long he doesn't "go stiff" (a sign a dog can bite), growl or snap, or show extreme fear with symptoms like shaking, drooling and glazed eyes, you can proceed slowly. Don't try everything in one day. For pups with serious grooming fears, just getting near the brush or comb may be a sign of success. So stop there on your first session, and each day aim for a bit more as long as the pup stays comfortable.

#23 "Shell Game"

Known for: A family favorite mental game for dogs and owners
Helps: Fun basic game that makes pups think & engage with owners
Which pups? Good introductory game even for young or distractible pups
Which owners? Everybody, including kids
Time, Effort, Cost: Minimal, more fun than effort. If you can't get down on the floor, present the game to the dog on a little table
Cautions, risks: Negligible, unless pup starts out food aggressive

Instructions:

This game is modeled after the "shell game" where street hustlers ask passersby to bet on whether they can find an object under one of three shells that the huckster shuffles around. It's a gambling game that naive tourists to New York City are known to lose. But the version of the game you play with your dog depends only on the power of his nose.

Start with aromatic treats and either three identical upended small plastic flowerpots, three upended plastic bowls with holes punched in the bottoms or the classic equipment- three large shells wavy enough to allow scent to waft out.

To play, show your pup a treat, then place the treat under one of the "shells" and move the shells around a bit until he loses track of where the treat is hidden.

Now say something along the lines of, "Find the treat!" And then allow your curious pup to move forward and sniff around until he finds the shell that he believes hides the treat. Some dogs will push at their choice with their nose, while others will yap or touch the "shell" with their paw.

If your pup makes the right choice, lift the shell and allow him the reward of eating the treat. If he makes the wrong choice, shake your head and say something along the lines of, "Sorry, wrong choice. Let's try again!" The words you use are not vitally important, just as long as your dog understands the rules of the game. Now shift the shells around again and give him another try. This is not a difficult game to master and it almost instantaneously helps flighty dogs and pups increase their focus.

The game is an even bigger challenge if your puppy doesn't use his nose to play, preferring to choose shells based on his observations. Or he may actually enjoy the feeling of letting luck and fate determine if he gets a treat. For pups that prefer to play the game by thinking, rather than sniffing, you can eliminate the nose holes entirely. And some pups will play without food treats, just for the fun of finding a small toy under the "shells."

Hint: Your kids will enjoy playing the shell game with your pups, and you can add it to the agenda on games night. Adults have a lot of fun with the game as well, as long as you don't mind if your pup's skill beats yours occasionally!

#24 "Slow Motion"

Known for: If you don't believe your pup can slow down, he needs this game
Helps: Can be the first way your pup learns to control his body movements & speed
Which pups? Ideal for hyperkinetic pups; this activity is interesting enough to provide a challenge, while resetting the pups' speed to be more effective & functional
Which owners? Owners who're at the end of their rope because they can't make their pup slow down for a second
Time, Effort, Cost: Minimal; the handler should be able to control an unruly pup on leash
Cautions, risks: An able-bodied adult should first introduce this to the puppy to gain control before other family members practice; not recommended for kids younger than preteen or any owner with physical problems balancing or controlling the pup on leash

Instructions:

This is a game for people whose dogs act like tornados in the home, running at visitors as they come in the door and knocking them off their feet. One pit mix Emma knew growing up ran around the house so fast the dog literally left the ground and pushed off the walls! If you know a dog like this, you definitely need this game.

Think about nature shows featuring wolves. It's amazing how wolves can deliberately move so slowly that you almost can't tell they are getting closer to their prey, and then they spring forward with a tremendous burst of speed to catch the animal. Unfortunately, if these wolves just ran out into a field like some of the hyperactive dogs we encounter in society today, the species would quickly go extinct because the prey would always know they were coming!

The game of "Slow Motion" is a way to slow overexcited pups down. First leash your dog or puppy and ask him to sit. Then tell the dog, "Slow," and take a step forward. If the dog moves along slowly next to you, allow him to continue moving with you. But if your dog shoots out of the sit like a rocket, just bring him back to your side. Repeat the cue, "Slow," and give the dog another try. Practice with your dog on leash, until he exhibits perfect control.

Once your dog performs the cue well with the leash on, you can start practicing off leash, holding a treat to encourage your dog to walk along close to your side. If your dog makes a mistake, and lunges ahead too fast, just bring him back to where he started. Give the cue again and, when your dog gets it right, offer a treat and lots of praise. (You will eventually phase out food rewards for all but the most stellar performances.)

The next step is to practice with a helper to teach your dog to move slowly rather than to run when he approaches guests. Use the same methods, starting with your dog on leash. First practice with a guest your dog is already relatively comfortable and relaxed with. (If he usually acts like a kamikaze pilot around unfamiliar guests, introducing a new person at his first practice session would certainly set the dog up for failure.) Once he learns "slow motion" in the presence of the first helper, practice with additional guests. Depending on your dog's progress and your degree of control, **and assuming your dog is always friendly to strangers**, you can eventually practice with your dog off leash, even when unexpected guests arrive.

Hint: It's obvious how teaching your dog "Slow Motion" will improve your dog's behavior. But "Slow Motion" also works as a great mental game because it hones concentration. Many owners struggle to provide adequate aerobic exercise for their dogs, never knowing that adding *mental* exercise can increase intensity and reduce frustration. It's natural for dogs to want to run, but learning to control their bodies adds a whole new dimension. Practice "Slow Motion" frequently at all times of day, including during play and during walks, and you'll soon notice your dog acting happier and more balanced.

#25 *"Play Hide & Seek"*

Best known for: Customer favorite; inspires even adult dogs and owners to get up & play

Helps: Teaches a pup concern about what his owners are doing; but is more civilized, safer and serves higher purpose than traditional "chase" games

Which pups? Start when your pup begins to be curious- usually about 16 weeks. This game works for any patient & gentle pup that understand it's a game. But not for pups whose prey drive (or need to chase moving things) is too high

Which owners? You'll need enough physical mobility & fitness to move around quickly and hide. Kids love this game the most, but parents should carefully supervise.

Time, Effort, Cost: Low cost and easy. Requires full attention for at least 15 or more minutes consecutively

Cautions, risks: Never let kids play if they might get hurt by your puppy or if your pup has ever showed dominant or aggressive behavior. And don't allow kids to overwhelm shy, frail or very young pups with this game.

Instructions:

This is a classic indoor game that most families and most puppies can enjoy. First tell your pup, "Let's Play Hide and Seek," and then hide somewhere in your house to see if your pup can find you. At first make it easy. Just hide around a corner and call the puppy. When he finds you, give him lots of praise and and/or a few treats.

Later you can make it harder and harder for the pup to find you. Ask a human helper to hold the pup when you go to hide, or you could put him in a stay. (See full instructions for "Training Stay" in Part 2). Playing Hide & Seek will also improve your dog's stays and recalls.

Once you're adequately hidden, release the pup from a distance by calling out his name and saying, "Okay, come and find me". Don't change your hiding spot, and don't step out into sight, although you can make some noises to get his attention if he's a small pup that seems to be having problems finding you at first. As soon as your pup successfully finds you, reward him with praise and/or treats.

Next your pup gets to have the hiding fun! First you will teach him to hide. Select an object or piece of furniture that you'd like him to hide behind and then tell him to, "Go hide." At the same time, walk the pup to the hiding place you have selected and then tell him to "stay". Allow the pup to "hide" for just a moment at first. If he remains staying in the spot, show up and enthusiastically say, "I found you!" and offer a few treats.

Alternate turns with you hiding and with your puppy hiding, until he learns that when you say "Go Hide," he is free to wander and select his own hiding place while you wait. Once your pup or adult dog gets the idea of the game, he might find some spots you never thought a dog could hide in. So you must have him trained perfectly to obey a recall command in case he ever takes Hide & Seek too seriously and you really can't find him! (See instructions for Training "Come" or "Recall" in Part 2.)

Don't make the mistake of calling out your pup's name while he's hiding and you're looking for him. You must look for the pup in silence as part of the game. This way, even though your pup understands he's having fun hiding from his owner as part of a mutual game, he still doesn't forget that he is trained to come the second his owner calls.

After your pup masters the game of "Hide and Seek", you can allow your kids to play the game with him. (To play with children your pup should be gentle and non-aggressive, and he should not have a habit of jumping on people.) Several children can hide while you hold back the pup. And then you can release him and tell him "Go find", and add the child's name if you have already taught the pup #15 Identify Family Members" in this chapter.

You can have your pup search the house, finding each of the kids in turn and then have each child give him a treat and praise when he finds them. If your kids want to "seek" out the puppy, advise them to play nicely and gently. You want your dog to always enjoy playing the game and never to fear getting disturbed by people.

Keep this game playful, but never overly wild. If children act too loud or rough while searching for the puppy, he may not want to play anymore. And while it is okay for your pup to have lots of fun with the game, you also don't want him to act too wild as he searches out your kids. If you things get out of control in your home as puppy and kids play this game, it is time to stop for a while and alternate with some mellower activities.

You can always try Hide & Seek again on another day. But if puppy and kids still act too boisterous, you may have to shelve the game for a long time. You can always try several years later when your children are more mature, and when your dog has entered a slower phase in life when he may need some perking up.

Hint: Playing the simple game and joyful game of "Hide and Seek" when your pup is young will get him in the habit of being curious about where your children are at all times and then using his nose to find them. At this age Hide & Seek is only a simple game. But practicing can become an essential building block for lifesaving skills like search and rescue, and feeling concerned each time one of your children momentarily goes missing.

#26 *"Play Basketball"*

Known for: Good indoor exercise; more challenging & adaptable than Fetch
Helps: Helps boredom; builds coordination, concentration & drive to accomplish a task
Which pups: Any fun-loving breed that has energy to burn & enjoys carrying things, including retrievers, terriers & Pit Bulls
Which owners: Family friendly; but small kids shouldn't try to force a pup to relinquish the ball
Time, Effort, Cost: Challenging to train & some dogs can't learn this. Low cost to buy or make the equipment.
Cautions or risks: Minimal; use the right ball that teething pups can't chew up

Instructions:

Basketball is good for pups of any age or physical fitness level- simply adjust the size of the equipment based on the size of the pup. You can play indoors or outdoors (even at picnics or on the beach), the equipment is inexpensive and your kids will enjoy teaching this game.

Start by purchasing (or building) a miniature basketball hoop on a stand that is the perfect height for your pup (you can find kids' versions in stores). Then choose a dog-friendly ball (you can buy one that looks like a basketball) and teach your pup to lift it in his mouth and drop it through the hoop. Reward him with tons of praise, and perhaps a treat or two the first few times he makes a basket, until he learns to love the game solely for the challenge.

There are several different ways to teach your dog to place the basketball into the hoop. Some highly alert dogs will mimic your actions if you demonstrate how you put the ball through the hoop and associate the action with a command like, "Make a basket!" But this method is challenging, and the average dog may not learn this way.

Another way to train is by "shaping". This means your dog doesn't need to be perfect the first time to get a reward. He just has to get a little closer to the final behavior on each attempt. For example, first reward him for simply holding the ball in his mouth. Next reward him for carrying the ball towards the hoop, then for standing there and dropping the ball, then for dropping the ball into the hoop, then for walking over and dropping a ball you give him into the hoop- and, finally, for picking up the ball on his own and making a basket.

Another way you could teach the trick is if your dog already knows the command, "Drop it". Just tell your pup to "drop it" after leading him to hold the ball over the hoop. You can find full instructions for "Training Drop It" in Part 2, Training, Section C, #7).

Or if your pup doesn't know the command "drop it", you can teach him using the basketball hoop. Lead the pup over so he's holding the ball over the hoop. Then unexpectedly hold out a very yummy treat. Say, "Drop It" as he's relinquishing the ball. Once you have him dropping the ball, he will generalize the useful command to dropping other items. And you can always teach the

"Make a Basket" command later. You can also simply point to the basket to indicate where you want the pup to go and, once he gets there, command "drop it".

Having your dog make baskets is a great party game, and a more pleasant way to first introduce your dog to guests than having him jump up on them with muddy paws. And most dogs really enjoy this coordination-building game. You can teach your dog to run up to the basket from a distance if you want to increase his abilities and give him more exercise. And you and the kids can join in the game with him.

Hint: Soon your pup will be making baskets not just for treats, but for fun. You may even catch him "shooting hoops" when you're not home. So, why not secure breakables and leave your hoop and ball available when you go out?

#27 "Walk a Straight Line"

Known for: Easy & quick intervention that works surprisingly well
Helps: Improves pups' balance & slows dogs that pull
Which pups? Best with medium to large breeds that need to learn to slow down & think
Which owners? Any owner that can walk their pup on leash
Time, Effort, Cost: Truly minimal
Cautions or risks: No more risky than walking a puppy on leash

Instructions:

Learning how to walk a straight line is important for building your developing puppy's balance. And the exercise is especially important for calming down wild high-energy puppies that have trouble controlling their bodies and their overexuberance. The straight line exercise can also help cure dogs that pull their owners down the street on walks, because regular practice teaches your dog to think about every step he takes.

It might take a playful puppy a while to catch on how to "Walk a Straight Line". But once your pup gets the point of the exercise, it is very easy to do. You can practice anytime and anywhere as long as you can mark a straight line for your pup to follow.

To start, first lay a long strip of colored tape down on a floor, carpet or anyplace outside. Or, instead of tape, you can simply lay down string, clothesline or an old 20 or 30 ft. nylon dog leash to mark the straight line. Now stand immediately in front of your puppy at one end of the straight line with your pup on leash, and start coaxing him forward as you move backwards. Command your pup to "Walk the Line" while holding the leash somewhat taut but not uncomfortably tight-just tight enough to guide the pup without allowing any slack.

As your puppy starts to walk with you standing in front of him and coaxing him forward, watch that he stays on the line. If he steps off too far line off the line, bring him back to the beginning, shaking your head to indicate that you are disappointed. Then try again, as many times as necessary without allowing practice to become tedious. If your pup still doesn't seem to get it after ten or so minutes of trying, you can call it a day and give him some hugs and verbal affection (but no treats for the imperfect performance) and try again tomorrow.

Try to coax your pup happily for every step he takes correctly. And, if your pup stays on the line properly for the entire length, say enthusiastically "Good, walk the line!" Then immediately give him a few tasty treats and a lot more praise. Now repeat the process, walking along the line in the other direction.

As your pup gets better at staying on the line, try walking at his side (which is a little more challenging) rather than walking directly in front of him. Next you can graduate to leaving the leash completely slack, moving off a bit to one side and letting the pup walk the line alone. He'll walk with more focus and build more coordination and balance.

Hint: Your pup can also learn to "Walk a Straight Line "off leash". This is a perfect challenge for high-energy and highly trainable breeds like Border Collies. So prepare to be impressed.

#28 *"Stand Like a Show Dog"*

Known for: This is how dogs learn the classic "stacking" position seen at dog shows
Helps: Helps posture & muscle tone, while building restraint & respect for owners
Which pups? Physically healthy pups that don't show aggression
Which owners? Owners with a gentle hand & good judgment who can stop immediately if the pup feels uncomfortable
Time, Effort, Cost: No cost, but requires patience, sensitivity & full concentration
Cautions or risks: Relatively low, but never hurt a pup trying to push him into a painful position. Also, some dogs/pups with unknown history or temperament could bite when you try to move them. So use extreme caution as described in more detail below and don't let kids practice this until adults are 100% sure how the pup will react.

Instructions:

"Stacking" in competition stance occasionally will improve your dog's posture and his muscle tone, self control, mental focus, attention span and calmness. This is the classic stance that shows the incredible beauty and magnificence of show dogs as the judges look them over. And, even if your puppy is not a show dog, he can learn to stand up regally in the same fashion. Holding a pose like this occasionally can also increase your pup's sense of pride, purpose and self-esteem while improving his connection with his handler.

Only attempt this activity with a healthy puppy (and don't try it with extremely young puppies). If a pup has any physical discomfort on his body and you attempt to move him around and place him, this could cause him pain or even physical damage. You should, of course always have your pup's health cleared by a veterinarian before doing any activities. But also respect your pup's cues. If he usually does okay when you try to pose him, but one day he is unusually wiggly or he snatches away one body part, he may be trying to tell you something. He might have a little injury hidden somewhere under his fur or one of his joints may be sore, so check out his health before proceeding.

When you start practicing "stacking", or show posing, your pup should already know how to walk politely on a leash (see "Training Heel" in Part 2 for full instructions. It can also help to teach your pup "Wait", also described in Part 2). Make sure the pup is exercised and loosened up before posing, but not too tired. Keep him on leash and walk him in a few precise graceful circles as you would in a show ring before bringing him to the spot where you want him to pose. This could be in front of a friend who can act as a mock "show judge" or in front of a mirror. Now, get down on his level, either by going down on one knee, sitting on the floor or sitting on a low bench or ottoman.

Command your dog either "Stack", "Pose" or just, "Stand" in an encouraging tone of voice. Meanwhile, gently adjust his stance and every aspect of his pose into the formal show standard for his breed. You can easily research show poses if you're interested, or if your plan to exhibit your pup in dog shows later in life. If your pup is a mix and/or you don't care that much about official show standards, you could just watch a dog show judging on television, DVD or YouTube to get a general idea how a show pose looks.

Or just use this exercise to have your pup stand proudly in a stance that looks attractive to you instead of constantly jumping around. (This will give you the chance to take some nice photos of your pup without the constant blur!)

Support your pup carefully as you adjust his body, murmuring "Stand" or "Look pretty!". And then say "What a pretty dog!" when he's in a satisfactory position.

Some pups are just too young for posing! You'll know yours is too young if he collapses with his belly supported in your hand, goes limp like jelly or falls asleep. Reward your pup anyway for his valiant effort, and don't try anything that could cause him distress.

Start easy. For a young pup, just standing still for a few minutes can be an accomplishment, so give lots of praise. Over a number of years, you can refine his presentation, challenging him to remain posed longer and to improve in style just like a real show dog.

While you make miniscule adjustments in your pup's stance, you can murmur words like, "Look pretty". Then, as he achieves the perfect pose, say something like "What a pretty dog!"

Stacking is healthy for most dogs since it provides a good stretch and improves body alignment. But, before you try it, make sure your pup has no illness, injury or chronic ailments like hip dysplasia or arthritis before you attempt to physically adjust him. You should learn to distinguish true discomfort from impatience or stubbornness. If your pup shows real pain, you should get him veterinary attention. But if your pup appears relaxed and resists only *slightly* as you attempt to pose him you can gently work to increase his comfort zone.

The best way to get your pup into the pose you want is to first lure him with treats or a squeaky toy. (Observe how show handlers do it.) Then make very gentle adjustments to position him into the perfect show stance. Also practice lifting your pup's gums and gently palpating his abdomen because a judge would do these things at a real dog show.

If your pup strongly resists, squeals or shows any signs of distress when you attempt to adjust him into a pose, stop immediately. It's possible that he's feeling real physical pain. The fault might also be yours if you're not moving him correctly.

And be ultra cautious about adjusting your puppy's pose with your face near his. Increasingly, people obtain pups without knowing their exact background or their exact temperament (this includes pups purchased from pet shops and over the Internet. These pups almost always are bred in cruel puppy mills, where they are abused or neglected and never receive proper human contact.) When a puppy without proper socialization with humans is handled in certain ways, it may bite. And even small breeds and very young puppies can seriously bite.

We adults should do the posing practice first a number of times to make sure of their pup's temperament before ever allowing children to try it. Since children constantly manipulate puppies bodies, whether encouraged to do it as a formal game like this or not, parents should always train the pup to endure this kind of touch with no aggression.

You should always supervise your children when they handle the pup and teach them safety basics. For example, everyone in the household should angle their face safely away from a pup's face whenever they adjusting his body. Stop any activity immediately if your pup ever growls or snaps, and don't allow that animal any more contact with children until you receive a professional assessment by a high level behaviorist.

Also beware if your pup ever becomes stiff, because this is a precursor to biting. It might happen because someone handled the pup too roughly, or because his body felt tender from an injury you couldn't see. Or he might have serious dominance issues. Whenever a dog stiffens, it's a serious warning that gives his handler only a few seconds to diffuse the situation or get out of harm's way. You can then talk to a high level behavior expert who can help assess the situation.

But children can't be expected to handle potentially aggressive pups. All young children need to know is to always handle the puppy gently and never put their faces near his teeth while they work with his body. But if the pup ever stiffens, the child should release him and confidently move away to get adult assistance- *without showing any panic.* Adults should always supervise while their children are working with the pup.

When practicing show poses at home, you may wish to allow your helper, the "mock judge", to handle your pup like a show judge would. **But first test that your pup won't bite the "judge"** Accepting handling by a friendly stranger is a sign of a dog with a good balanced temperament, but no one should make assumptions about their pup's behavior. Dogs have bitten judges in show rings. And you certainly don't want this to happen to a friend or neighbor who has kindly volunteered to help with your puppy.

But if your is wonderful about letting a pretend " show judge" handle him, he may also be a candidate to pass the Canine Good Citizen Test. Canine Good Citizen is an AKC designation offered to dogs that can behave well in the face of dog and human distractions. These standardized trials are offered at many dog shows and events at the local level, and mixed breeds as well as purebreds can earn the Canine Good Citizen title.

Whether or not you plan to show your pup off in a dog show ring, once he learns the skill of "stacking", you will certainly want to show him off at every family reunion; and you can expect him to make a better impression on relatives than if he jumped on them!

Hint: Once your pup masters a nice show pose, you may want to hire a professional dog photographer or an artist who paints canine portraits to depict him. And then display the magnificent work over your mantle for many years to come.

#29 *"Jump Through Hoop(s)"*

Known for: Good first activity to start interacting with your pup, directing his activities and setting a prototype for further training. Hula hoops are cheap, easy, popular & fun.
Helps: Dogs learn to happily focus on doing what you want while quickly burning off energy indoors or out. Helps dogs trust their owners & helps owners gain confidence directing their dogs.
Which pups? Can be a good first physical game for new owners to play with pups; especially good at focusing unruly energy

Which owners? Great for owners without previous experience training dogs. Also a safe, fun activity that allows kids to direct dogs' actions without confrontation.

Time, Effort, Cost: Minimal. Ultra cheap and easy to try, anywhere, anytime and by any family member

Cautions, risks: Varies. Minimal risk unless you hold the hoop too high for your dog's physical condition, which could hurt him badly. There's no reason to make any pup jump higher than knee-height & keep the hoop extremely low for tiny pups, giant-breed pups and pups with bone or joint problems. Parents should help small children play.

Instructions:

Teaching your puppy to jump through a hoop is more than just a fun and easy way to pass time and a cute trick to show off to your friends. It can also focus your puppy's mind, get him in the habit of obeying his family members and teach an alternative behavior to discourage jumping up on people. "Jump Through Hoop(s)" is, of course, a good trick to show off at parties, and your kids will enjoy it. But the best part is that your pup will learn when you *do* want him to jump, so he won't be as likely to jump at every random moment when you *don't* want him to.

This game is especially great for small high-energy breeds like Jack Russell Terriers, and all breeds that naturally love to jump. It's also good preparation if you want your dog to compete in agility trials later in life.

You can buy inexpensive hula hoops at discount department stores, and we've bought small hoops for a just a dollar at some Dollar Tree locations.

It's easy to teach most puppies to go through a hoop, although some shy pups may need patience and coaxing. NEVER HOLD THE HOOP UP HIGH, even when your pup has perfected the activity. Start by holding the hoop with one end resting on the ground. Lure your puppy through using a treat while calling his name excitedly and saying "Jump". Most likely your pup will walk through. When he does, praise him and reward him with the treat. And then try again in the opposite direction.

Once your pup seems to understand the meaning of the command "jump", you should stop using treats to lure him through the hoop. Just hold onto the treat and use it to reward him after he's made it through the hoop successfully. Eventually, you should reduce the amount of treats you use, allowing your pup to go through the hoop several times before you reward. Pups learn to enjoy the fun of the game, and some will happily "play" for no rewards at all. For pups like these, you can wait until the session is over to give a reward, or you can simply reward with affection.

As your puppy learns to walk through the hoop without fear, you can bring the hoop a little higher if desired. When your dog grows up, and with your veterinarian's permission, you may wish to get more ambitious. But ambitious jumping activities where the hoop is held high- including the photos commonly shown in other dog activity books- could be dangerous for certain dogs or pups. **For safety, we recommend that readers of this basic puppy book never force** their puppy to jump through a hoop that is too high. Be especially cautious with large/giant breed pups that tend to have susceptible hips. "Jumping" through a hoop that you hold low is just as therapeutic, just as much fun and just as good for exercise as if you hold the hoop higher.

A hula hoop can help you exercise your pup indoors inside in bad weather, or you can use it outdoors for more vigorous exercise. And bring a hoop to family gatherings so kids can play with a vigorous pup in a channeled activity, rather than simply letting him chase them.

After your pup learns to go through a single hoop, you can bring the game to a different level by introducing a second hoop. Gracefully moving two hoops in sequence as your dog jumps or climbs through makes the activity faster-paced and more challenging. Your pup can twist his body around, doubling back to the second hoop after he has climbed through the first. Or you can have a partner hold one of the hoops.

Hint: If you own two dogs that work well together, you can teach them to intertwine with each other, alternating hoops. Watching the dogs "perform" like this is entertaining and invigorating. You may even want to videotape your dogs moving smoothly and perfectly like this.

#30 "Calling Multiple Dogs"

Known for: Good for teaching a dog to obey when he's around other dogs
Helps: Control dogs even in a pack situation; teaches pups restraint and how to pay attention & increases their mental concentration.
Which pups: Necessary in all households with multiple dogs or pups; all pups should practice commands around other dogs to get their behavior right when they are young
Which owners: Everyone in multi-dog households; most adults & mature young people benefit from the confidence of knowing how to control dogs in a group
Time, Effort, Cost: Slight; requires a little patience & practice & is easier with a helper
Cautions or risks: There are always some risks around multiple dogs, who often act rougher with people than single dogs. Practicing this exercise helps those risks. But carefully supervise any young children who could get knocked over by running dogs.

Instructions:
You can do this alone or with helper(s) and any number of puppies or dogs. First, train each dog to know its name and teach the "come" and "stay" commands. (Find full instructions in Part 2, Training, Chapter 5). Then put each dog in a long stay (a "stay" in the lying down position). Or you could have a helper hold each dog.

Now, call out one of the dogs' names, along with the command "come" in an excited positive fashion. If you have a helper, he'll now release the dog you called so it can come to you. (See full instructions for teaching the "come" command in the Part 2, "5. Training Come or Recall"; also check "#40 Learn to Love to Come to Everyone" in this chapter for hints on how to inspire your dog to come.)

The dog that you called should come happily running to you. But no other dog should move. Interrupt any other dog that tries to get up with your palm up in the air and a sound like "Uh-uh" and that dog's name.

Reward and praise the dog that you called when he gets to you. At the same time, gently take hold of his collar. (This is practice for real life, because you always want to be able to take hold of your dog when he comes to you.) Now, put the dog in a "stay".

Leave him, walk around the room and select another name to call. Or, if you are working with a helper, you can take turns and your helper can call the next dog. Only the dog that is called by name should come running, and all the rest should remain staying. Now alternate as often, and in any order, that you like.

This exercise teaches pups restraint and how to pay attention, and it increases mental concentration. Practiced slowly and carefully, it's a good obedience exercise. If you want to make it more complex, you can add in different commands, such as "sit" or "down" or "heel" rather than just "come". (Find instructions for all these commands in Part 2.) Direct each command to only one dog at a time by first saying the dog's name, and only reward a dog that reacts correctly to its name and the command you've given.

If you wish, speed up the process. Humans and dogs will get a good mental and physical workout and have a lot of fun if you play very fast with a large group of dogs. "Calling Multiple Dogs" sharpens communication, and your dogs learn to work with you just as they would orchestrate their actions with a canine pack leader during hunting. Practicing this exercise will prevent your dogs from always trying to push forward at once. Instead, they will wait for your command to come forward at times like mealtime.

Hint: For more exercise, you can have your helper line the dogs up at one end of a large fenced yard. Then you and your helper can call them back and forth between you by name.

#31 *"Jump Over/Crawl Under a Bar"*

Known for: Exhilarating mini indoor agility practice- without much equipment or space
Helps: Teaches pups mental discernment, bodily coordination and split-second obedience to their owner's commands.
Which pups? Physically healthy pups that like to have fun; also bored pups. Not ideal for extremely young pups
Which owners? Owners who like their work with their pup to be fun; also children with mature judgment
Time, Effort, Cost: Easy; you can play for only a few minutes or longer if you like
Cautions or risks: Use caution. Don't raise the pole too high. Dogs with medical conditions & some breeds with short legs and/or long backs or large/giant breed puppies shouldn't jump & some dogs with medical conditions can't crawl.

Instructions:

"Jump Over/Crawl Under a Bar" is a simple jumping/crawling game, played with one or more dogs or pups, which has the benefits of a mini agility practice. In this game pups learn mental discernment, bodily coordination and split-second obedience to commands. The only equipment you need is a long stick like a broomstick, curtain rod or bamboo pole and two willing people to hold the pole up for the pup(s) to jump over or crawl under. Or, if you're alone, you can wedge one end of the pole safely against a piece of furniture.

Start by teaching "over". Call your pup to you, hold the pole very close to the ground and lure the pup over with a treat as you command "over". Once the pup steps over, praise him and let him eat the treat. Then call him back over the pole in the reverse direction; and practice with him going back and forth a few times at your command.

Next you and your helper can raise the pole a little higher off the ground so that the pup now jumps over it. Use discretion about how high to raise the pole, especially with large and giant breed pups, pups with long backs and short legs and pups with existing physical conditions. (If in doubt, check with your veterinarian about how high it is safe for your particular puppy to jump.) Even the healthiest pups shouldn't be jumping too high. And it's not necessary for the pole to be more than a few inches off the ground to make going "Over" an enjoyable challenge, even if your pup can only step over, rather than jumping. This game is more about discernment and control than it is about athleticism.

Once your pup masters the "over" command, stop using treats to lure him over the bar. Just give the command, "over" and then wait to offer praise and treats after he jumps or walks over the bar on his own. Next, start rewarding with treats only intermittently. Eventually the fun of playing the game, along with your fervent praise, will become its own reward and you should only offer treats at the completion of a successful session.

Now go back to the beginning and teach the "under" command. Lure your pup with treats again and start with the bar held high enough that your pup can walk under. If your pup is completely healthy, you can eventually lower the bar so that he has to crawl under.

But keeping the bar this low is not necessary for having fun. Always use care that your pup remains physically comfortable when asking him to go "under" the bar and make sure his health, breed and physical condition allow him to crawl safely. If your pup has physical limitations, you can have him walk underneath the bar rather than crawling or choose not to play. (Consult with your vet for what's healthiest for your puppy.)

Once your pup has learned "over" and "under" individually, next teach him how to alternate "unders" and "overs" at your command. Some little puppies' brains might "lock up" a little when they first attempt to alternate "under" and "over" on command, or they might seem to acquire "four left feet". But be patient. **This activity is meant to build coordination and mental acuity, so it should be somewhat of a challenge at first.**

Eventually, with practice, your pup's skill will build and this can be a great game to occupy bored pups and bored family members. Quickly alternate the commands "under" and "over" with no predictable pattern, and try speeding up the pace. After playing this challenging game for a while, reward your pup lavishly and take some time for a mellow cool-down.

Hint: If you add more dogs/puppies and speed up the pace, "Jump Over/Crawl Under a Bar" can become a serious obedience challenge or an intense party game. Yet you can still play in your living room.

#32 "Wait"

Known for: Teaches a pup self control in varied situations when used as a command.
Helps: Makes everyday tasks, like locking the door behind you, easier. Calms your pup, stops inappropriate energy before he disembarks from your vehicle. And it could save your pup's life by teaching him not to dash out the door without permission.
Which pups? Critical for every pup- especially those that don't seem able to wait.
Which owners? Every owner- having control in this sense eliminates much frustration
Time, Effort, Cost: None- teaching this is easier than living with your dog if you don't
Cautions, Risks: None, but the pup may not obey if young children try to teach this

Instructions:

This is an important exercise to make your dog think and learn greater self-control. Teach your pup to wait any time you want him to stay calm and wait for you. This can help on those mornings when you're on your way to work and your pup runs out for a run you didn't plan for! You may be late for work or have to take the day off as you travel the town frantically looking for him.

But it's easy to change this behavior, when you start with total confidence and the knowledge that it's dog's deepest nature to want to follow their owners and look to their owners for directions, rather than pushing past owners and taking the lead themselves.

To first teach the "Wait" command at the front door, start with your pup on leash. Start with your pup in either the standing, sitting or lying down position and say "Wait." Then open the door just a little, while blocking the passage with your body. If your pup breaks from his position, block him with your body and close the door behind you. (You can also use the leash to hold him back at first if you need to.) And make sure to send out your strong personal energy to hold him back. (See "#4 Forcefield (Control Your Pup With Your Psychic Energy)".)

Once your pup remains still repeat, "Wait," and try opening the door again. If your dog waits this time, leave him inside while you step out the door first. If he remains waiting appropriately, you can now tell him, "Okay," and invite him out the door. Now practice this exercise as frequently as necessary until your pup reliably waits for your invitation before he steps out the door.

The "Wait" command is versatile. You can use it during walks anytime you want your pup to slow down, and during play any time you want him to hesitate. Use this great command anytime you need your dog to hesitate at a doorway, including in public places and when you are allowing him to get out of your vehicle. You will probably find hundreds of different situations each day when you will want to use the "Wait" command.

Another important reason to use the "Wait" cue is to stop your pup from running up and jumping on visitors whenever they step through the door. Teach your pup that when a guest enters your home, he must wait and only approach them when you release him with the word "Okay".

The best way to practice proper greetings is with the help of somebody the dog sees frequently, but still rushes to meet. Have this guest knock on the door or ring the bell, and then continue to wait outside. You walk to the door and, if your pup attempts to follow you, tell him, "Wait," and hold up your hand, palm facing forward. (This is the same gesture as you would use for "Stay", but you can hold your hand a little looser and more forward in a gesture that feels natural to you. Some people will actually touch their pup with the tips of their fingers, as if gently holding him back when they make this gesture.) Your pup does not have to sit or lie down. He can remain standing, or in whatever position he is comfortable in as long as he does not lunge forward.

While your pup waits calmly, you can open the door and admit the guest inside. If your dog attempts to come forward to greet the guest before you give permission, ask the person to step back out the door again. Now again command your pup to "wait". Once he does, open the door and invite the guest inside again.

You may have to repeat the exercise quite a few times. When your dog waits appropriately for a few minutes, you can release him with the "Okay" command. Your guest can then call the pup to them, ask him to sit and then pet him or offer him a treat as a reward for his patience.

Hint: Ideally a pup should learn to automatically wait just to be polite in certain situations, such as always allowing humans to walk out a door before he does. Personally we prefer a puppy to develop a consciousness of when it is proper and polite to wait, and then make the choice whether or not to wait on their own, rather than obeying "wait" as a formal command. But regardless of whether you train "Wait" as a formal command, every young puppy should learn the habit of willingly waiting.

#33 *"Teach Your Pup to Crawl"*

Known for: Adorable & easy command that comes naturally to puppies
Helps: Helps puppies calm down, while practicing coordination
Which pups? Pups that are hard to slow down; ideal for small breeds
Which owners? Owners looking for fun alternatives to regular obedience; also good for most kids
Time, Effort, Cost: Almost none
Cautions, risks: Minimal. Don't try it if your pup has physical problems or pain.

Instructions:

When your puppy gets down and crawls towards you, your heart will likely melt and you may want to give him anything. And this activity can help control a pup that's rough with his body and has no idea what grace is when he wants you to pay attention to him. Everyone runs when they see this pup coming, knowing he'll run into them like a load of bricks. But a pup can't hurt people or do much damage when he's crawling. And this exercise can sometimes be the first way to break through to your pup and slow him down while he's still enjoying himself.

There are many ways to teach a pup to crawl. The first method is to first put the pup into a "down" (see full instructions in Part 2 "Training (Lie) Down"). Then hold a treat just out of his reach, luring him and asking him to "Crawl". If he moves even a few inches, praise him and give him the treat. Then repeat this, asking him to crawl a little farther each time you practice. Another way you can teach a pup to crawl is to sit on the floor beside him and use a treat to lure him to crawl under your legs.

For a more advanced challenge you can ask your pup to crawl under a long coffee table or to crawl through a tunnel (see "#17 Explore a Tunnel" in this chapter). You can even "play soldier" and you and your dog can crawl under a net stretched a few inches off the ground like they do in the army, pretending you are both commandos. Or your pup can learn to crawl under a bar (see "#31 Jump Over/Crawl Under" in this chapter.)

You may notice that some dogs and puppies will even crawl on their own, because it is so endearing to guests. This trick is a better alternative to jumping when your pup wants the attention of new people.

Hint: Be cautious about asking a pup to crawl if there's a chance he has physical problems. If you pay attention, your pup will usually let you know if a movement feels uncomfortable for him. If your pup enjoys crawling on his own during play, then crawling is probably comfortable for him. But if he shows really strong resistance to crawling, even when you lure him with highly appealing treats, he might feel pain. So don't attempt to physically push him down. If he also shows distress or stiffness when he tries to lie down or get up from a lying position, you should mention the problem to your veterinarian.

#34 "Get Excited; Then Calm Down"

Known for: Dog and owner jumping around like fools- then suddenly calming down
Helps: Teaches a pup to fine-tune his excitement, and only act hyper at playtime
Which pups? Playful large pups that need to learn to read people's signals
Which owners? Reasonably fit adults who can jump around, but don't want their dog jumping on people; NOT recommended for children or homes with kids
Time, Effort, Cost: Minimal; owner has to be able to physically jump around
Cautions or risks: Never play this around kids. Any game that involves large pups jumping could hurt kids, so never let kids try this. And don't teach your pup to do this if you have young children whose jumping around might confuse him

Instructions:

This is a good learning game for owners who have trouble controlling bigger pups when they get excited. In this game, the owner goes from acting relaxed to suddenly busting loose and jumping, dancing or spinning while encouraging their pup to jump around with them. Then, after the dog is slightly worked up, you suddenly command, "Stop," and both of you come to a complete stop. Make your pup "sit" or lie "down" until everything is completely calm and controlled again. (Find detailed instructions for training these commands in Part 2.)

Once your pup calms down fully, once again give the cue that it's okay to get up. And both of you can start jumping around and having fun again for a few minutes. Practice stopping and starting this game frequently so that your pup learns how to quickly turn his excitement on and off. This gives him better control over his body and his state of mind and it also assures you that you can bring him back into control even when he's highly worked up.

Often, the owners who need this exercise the most have large pups and they play the game on their feet. But you can also play with tiny puppies of any age on the floor. Whenever you want your puppy to play, simply imitate the play posture other dogs use by leaning over, spreading your arms, and slapping your opened palms against the floor a few times. You can also hold a toy. Just act excited and move around a bit. Get your pup to chase you around a little. If you are not sure what canine playfulness looks like, just watch your pup and try to imitate some of his movements when he runs around tossing around a toy.

Once you have your pup playing with you, suddenly stop moving, call his attention to you with his name and then give him a command like "sit", "down" or "stay" to settle him down. Once he settles down appropriately for a little while, the two of you can play again.

Hint: Most owners like this game to teach self-control to pups that jump around too much. It also introduces fun to shy dogs and dogs that show too much self-restraint. And the game can be a reward after demanding work or obedience practice.

#35 "Puppy Massage"

Known for: Lifelong health and emotional benefits when practiced with care
Helps with: Ideal dog/owner bonding activity for all pups; keeps pups centered and calm
Which pups? Especially helps nervous, jittery pups & those with physical discomfort
Which owners? A healthy option for owners who constantly like to pet their pups; mature children of all ages can also do it with caution & supervision
Time, Effort, Cost: Versatile & relaxing, but remain attentive & use correct techniques

Instructions:

These days more people are learning to appreciate the holistic health benefits of massage, both for themselves and for their dogs. Massaging your adult dog can help protect him from joint pain when he's older, help him exercise without injury and help center his mind and emotions. It's also a good daily bonding activity for dogs and owners. And a purposeful technique like massage can actually improve dogs' behavior as a substitute for some of the aimless petting that many owners do with their dogs.

Rather than giving in and petting your dog whenever he pushes on you for attention, when you massage your dog it still provides positive physical touch. Yet massage shows your dog how to be centered and cooperative around his owner's touch rather than demanding.

And massage isn't just for older dogs. You can start massaging your dog the day you bring him home, no matter what his age. Massage can also help calm your puppies, which is something many pet parents beg for. Massage can demonstrate to older children (always supervised) a healthy way to show love to a pup rather than constantly overstimulating him. And, if you combine regular massage with other healthy lifestyle changes, you may even be able to prevent joint and muscle problems from ever happening in your dog's future. Massage also keeps your pup limber and comfortable before and after exercise.

Most pups won't need massage for therapeutic medical purposes. But if your pup has physical problems or is rehabilitating after injury, the right kind of massage can help. For therapeutic purposes, we recommend first checking with your veterinarian for recommendations about specific types of massage or if you should avoid particular movements.

For general purposes of bonding, limbering up and relaxing together most people will use basic massage where they simply run their hands over the pup's skin. This type of massage makes a puppy start to relax and loosen his muscles. All you need to do is to get settled with the pup in a comfortable position, run your hands slowly and GENTLY all over his body and relax as he starts to fall asleep in your arms. Massage like this, which you can do daily or even more frequently, sets a future precedent for dog/owner bonding in a calm and positive atmosphere. It also keeps the puppy limber and keeps his joints loose to avoid injury.

Additional massage techniques work differently, targeting specific problems. One massage technique called Tellington Touch, or TTouch, that helps both physical and emotional healing, has gained tremendous popularity recently. Tellington Touch is a gentle intervention that not only works with dogs, but with cats, horses and zoo animals, as well. Tellington Touch massage is much more involved than the basic massage. And a specifically trained practitioner will use many different hand positions and move their hands on the dog's skin in specific patterns while performing TTouch, starting with extremely light pressure and carefully matching the amount of pressure to the animal's therapeutic needs. You can find more information about TTouch in books and online. There are also now many professional dog masseuses who you can hire to work on your dog for specific purposes. But since the field is not regulated, you may want to first clear with your veterinarian that your puppy is healthy enough for the specific type of massage, especially if any deep manipulations will be used.

If you are using basic massage that's only skin-deep at home, and your puppy is healthy, you don't necessarily need to clear it with your vet, but you should always use caution and common sense. Start your first session simple, and work within your pup's comfort zone as you cover every part of his body. Some areas respond particularly well to gentle massage- including the ears, a little spot in the center of the dog's forehead and the feet. But these same areas are highly sensitive and your pup may not like them touched at first if he is not used to it. **Go slow, never push things and always respond to your dog's feedback. If the puppy pulls away from, or winces, when you touch a particular spot, it's a cue to ease up the pressure and/or move away from that area.**

Serious signs of discomfort when you touch a certain area might indicate illness or injury, so you should stop massage immediately and report the symptom to your veterinarian. You can use massage to cure minor discomfort like stiffness, but you should always watch your pup's expression. The more you touch, the more he should relax, even looking a little sleepy.

If the puppy ever squeals when you touch him, stop immediately. Pressing certain areas on your dog's body could hurt or even kill him. Your veterinarian can advise you in detail, or you can research more on your own. **Also never force massage on a pup that appears to be unfriendly, angry, growly or snappy or any dog or pup with an unknown history (such as a stray or shelter dog) until you are sure of his reactions in all situations.** The safest rule of thumb for any pet owner who wants to massage their dog of any age at home is to never push hard and never force anything if the dog appears to be in discomfort!

Always leave any deep massaging to qualified adults in the home and supervise your children carefully if you want them to practice basic massage on your puppy. **Only individuals that are calm, unpreoccupied and possess a gentle touch should massage the puppy.** Their calm gentle touch will lead to him becoming calmer and gentler as well.

Hint: We frequently have to slow down pet parents who try massaging their dogs too quickly and too hard. Yet we've never had to correct a person for massaging too slowly or too gently. If you notice your pup getting *more* wiggly rather than calming down when you first try massaging him, it's likely because you are stroking too fast or too hard.

#36 *"Play In the Leaves"*

Known for: Pups do this on their own but it's better with your supervision

Helps: Cool game to stimulate shy, timid and listless dogs to act vibrant

Which pups: Puppies that need to explore new stimuli to combat fears; bored pups that get underfoot when you try to do yard work

Which owners: Owners who want an outdoor physical activity for pups without extra physical effort for them

Time, Effort, Cost: Minimal

Cautions, risks: Some risk of hidden hazards, which could be serious in snake country, so go through the leaf pile carefully with your rake before letting your pup play

Instructions:

Pups are fascinated with the mysteries hidden underneath piles of autumn leaves. We can't help but smile, as our pups dig through piles of leaves in great spirits, sending colorful leaves flying in the air. Digging through leaves like this is more than just fun. It can help keep a young puppy occupied while emboldening him and encouraging him to explore the world with several of his senses. It builds acuity of touch, sight, sound and smell and provides plenty of healthy exercise. Playtime in the leaves can also serve as a "real world reward" after your pup completes tasks like successful obedience sessions. And if he plays with another dog, it's better than more violent games that mimic fighting.

To make the game more challenging, you can hide an object, or a scented object, amongst the leaves and make your pup try to find it. "Play in the Leaves" is also good for fearful or timid pups because it tempts them to come out of their emotional shell and take action. And every pup should learn to confront and conquer new stimuli like crackling leaves at the urging of his owner. Playing in leaves can also focus overly wild or bored pups and take them away from destructive alternatives, such as mutilating your trees or digging up your flowers.

It's also a truly fun way for dogs and adult owners, or dogs and kids, to play together. But for safety you should check each pile of leaves before your pup (or children) start playing in it to make sure that there's no hidden hazard, like a snake or barbed wire.

Hint: Your pup is only young once and this game is so cute you'll probably want to videotape it, especially if your pup can get your older dog playing with him!

#37 *"Weave Through Poles"*

Known for: Easiest, cheapest, most versatile agility move everyone can use at home
Helps: Fine-tunes control; teaches pups to walk well on leash, good yet mellow exercise
Which pups? Almost every pup
Which owners? Almost every owner, including children
Time, Effort, Cost: Low if you make "poles" yourself or improvise with household objects; higher cost if you order regulation equipment
Cautions, risks: Low. Almost every dog & owner are safe working with weave poles at a relaxed pace

Instructions:

Picture a line of up to twelve narrow plastic poles each a few feet high stuck in the ground with a couple of feet separating each pole. Now envision a dog progressing through these poles by weaving his body between them, as in an obstacle course, while his owner runs along bedside him, cheering him on to move as quickly as possible. If you can picture this, you can picture the "weave poles" portion of formal dog agility competition.

Another use for weave poles is with both dog and owner heeling together and winding through a line of poles or cones, taking care not to touch any. The faster the dog/handler team move, the more difficult clearing the poles or cones without touching them becomes.

Both options provide great exercise for dogs; help teach dogs self control, aid dogs in learning to heel properly and provide healthy exercise and sensory stimulation. Working with weave poles is also fun for most dogs and owners.

And owners don't need to enter formal agility competition for their dogs to practice with weave poles, or similar obstacles. Weave poles, or similar, work just as well in every back yard. And if you use the "cone", or crossed bottom PVC variety and you have sufficient floor space, you can even set up indoors.

Weave poles work well for puppies because (unlike with some other formal agility obstacles) the dog (and handler) can weave through poles at any speed and intensity. And the activity doesn't pose any special risk of injury because the dog doesn't put much more sudden pressure on bones or joints than he would with regular walking. Weave poles (or cones or similar objects) arranged for your puppy to wind through are good for many things. They help a puppy's coordination and proprioception (knowledge of the body's position in space) and we feel they are one of the best ways to practice heeling so that a dog learns to enjoy being "glued to his owner's side".

We tell almost every family to try weave poles with their pups and to use poles or cones as a "go-to" solution if you ever want something fun and easy to do that will burn off a little puppy energy. Practice also helps pups learn how to heel without pulling. When a pup learns to walk through weave poles beside his owner it gets him in the habit of always glancing toward his owner to know what next move to expect, rather than just forging ahead.

Knowing that your pup will stick close to you even winding through the poles builds confidence in owners who are afraid that their pup may not heel correctly out on a public walk. It's also an excellent activity for children to try, even if they are not mature enough to take their large breed pup out on a walk alone. When the pup walks through the poles, or cones, with a child, he is challenged to stay right by their side, rather than pulling straight ahead as he might if the child tried to walk him out on a public street.

Practicing walking a puppy through the poles is fun and challenging for every family member and makes people of every age smile. And you get more intense feedback about your pup's ability to behave than you might if you always take him for the same boring walk around your block. You or your kids can practice walking the puppy through obstacles on leash, or you can make it more challenging for yourself and the dog by removing the leash, and still expecting him to stick by your side. Next you can try increasing the pace.

In agility competition, the handler has to teach the dog to enter between the first two poles on the right and weave his body around each pole until he comes out at the last pole, moving as fast as possible. The dog must not miss even one pole or he must start at the beginning again. If you want to approximate this at home without walking through the poles yourself, teaching your pup is easy. First take him through quite a few times on leash so that he gets the feel of it. Start out giving him treats for performing well and gradually phase out treats- except occasionally.

Then remove your pup's leash and have him move through the poles or cones with you off leash, giving him treats when he gets it right. Now, start phasing out the treats. For his next trial, give your pup the opportunity to win treats again, but only if he can wind through a few poles on his own.

Say a command like "let's go" and start luring him through the poles with a treat. Once he gets through a few poles on his own, give him the treat. Try a few more poles and give him another treat. Soon the pup will be able to do all the poles or cones in one shot as you lure him. When he finishes, give him lots of praise and the treat you've been luring him with. Eventually, your goal is not to have to lure him with the treats, but to let him follow your hand signal as you step back a tiny bit. Getting it right at this point takes a little finesse for dog and handler, but your pup should improve every time you practice.

Eventually, you won't even have to give your pup direction with your hand at all. You can just sit in your lawn chair and give him a command like "go through the poles". Your pup will get great exercise for body and mind, you will impress anyone who sees your performance, and you won't even have to get out of your chair. And, if you ever want to win a formal agility competition, your pup will be ready.

Hint: Agility on a budget: Some people briefly consider trying agility with their high-energy dogs in their backyards, but then they give up because of the high prices of formal agility kits sold in some stores or online. But you don't have to spend a lot for equipment. As long as you're not practicing for formal agility competition, you can create your own weave poles that are easy to move around the yard. Use discarded traffic cones or cheap "mini" cones, PVC lengths attached to a crossed base or any similar homemade obstacle that won't fall over on your puppy. We like cones or homemade PVC poles because they are easy to move around and stow away, and because they are suitable for indoors.

#38 "Kiddie" Pool

Best known for: Owners always say, "Why didn't I think of that?"
Helps: Unique physical & mental stimulation for almost every pup; positive intro to water
Which pups? Curious, playful high energy pups with lots of energy to burn (such as terriers), water loving breeds (such as Labs or Poodles); also helps any pup that needs to come out of their shell for some fun
Which owners? Every owner; but follow cautions below for children
Time, Effort, Cost: Minimal. More fun than work, but you must empty pool after use
Cautions, risks: Serious, life-threatening drowning risk if young children are left unsupervised around a full-kiddie pool or if they enter the yard without being seen, plus other dangers. See "Safety Note" below.

Instructions:

A "kiddie pool" can be one of the easiest, cheapest and most stress-free ways to entertain your pup in the warm weather, and dogs love it! You can buy a kiddie pool in discount stores and some pet stores for less than $10 and you can use it to acclimate your pup to water and stimulate all of his senses.

Start with just a tiny amount of water in the pool so that your pup can first get comfortable just walking in it. Once he achieves this milestone, you can gradually increase the water depth as he tolerates it. You can even start to teach him to swim by gently cupping his body. (If your pup is a small breed, you should also provide a little step to set a precedent for your pup to learn how to swim to the step in order to safely climb out of the pool on his own.)

It's a lot of fun to watch puppies playing in the kiddie pool, especially if you have more than one. You may also want to get creative. Buy some interesting water toys and teach retrieving from your lounge chair. The water entertains the pups, and keeps their minds and bodies stimulated, even when you don't feel like expending a great deal of energy. This is also a healthy activity for a pup and an older dog to play at together.

Another nice benefit of owning a kiddie pool is that it provides your pup the chance to cool off in hot weather, allowing him to play outside a little longer, in slightly hotter temperatures.

If you feel inspired, you and/or your kids can splash around in the kiddie pool with your puppy, and you may want to help him when you first introduce him to the pool. Just use clean water of a moderate temperature, and make sure the pup is clean, healthy and pest and parasite free. **Your children must never get the water in their mouths when the dog's been in the kiddie pool, and you should always provide adult supervision for kids and dogs whenever they play in water. For safety purposes, you should also make sure to empty the pool when not in use.**

Kiddie pools are also a solution for owners with limited mobility and for seniors. You can give your pup his daily kiddie pool playtime in your back yard while you sit next to him on a lawn chair to supervise.

Safety Note: Always secure your yard so children can't get in the pool unnoticed, and empty the pool whenever adults aren't present to protect children, small pups and other pets from drowning. Supervise your kids carefully around the pool at all times, especially when they play with your pup. Don't let kids swallow non-sterile water that dogs have been in. Use low water level with tiny pups, test water temperature, never force terrified pups into water; and provide steps for small pups to climb out.

#39 "Bark for Help"

Known for: Helpful barking, the opposite of problem barking, could save your life

Helps: Your dog's barking could scare away intruders, alert you in an emergency or let you know if a family member's in distress

Which pups? Any dog can be a watchdog or bark when their owner is in trouble, and this skill is always helpful when it's done right. It's important to channel your dog's barking correctly when he's young, especially with large guardian breeds

Which owners? All owners should learn to recognize when their dog is barking to alert them of danger. A dog that barks to signal that a person is in distress can be especially helpful in homes with elderly family members or children

Time, Effort, Cost: Takes patience and responding correctly without frustration

Cautions or risks: You should encourage your pup to be watchful and helpful, but never to act aggressive. Each situation is different. A true problem barker may need professional help if he's dangerous to people or himself, or if his barking violates the law

Instructions:

Barking for help is a lifesaving skill. And you may not know your pup could save your family's lives until the day he's called upon to do it. Acting as a watchdog and sounding the alarm when danger threatens comes naturally for dogs, especially certain breeds. Many dogs (not all) will bark whenever a potential intruder approaches the home, or in other situations where the dog perceives risk to human family members, and most families trust their dog's superior senses and ability to perceive danger.

Sometimes dogs bark for other lifesaving reasons. For example, your dog may come running to you for help if your toddler falls into the swimming pool. In an emergency like this, your dog's bark will sound agitated and insistent. He may also "dance" and toss his head as though leading you or even attempt to drag you by the sleeve or pantleg. You should never ignore a summons like this, especially if it comes from a usually placid dog!

A dog with an elderly owner may tend to watch over their owner. If she falls asleep with a pot boiling on the stove, the dog may bark frantically or grab her by the sleeve to try to wake her. If this doesn't work, he may run to alert another family member or even try to get out of the house to bring a neighbor to help.

Unless your pup is professionally trained in protection or as an assistance animal, he will bark to help you out of natural instinct. There is no way to one hundred percent proof that he will act to save your life, especially if he's not professionally trained. An untrained pet dog will bark to help a family member in a life threatening crisis only if instinct, and experience, tells him he should.

Some breeds are more apt to be protective or nurturing with their owners, but this rule has many exceptions. In the end, how your dog reacts in a real crisis depends on the right training, the right dog and the right relationship with the family. You can't *force* a dog to act heroically on the day a real crisis occurs. But you can *encourage* him to act like a hero. And even tiny toy dogs can bark for help.

Another way you can encourage your pup to bark at intruders or to alert you when a family member is in trouble is to train him to bark on command (see "Stop Barking On Command" in this Chapter) and then praise and reinforce him whenever he barks at appropriate times. Some pups may bark to alert the family of possible intruders from a young age, but don't expect too much until your pup approaches one year, when most breeds start to develop adult temperament and judgment.

To encourage a puppy to develop into a heroic dog, you must raise him with love and respect. You should also actively build the pup's confidence while teaching responsibility. Basic obedience trained with gentle methods is essential, and all family members should be involved in the training. **If you want your dog to someday use his own judgment to save your family, you should never train him with harsh corrections or by intimidation or he might feel too afraid to act if there is a crisis. You must also expose your puppy to varied environments and stimuli that challenge his mind.**

A puppy that is raised feeling he's an essential member of the family will more likely take responsibility in an emergency. So, to raise a capable dog you should ask a lot of your pup every day. Dogs are proud to do small tasks like carrying items from one family member to another or retrieving small items for an owner who has trouble bending, and they also enjoy practicing obedience. Training your dog to do any type of helpful task will teach him that he has a real part in his family's well being.

One of the most illustrative examples of helpful barking we've seen involved a 5- month old Presa Canario pup that we knew from the time he was abandoned at just 6 weeks in a South Florida grooming shop. It was likely the young guys who abandoned him had bred him for fighting because the breed has such a dangerous reputation. But no one will ever know because they simply dropped the pup in the shop, leaving phony contact information, and never returned. The owner of the grooming shop took a chance on adopting the pup after asking for our opinion about the pup's temperament. While this breed is absolutely *not* for most owners because of their natural highly defensive temperament, there is often a connection between Presas that attack and the wrong kind of shaping by their owners. But, by 20 weeks, this little pup clearly loved his adopted family and was already showing extraordinary judgment.

One day we dropped by to say "hello" and take him out for a little walk. Emma was walking along with him when suddenly the little Presa came to a halt, looked back and started barking intently and staring fixedly at something on the pavement. He was barking at Emma's umbrella. She had dropped it ten feet back without realizing it while they were walking. And the pup's tone and message was as clear as if he were a human friend telling her she had dropped something. What a little gentleman! And what a testament to how helpful a dog can be with no formal training, even at a young age.

This story shows how, even in a breed that has made some extremely bad headlines, an individual dog can have people's best interest in mind even without prompting. We always advise that, if your dog or pup ever gives a few alarm barks if a strange car pulls up outside your home at ten in the evening or if a stranger steps up on your porch, you shouldn't punish the dog or get angry at him. First take a moment to check if anything is actually wrong. If there's no real danger at the moment, respectfully signal your dog that everything's okay and that it's time to stop barking now. Or distract him to a different task. (You can use commands like the "Sit", "Look" and "Go to Your Place" described in Part 2.)

Never use frightening or hurtful methods, like shock collars (or "e-collars") to stop a puppy's barking, or he may never bark when you need him to. If your pup ever barks, not as a nuisance, but to alert you of some problem, you should reinforce the behavior. For example, if your teenaged daughter screamed because she saw a spider and your pup comes to you barking, this would be the perfect time to praise and reward him for an appropriate reaction to her distress even though there was no actual danger. You could say the dog's name and something like, "Good Bark for Help".

Many families these days, at the advice of terribly misinformed dog professionals, are wasting their protective breeds' natural ability to take care of their families and their homes. These families are locking dogs like adult German Shepherds, Dobermans or Pit Bulls- even Mastiffs- up in cramped dog crates for almost every waking hour and all night, when the dog would naturally patrol the house and protect the family. Dogs are able to hear and smell what goes on outside in ways that humans cannot, and their bark alone is sometimes enough to scare off dangerous intruders. **If you want your dog to protect and watch over your family and your possessions by barking, he should have as much free access to all areas of the house as possible as long as he does not have direct unsupervised access to infants or small children unless adults are present.**

If you can't trust your adult free in most areas of your home, even after you carefully attempt to train him yourself, you should get professional treatment from a high-level behaviorist so you *can* trust him around family and possessions.

Both dog and family are happier when the dog is actually helping. And protecting you and/or alerting you to danger is one of the most important things your dog can do to help you. There is no substitute for the peace of mind you will feel when you know that your dog is roaming every corner of the house all night long, checking every family member, every door and every window, checking for any bad sound or smell and never waking you until that one night when you need it. There's no absolute guarantee that your particular dog will react by barking and save your life in a crisis. But there *is* an absolute guarantee that **a dog in a crate CANNOT bark to save your life if he's not free to roam your home and evaluate the safety of every situation.**

Hint: The difference between healthy and problem barking:
In "healthy" barking, for example during play or to sound the alarm, your pup communicates with you for a specific purpose and intent (as shown in the story of the Presa puppy and the umbrella.) **In contrast, unhealthy barking is so extreme it hurts the dog or interferes with other healthy activities, and there's no communication** (for example, a pup might still be barking an hour after the mailman has gone away. Dogs barking like this appear to have glazed eyes; they don't look at anyone or anything and they simply lift their heads and bark

incessantly, resembling wind-up toys. Owners should help by interceding and treating this problem before it gets worse. Some dogs or pups, especially outdoor dogs, bark when they're in physical distress. If your dog barks excessively, first check that he's not hot, cold or sick or that he doesn't need more comfortable shelter or more room to move around. **There is no such thing as "problem barking" in a crate, since crates/cages inherently cause physical and emotional distress. A pup that barks while he's crated may just need more spacious housing- or he may need water.** Dogs may also bark because of extreme boredom. Sometimes increased exercise, interactive toys or stimulating activities may solve the problem. (Read "#16 Interactive Toys" in this chapter for more information.) Clinical separation anxiety is different from frustration barking. It is a serious syndrome where a dog that's left alone may bark all day to the point of hurting himself and may hurt himself in other ways, such as destroying furniture and ingesting dangerous materials. Mild cases of separation anxiety sometimes respond to increases in stimuli and exercise, just like boredom barking, but more serious cases often require the help of professional behaviorists. And, finally, some dogs, especially those in multi-dog households, may bark for social or dominance issues in their relationships with each other and with their owner. Sometimes, just training the "Look" command, or even to "Sit" at the door when visitors come may be enough to break this cycle (see instructions in Part 2). But more serious cases of dominance-based and/or multi-dog barking may require professional assessment and/or treatment.

#40 *"Learn to Come to Everyone"*

Known for: Highly recommended; easy & enjoyable game to teach pups to want to come
Helps: Teaches from an early age that coming to you brings rewards. Shapes the psyche of all dogs & pups, especially those that get distracted when called
Which pups? All pups-this skill could someday save a dog's life! But don't get the pup so excited that he runs too fast or knocks people over
Which owners? Any owner who doesn't know how to get pups to come. Since you'll be use a long leash or line, you should be physically able to manipulate the line and make sure you don't get yours or your pup's legs entangled. Children can practice with adult supervision with small and/or mellow pups. But kids shouldn't practice unsupervised.
Time, Effort, Cost: Low effort, low cost & only takes minutes at a time. Requires one or more helpers and a long lead or light rope.
Cautions or risks: Considerable risk. A long lead handled incorrectly can catch on legs if the pup starts to run wildly or the pup could "run someone over". For safety, practice only with adults or

older kids/teens that are nimble enough on their feet to dodge a moving line or a running puppy. Small children should be supervised by parents & this activity is not recommended for anyone with balance problems.

Instructions:

Getting your dog to come to you reliably may be the most important thing your dog will ever learn, and it could save his life. But if you try to rush it or force it you could make it so the dog never wants to come to you or your family. **You should start teaching your puppy to love to come to you from the day you bring him home and your pup should always associate coming to his family with happiness and reward.**

Many owners have no idea what happened to their pup in his former environment before he came to them. If you were careful enough to buy your pup from a great breeder, the pup may already know how to come when called when you get him home. If so, you are quite fortunate and you should continue to keep the experience positive throughout the pup's life by only calling him to you for pleasant things.

Unfortunately, bad breeders just breed dogs to make money; and they make things difficult for the new owners by not interacting with pups at all during the critical early weeks of life and not teaching skills like coming when called.

Uncaring puppy-mill breeders or abusive former owners may have scared or hurt your puppy whenever they called him and this makes it harder to teach the dog to come to you later in life. But if you're gentle and patient, you can eventually teach even an undersocialized or skittish dog that the greatest things in life happen when he comes running to you.

To make sure your pup will learn to come to you, first address any stress or fear he might feel overall. And make it a habit to never call him to you for anything unpleasant (for example, don't call him to have his claws cut; simply pick him up and do it). Also **change when you lavish attention on your pup so that you don't reward him with hugs and praise every time he pushes his attention on you when you are busy; but rather reserve the big shows of affection only for when he comes after you call**. (If you give too much attention to a dog all the time, he'll learn not to value it, and he'll see no need to run to you when you call. But once you make your attention scarcer, he'll value it more and he'll quickly come running.)

We recommend first teaching your Pup to come with treats. (See detailed instructions in "5. Training "Come" or Recall", Chapter 5, Part 2.) Get your pup's attention and call him to you from a short distance while he is on lead while showing him a treat. Make your voice excited and upbeat and crouch down or backpedal a few steps to get the pup interested, if necessary. The fact that you have control of the lead will mean that you can guarantee the puppy comes, so if he still lags you can gently draw him towards you. Don't give him a reward for coming to you this way. But the first time the pup comes to you on his own, give him tons of praise and offer him one or more yummy treats.

Another enjoyable and highly effective way to first teach a pup to come is a game where two or more family members teach the pup coming to people brings reward:

The family should form a small circle around the puppy, with the pup on a long standard width leash or line that is fifteen to thirty feet long. (Don't use thin, filament-style retractable leads, which can be dangerous when your dog runs.) Each family member or each partner should hold a handful of small soft treats. You start with one person holding the leashed pup, while another person holds the looped end of the long leash which is stretched across the distance between them.

The person holding the end of the leash then calls the dog to them, acting extremely happy and enthusiastic and backpedaling if necessary to make the dog run towards them. Meanwhile, the person holding the dog releases him. When the dog reaches the person that called him, the person should first touch his collar (imitating grabbing him if he was off-lead) and then they should warmly praise him and offer a treat as a reward.

Now it's time to switch. The person the puppy first came to should now hold onto him and toss the end of the leash to a different person (or your single partner). And the person who originally held the pup now calls him. Each person then repeats this process, alternating and taking turns.

Since your pup gets loads of treats, attention and exercise, you can see why he'd enjoy this activity. But if he ever refuses to come, just gently reel in the leash to bring him to you, to reinforce the fact that he can never refuse a "come" command.

Start with a small circle. As your dog or puppy gets better coming to you from short distances, you can make the circle bigger, so he has to come farther to get to you. To make it easier for your pup to come to you when you first practice "Learn to Come to Everyone", simply get closer to him and pick up much of the leash to allow less slack.

Don't play too long, because you want to keep the puppy interested and energized. If his energy or yours starts to drop, it's time to call it a day and practice again the next day. But practice frequently and continue throughout your dog's life, as this technique is one of the basics to get pups and dogs coming to their owners on command.

If you have a fenced-in area, also practice taking your puppy off the leash and calling him from all corners of the yard once he has gotten good at coming to you on lead. But never try without a fence, or you may defeat your purpose and the puppy could run away before he's fully trained. Practice this activity frequently, including around distractions. If, at any point in his life, the dog starts getting lax about coming to you off lead, resume practicing the game with the leash and the family in a circle. Pups love this game. And older kids and preteens love it too.

This game is also a positive way to include your pup at family get-togethers, rather than chasing him away from human sports and games. Practicing outside with a long lead and a big circle of participants is good exercise for your pup. You can also practice indoors, using the lead. Remove the leash once your pup is coming reliably and have family members call the pup from different parts of the home. If you practice enough, you'll notice your pup coming to you faster, no matter where you are.

Hint: Sometimes people don't know they can train their pups to come this way because they don't realize they can purchase regular width leashes 15, 20 or 30 feet long at pet stores and discount department stores. A full-size long lead (which is safer than the nylon filament style used in most extend-a-leads) also has many other important uses. These are detailed at length directly below in "#41 Long Leash" in this chapter.

Safety Tip: Take care not to trip on a fast moving long lead or let it catch your pup's legs. See additional cautions above and in "Long Leash".

#41 "Long Leash"

Known for: Highly recommended, yet underused tool; greatly improves life for every family with a dog

Helps: Reinforces obedience commands while pup feels free; makes exercising easier

Which pups? Essential for pups in homes without fenced yards; highly important for high-energy pups that needs more exercise than their less fit owners

Which owners? Important tool for owners who lack the physical endurance of their frustrated high-energy pups. Helps all owners with important commands like the recall.

Time, Effort, Cost: $10-$35; requires significant effort to keep lead from entangling

Cautions or risks: Serious physical risk whenever a pup runs on a long lead. The lead could hit the owner's legs, knocking the owner down. Or it could wrap around a pup's delicate leg and break it. A handler can avoid this risk by continually adjusting the leash and discouraging fast running. Thin, filament style adjustable extend-a-leads that are currently popular are even more dangerous and can cause serious injury to owners' fingers and serious injuries to tiny dogs' legs, including amputation. We only recommend full-width long leads or extendable leads. (See details in the "Hint" below.)

Instructions:

A long leash is absolutely one of the best tools to help anyone to exercise their dog or pup, and it's particularly valuable for puppy owners with physical limitations. It's also quite inexpensive and easy to find. You can purchase a full-width nylon leash of 20-30 feet for between $10 and $25 in pet stores, pet catalogs and discount department stores.

One important use for a long lead is practicing the recall or "come" command (as described in "#40 Learn to Come to Everyone" above). If you don't have a fenced yard, you can also use the long lead to practice other obedience commands at a distance to increase the challenge. And you can bring the lead with you to practice commands when you and your pup go to public places. Sometimes you can get a dog out of the habit of pulling by first teaching him to walk with you on the long lead with a great deal of slack.

For an owner with limited endurance a long lead can "magically" enhance your pup's exercise and overall experience when you go for walks, especially at the park. The long leash allows a well-trained dog to literally run circles around their owner, wearing himself out, while you simply revolve in one spot, enjoying the fine weather. Or, you can amble along walking paths and trails at the speed suited to your physical abilities, while your puppy gets to weave back and forth on the long lead, taking thirty steps to each of your steps and sniffing around as much as he likes. Just follow regulations, because some parks only allow 6 ft. leads. And, for courtesy and safety at public parks, you should reel your pup in closer to you whenever you pass other people and dogs.

A long lead can also help you at home because it allows you to supervise your puppy without having to walk a lot while he spends hours exploring the backyard. A well-trained dog of any age can stay attached to you on a long line and sniff around for as long as he likes in your unfenced yard or patio area. He'll have a feeling of freedom. And you can rest, relax and remain seated as long you as you can stay attentive and control the leash.

Dogs can even play Frisbee or catch while attached to a long lead, as long as you are extremely careful that the lead doesn't get entangled in anyone's legs. Of course a fenced area is an infinitely better choice for these games so your dog can run freely and so you do not have to face the risk of the leash getting tangled. But, if you're like so very many new puppy owners who have absolutely no access to any fenced area, a 30 ft. lead can give your pup a completely different feeling of freedom than a standard 6 ft. one. And it also gives your pup more room to stretch his legs for a little aerobic exercise.

Another important use for a long lead is to let a pup out for the dreaded late night bathroom break when you're dressed in pajamas and don't want to step outside. Stretching the puppy out on the long lead is no substitute for "real" walks during the daytime that include exercise, exposure to outside stimuli and dog/owner bonding. But it can make life much easier on rainy nights at two or three in the morning when your tiny puppy has an uncontrollable need to relieve himself and you need to keep tabs on him.

Because of nighttime hazards like snakes, owls, scorpions and feral cats, you should always keep the pup in sight when he's out at the end of the lead. Don't let the pup get into any bushes and don't allow much more slack than the pup needs to relieve himself. If you spot a hazard, immediately reel your puppy in or go to him, using the leash as your guide. This can be a lot easier than trying to chase him down in a dark, wet or snowy yard!

Hint: For safety, avoid popular extendable or retractable leads with a long narrow cordlike line. Although these seem convenient, they endanger owners and dogs and have been known to cause injuries including amputations of fingers and dogs' paws. Thin retractable leads are also dangerous and impractical for owners with limited manual dexterity who might have problems controlling the leash if the dog runs or lunges abruptly. If you still want to use an extendable leash as your long lead, you can buy sturdier versions made of solid, full-sized leash without filament.

#42 *"Toy On a Line"*

Known for: Keeps your pup on his toes having fun, while you remain comfortably seated
Helps: Small prey-driven pups that love to chase things instantly exercise and blow off steam indoors or out
Which pups? Only for pups under 25 lbs. that aren't strong or wild
Which owners? Helps owners with difficulty running around or bending play with pups. But you *must* have full physical control of the line to keep people, pup & breakables safe
Time, Effort, Cost: Minimal; cheap supplies & it's easy to do anytime
Cautions or risks: SERIOUS risks of entanglement in the line if you disregard instructions. If you only play with dogs under 25 lbs. that you can completely control, the risks are quite low. Choose a toy that won't harm your pup in case he chews it up or swallows it. Also, be extremely careful manipulating the line so it doesn't catch human legs or your pup's tiny paws. Children really enjoy playing this game, but must have adult supervision.

Instructions:

This one extremely simple activity can sometimes enliven a lackluster dog/owner relationship and immediately fill an afternoon with fun and laughter. And this activity is particularly suited to certain breeds of dogs. If you have a pup that is known as "prey-driven", you may already know it. He's the pup who madly chases butterflies and dandelion fluff and always goes into overdrive every time anyone rolls a tennis ball across the floor. If you own a pup with high prey drive, whenever something moves, he goes crazy to catch it.

Many retrieving breeds have a high-prey drive, because chasing after faraway objects is the life-work they were bred for. Some terrier breeds also have extremely high energy, coupled with extremely high prey drive. And this includes breeds like Jack Russell Terriers and Yorkies. These particular breeds are often owned by seniors who cannot comfortably bend or throw balls, etc. to meet the dog's exercise needs. Even if you walk your pup daily, walks usually aren't enough to meet the exercise needs of an active breed- a dog that would happily chase after moving objects all day.

Some owners are naturally energetic themselves and have ample free time to enjoy playing with their high energy puppy. These owners already know their little pup has high prey drive- because his reactions make it even more fun to throw things for him and watch him chase. Other owners don't have the time, energy or physical capabilities for extended play sessions with their high-octane little pup. And so they may find out about his extraordinary prey drive the hard way- when he starts getting into mischief chasing the neighbor's cat, or the broom they are trying to sweep with.

But watching your puppy engage his natural instincts can be a delight when you don't have to do much more physically than chuckle at his antics. "Toy On a Line" is an easy, but almost miraculous concept that allows you to exploit the laws of physics so you can sit, stand or walk slowly while your pup gets to chase around the toy, have tons of fun and finish happily exhausted. The concept is similar to how puppies are sometimes trained in Schutzhund, where pups are worked by chasing a towel, or a small stuffed cylinder attached to a line.

For a line, you can use regular string or rope, or use a full-thickness long lead, (as described in "Long Leash" in this chapter). Don't use a thin filament extend-a-lead. Tie the end of the string or lead to a toy that you know your pup will want to chase after. Then throw the line whatever distance you choose and then reel it in so your pup will chase. You can also use the line to move the toy in circles around you, or move it up in the air just out of your pup's reach. **Learn to tease the puppy and work the line so that he keeps chasing, but can never quite catch the toy.** (If you've ever played with a cat, you know exactly how it's done.)

Customize how you play to your exact dog, your physical condition and what you both enjoy. This game is perfect to exercise a small breed pup inside when the weather is bad. Some little dogs can chase after toys at speeds you couldn't imagine and they also have sharp little teeth, so make sure the toy you choose is not dangerous if the pup suddenly fastens on to it. And **be especially careful with line twisting around feet and knocking people over, or hurting your pup's legs.**

Ideally, you should play this game with a tiny young pup that's not overly fast or vigorous and won't instantaneously rip toys apart. With a pup like this, you can use varied toys, including some padded soft toys to provide a variety of stimulation. But be careful if your pup is particularly fast or "wild". **Only attempt this game if you have complete control of your pup and are sure neither people, nor the pup, will get entangled**. This is why we discourage playing with dogs over 25 pounds.

Don't allow your pup to become overexcited by playing too long at a time. "Toy On a Line" is more fun when you play at spontaneous moments, indoors or out for only a few minutes at a time. Try it whenever you feel you need to laugh or smile after a stressful day.

Hint: The game can also help shy, fearful, previously abused dogs and pups- and senior dogs- regain some inner playfulness.

#43 *"Chase the Bubbles"*

Known for: Pleasant, cheap and easy activity everyone enjoys
Helps: Coordination, alertness & focus; alleviates boredom & puts dogs in a mood for fun
Which pups? High prey drive pups that love to chase things, pups with extra energy; also helps engage listless, shy or tentative pups and healthy, but listless, senior dogs
Which owners? All owners, including kids and owners with physical limitations
Time, Effort, Cost: Minimal; more fun than work; no physical strain
Cautions or risks: Low, but use common sense; supervise and don't let bubbles rise too high if your pup is a large or giant breed or has joint problems that prohibit jumping

Instructions:

Most pups will immediately take to chasing children's toy bubbles. Equipment costs less than fifty cents and you can play inside or outside, for as short or long a time as you like. The bubbles look gorgeous and your puppy's antics will make you laugh. This is a fun way to redirect an inquisitive high energy puppy that might otherwise bother family or guests when he wants to play. Instead, with this easy activity, everyone can have fun and laugh. This includes pet parents with limited mobility, because they can blow bubbles sitting down, while the pup runs around to burn off steam. This is also a good game with no downside for all but the smallest children to play with their pups. And the fact that you can play indoors makes it a good choice for something to do with a frustrated and bored puppy during snow days or heat waves.

Instructions are easy- blow bubbles at whatever pace you like, inciting your puppy to chase them and burst them- either by bopping them with his nose or by biting or hitting them with a paw. How high you want your pup to reach to burst the bubbles depends on his physical tolerance for jumping. The game is safe for every puppy, including small breeds, senior dogs and dogs with limited mobility, but don't allow your dog to jump too high. And don't mind if your dog "talks" a little in his excitement as you blow bubbles to let you know he's having fun.

Although bubble mixture is intended to be safe for kids, it's made of soap. Ingesting too many bubbles could give your pup diarrhea. And never let him chew up the bottle and drink the mixture!

Hint: You can also buy flavored bubbles made especially for dogs in pet stores.

#44 *"Pup on the Table"*

Known for: An alternative for training small dogs & pups without constant bending
Helps: Physically easier for owners, while teaching pups to trust and not panic
Which pups? All pups, especially small breeds, should learn to stay calm on tables for later success at the vet & the groomer
Which owners? Good solution for owners with back problems or problems bending to train certain commands, especially with small breeds
Time, Effort, Cost: Minimal
Cautions or risks: Serious risk if pup falls off table. Clip a leash to a harness to catch him if he falls. Or train him on a soft piece of furniture.

Instructions:

This training trick simply gives you easier access to your small puppy when initially teaching some commands, particularly the often time consuming "down" command. First, gradually introduce your pup to surfaces off the floor to make sure he won't be nervous. Then find a wide solid surface that won't wobble (for example a picnic table, which also has a ready-made seat for you.) Lift your pup onto the table, keep him leashed, with the leash attached to a harness for his safety and train him the desired command(s) using treats.

You should also practice occasionally using a table to groom your puppy to rehearse real trips to the groomer. And using care, you should rehearse examining your pup on a slippery surface table while giving him treats and praise to prepare him for future trips to the veterinarian. (See full instructions in Mock Veterinary Exam, in this chapter.)

Whenever you work with your pup on a table carefully monitor him, especially if he tends to be "hoppy". Until you're confident your pup will stay totally calm on a table, use raised surfaces at lower heights. Always keep the pup leashed. And, if you think there's even a remote chance of the pup jumping and you having to catch him mid-air to be safe, attach the leash to a harness rather than a collar. If you practice with him a lot when he is young, your pup will be more likely to always stay calm on tables and never try to jump.

Hint: You don't always have to use a table to save your back when working with your pup. Placing the pup on any kind of platform, raised surface or step above you works on the same principle- just make sure that the surface is stable so that your pup feels confident and stays safe.

#45 *"Puppy Stairs"*

Known for: More owners should know about this wonderful tool

Helps: Pups (and older dogs) get up and down from high furniture and vehicles; helps dogs with physical problems feel more independent, while preventing injury.

Which pups? Good for loading dogs into a high vehicle, especially small pups, large/giant puppies and dogs of any age with hip or joint problems

Which owners? Owners with problems bending/lifting; any owner whose pup can benefit

Time, Effort, Cost: $10-$100 or build it yourself; takes some time to train pup to use the equipment, but makes life infinitely easier, and could someday save thousands in vet bills

Cautions and Risks: Doggie stairs and ramps are designed to protect dogs/pups from serious falls & serious injury. But, since the pup will use the stairs to climb to high surfaces, you should carefully train him to use them right & supervise that he doesn't fall

Instructions:

We strongly believe that most new pet parents should invest in a carpeted set of portable fold-up dog stairs available at pet stores, online, on television and at retailers like some chain drug stores. Prices for stairs start at approximately $20 (some are even less) or you could purchase a ramp designed for dogs (available from the same sources) or fashion your own sturdy, non-slip step or ramp for your pup.

The right set of stairs can protect pups from injury and aid them in many important ways. Stairs are also important equipment for senior dogs, small and toy dogs, overweight dogs and dogs with joint disorders or other disabilities. And they assist owners with high vehicles like SUV's and crossovers, owners with large dogs or puppies and owners with physical problems lifting and bending.

Dog stairs help your pup get up and down from furniture and safely climb into and out of your car or SUV. Stairs also help pups safely navigate any area in the house or yard where they'd usually have to jump. Using stairs (or ramps) can protect your pup from injury trying to jump up or down when a surface is too high. It can also make your pup feel more confident in potentially scary situations like getting into a high vehicle. And protecting a large breed pup from jumping too high is also important to help prevent future hip problems.

Hint: Dog stairs and ramps not only protect your pup's back- they can save yours as well. Many pet parents today strain their backs lifting their pups into high vehicles like SUV's. Or they may avoid outings and deprive their pup of critical socialization because getting him into the vehicle is so difficult. A ramp can easily solve this problem and make you want to take your pup on outings.

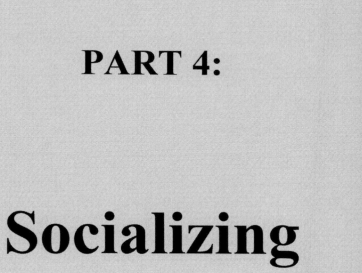

PART 4:

Socializing Your Pup

Chapter 8:

Socializing Your Pup to People & Dogs

Section A: Why & How To Socialize Your Pup
Section B: Socializing Your Pup to Different People
Section C: Socialzing Your Pup at a Pet Store
Section D: Play Dates to Socialize Your Pup to Other Pups

Section A: Why & How To Socialize Your Pup

Adequate socialization is important for your puppy to encounter the larger world and become comfortable in it. Proper socialization will help your dog mature without fears or aggression when he sees new stimuli. Unfortunately, we're often called to work with grown dogs that weren't socialized properly as pups and were never taken outside their backyards. Their owners then struggle for years with adult dogs that act crazy whenever they see other dogs or people on basic neighborhood walks or trips to the vet's office.

Owners can create serious problems when the only thing their puppy ever sees is the same block in the same neighborhood with the exact same stimuli every single day. The first time they attempt to take a dog like this out into the larger world, he may panic, lunge and act "rabid" in response to the sight of anything different- people of different ages or races than he's seen before, children on bikes or skateboards, babies in strollers, adults in wheelchairs- or even a man wearing a cowboy hat!

In contrast, a pup that encounters diverse people under relaxing circumstances when he's growing up will learn that people in his community are benign. And his owner will enjoy outings more in the company of a good canine citizen.

Unfortunately, people sometimes confuse the concept of puppy "socialization" with the kind of socializing humans do at a party. But a young puppy cannot tolerate too much sensory stimuli at this sensitive and impressionable time of life. Too many highly intense stimuli at one time can overwhelm a puppy, and overly ambitious efforts to make him like the larger world can backfire and *create* fears. You should keep all encounters with new people and places short and pleasant, and use caution if any "dog people" encourage you to throw your pup into social situations more vigorously.

Young puppies have not completed all their vaccinations, and their immune systems aren't fully developed. Therefore you should not allow your young puppy to come in contact with strange dogs or their waste. And you absolutely cannot risk your pup being bitten before his vaccinations are complete.

But even though you must protect your puppy from contagious diseases, you *should* make sure he *sees* all sizes and shapes of dogs at a distance during the impressionable window for socialization. This is the time he is still open to new experiences, like a baby. He will assume whatever stimuli he sees before 20 weeks are just natural and normal parts of the world. And he will grow up to show normal reactions around these stimuli. But if you don't introduce your pup to enough people and animals when he's young, he's likely to overreact whenever he encounters them when he is older.

Even though you'll want to protect your puppy from disease when he's little, you still want him to see the big wide world outside your home, including both dogs and people. And the best way to initially expose your young pup to the world is to carry or walk him where he can *look* at people and friendly dogs, but not necessarily touch them and reward him for a calm reaction.

Section B: Socializing Your Pup to Different People

The first people outside of your immediate family that your pup meets will likely be extended family and close friends who commonly visit your home. The best thing you can do before friends drop by and immediately start excitedly interacting with your pup is to first talk to them and get them to agree with your protocol for socializing and training.

No guest should ever give the pup attention if he is jumps around, acts overexuberant or doesn't keep all four paws on the floor. (Although it may seem difficult) ask your guests to ignore the puppy when they first walk in the door, and only give him attention once he settles down or sits or lies down politely. Your family members should do the same after any time away from home to keep the pup from getting too wild.

Awesome Puppy

Once the pup acts calm and polite, the guest can gently pet him on the side of his face or his shoulder. Visitors should avoid: bending over the pup and petting the top of his head (dogs can perceive this as dominance), "ruffling" him up or getting him overexcited, attempting to grab his collar, rapidly lifting him, hugging him tightly, allowing him to chase them or bite their hands or shoving their face directly into his. It may be tempting for people to immediately try to play with your pup or smother him with physical affection in one or all of these ways, but dogs can interpret any of these moves as confrontational. If too many people do these things to a susceptible pup too often, he could become nervous and "handshy". And sometimes people, frequently children, can get bitten when they handle a pup too roughly or use the wrong body language.

At the same time, it's very important that your young puppy meet children under pleasant circumstances. So supervise meetings carefully. If a young child or toddler is not yet mature enough to handle the pup properly, or if the child is small and you're afraid the pup might act too boisterous, the child can still interact with the pup without touching him. Have the child reward the pup with a treat for completing an obedience command like "sit" by throwing it on the floor, rather than trying to give it directly. This still serves as a positive experience for both child and pup.

Adults should supervise all encounters between pups and young children, even when the children are frequent visitors in your home. And never allow any physical contact if your pup has shown aggression- these situations require professional assessment and treatment.

In general, to keep your pup comfortable with people, ask visitors not to try to grab the pup but to instead let him approach them first, at his own pace. Also teach your guests not to inadvertently reward your pup with attention for pushing on them or jumping on them.

Having pleasant, non-stressful meetings with family and friends will help your pup before he goes out into the world to start meeting strangers. But in some cases where a family does not have many guests, strangers will be the pup's first meeting.

Before twenty weeks, it's important that your puppy meet different people; and it's okay for him to have physical contact with them under certain conditions. Since puppies are so cute, the people your pup meets will likely give him lots of friendly encouragement, but make sure they don't get too exuberant or hurt or scare him in any way. You can hold the puppy, or keep him on the floor. Keep him comfortable, and stop all encounters on a high note.

Many puppy owners may try to act polite to strangers and they may not realize that **not everyone you meet should be allowed to touch your dog. Your pup can learn to like people, and learn to be comfortable with them just by seeing them, so not every person that sees your pup has to touch him.** Walk or carry your pup past new people of all different races, ages, shapes and sizes and people engaged in varying occupations and leisure pursuits and past bikes, motorcycles and skateboards and reward him if he acts appropriate. But never put him at risk or stress him. Instead, make him feel comfortable around many different sights and sounds.

If a person you encounter knows how to pet a dog properly *and* if your puppy seems to like the person, you can invite them to pet your puppy. Pleasant encounters like this will show your puppy that people are his friends, and he'll learn to feel comfortable when people touch him. **Your pup should also meet children, but only if they are supervised and if they know how to handle dogs gently.** This cuts both ways. It's fine to let your active five-month-old Labrador "look at the nice baby". But never force your pup to physically sniff, lick or paw at a passerby's child just because you want your pup socialized. Both parties should mutually agree on any physical meeting involving a dog. **And remember that you can be legally and financially liable for anything your dog does!**

If you take your puppy out in public, he can see many people, but we recommend you limit physical petting sessions to one or two strangers a day. You can always bring the puppy out the next day for more. Make your pup's excursions out into the "real world" frequent, but never allow any outing to feel overwhelming.

For example, we recommend bring your pup to small, relatively quiet public events, like a local fair sponsored by your church, rather than huge regional art shows with hundreds of vendors, citywide street parties or county fairs.

And huge dog-themed events can also be overwhelming and dangerous places to take your young pup for his first introduction to new people and animals. Unfortunately, we've often watched owners overstress vulnerable young pups by allowing hundreds of people to touch them and many bigger dogs to sniff them at these giant charity events- and they most likely did it at the recommendation of dog experts they trusted.

If you're desperate to see the assortment of breeds and doggie costumes at these events, and if you want your pup to get some socialization benefit without him getting mobbed, there are two ways to do it. You can stay at the periphery of the event, rather than walking the crowded paths. An adorable tiny pup is a natural people magnet. But this way he can see the mob from a distance while only having a few individuals ask to pet him. And this will still keep the day a positive experience.

Or your precious pup can travel incognito in a carrier or in a stroller behind zipped up dark mesh when you enter areas that are heavily crowded with people and dogs. This will allow your pup to see, hear and smell many people and dogs while you can control how many people get to touch him by zipping or unzipping the mesh. In a stroller, your little pup can also get some sun protection and take a little nap if he's worn out. A small breed pup certainly has to learn to "be a dog", and we do believe pups should spend most of their time walking and interacting with the world, rather than sitting passively in a stroller or a carrier. But these can be useful tools for particular occasions like crowded streets and crowded dog festivals, especially with very young pups.)

And the truth is, it's usually better to take your puppy out with you on everyday outings whenever possible and then leave him home during highly crowded special events. Or stick to smaller, more manageable events, like church-sponsored picnics, local, rather than regional, art shows, small scale farmer's markets and smaller dog events. Many community events take place in huge, sun-scorched areas but try to stick to those that offer some shade. And never take your puppy to a fireworks display! This one experience is more stressful than most pups can tolerate and it may cause lifelong damage.

As long as you stay reasonable, the task of socializing your puppy can also be a great experience for your kids. While you supervise, your kids can think of new places the family could introduce the pup to people engaged in different activities for the first time. Maybe your kids will spot a pullover near the beach where the pup can observe skateboarders, a playground where the pup can watch smaller children or a quiet section of a local park where older gentlemen play checkers each afternoon. Or they can bring the puppy with them when they visit friends of different races or a child who uses a wheelchair.

With you supervising, your kids could politely introduce your puppy themselves to an older neighbor who uses a walker when she comes out to get her mail. Or the kids and pup could even say, "Hi", to the postman as he drops the mail off. All of these pleasant encounters meeting new people will help make your pup a friend, rather than a problem, when he meets people in different situations when he's grown. (And this includes the postman.)

Just remember that children younger than preteen age may not be assertive enough to fend away strangers that reach out to pet your pup or who allow their dogs to touch your pup without permission. Since a cute puppy is a magnet for all types of people and, unfortunately in today's world, not all strangers are safe, parents should always supervise younger children when they're out with the puppy. Parents should always make the final judgment whether to stop and allow a person to pet your pup or to just pass at a distance. You should always set a proper example and introduce yourself politely when approaching strangers and never force your pup on a person or their dog. Never invade a stranger's privacy if they don't encourage your approach or if they seem uncomfortable. Make every meeting short and pleasant and thank people for their time.

Some readers of this book own pups 7 months or older that are physically hyperactive and weigh 80-100 or more pounds, and these owners should remember that some people are afraid of dogs. Even if you feel that your pup "just wants to play", don't let him lick, sniff or jump on any person unless the adult or the child's parent specifically okayed it. Never force any person, including friends and neighbors, past their comfort zone and never force your puppy's physical greetings on someone else's dog.

Everyone should be smiling and every dog should be wagging during every social exchange. The best way to get your pup to enjoy the world at large without turning antisocial or defensive is to start when he's just a pup. Introduce him only to nice people. Only allow people to pet him when he acts polite. And make his every encounter with people and dogs positive.

If your pup jumps on, claws or nips at a person or if your puppy trembles, cries or if he submissively urinates during a meeting, it's time to leave and try again in a different situation. If he seems just a little tired or unsure when a particular stranger touches him, don't stop interacting with the person entirely, but back off on the petting for the moment until the pup regains composure. Doing this rather than pushing too hard will teach him that unfamiliar humans won't hurt him.

At first your puppy doesn't need to touch new people (or dogs). He just needs to *see* **them and experiences positive things (like your praise) while he looks at them and remains calm.** *Only once he is comfortable looking at many different types of people engaged in many different activities should he start meeting individual strangers up close.* **Your pup doesn't need to meet large numbers of people physically to gain the benefits of socialization. But each physical encounter with people must be a wonderful experience for him so he can learn to be comfortable and trusting of humans and always treat them gently.**

Keep meetings and greetings pleasant, and limit them to only one or two a day so you don't overwhelm your pup. Many dogs never leave their backyard for months at a time (or they spend almost all their time crated) and then suddenly one weekend their owners parade them out to huge seasonal events sponsored by the local humane society trying to "socialize" them. It's no surprise that these dogs act like emotional wrecks the first time they see a huge crowd like this, if they've never even been on a leashed walk!

If your pup is unusually young or cute, and you take him to a big dog event like this literally hundreds of people are likely to try to fondle him without permission *and* also force their dogs on him. Physically meeting one hundred people in a day is *not* the same as letting your puppy meet one-hundred people and dogs over the course of a year, which would be positive for him. **Social meetings for a dog are like vitamins- it's healthy to have them every day, but it's very unhealthy to get a year's supply in** *one* **day.** And, while it will help your pup to meet strangers because he must be comfortable meeting strangers as an adult, the first people he meets only need to be strangers to *him*, and not to you. You can invite friends to meet your pup that you know are gentle and good with dogs. This way you know that the very first people outside of your family that meet your puppy will actively follow all your behavior shaping advice, such as not giving him attention when he jumps, and not being overly "handsy". Once everything goes well with your pup and some carefully selected friends, you can start introducing him to strangers that show restraint and good judgment.

Of course, not everyone your pup meets will show perfect behavior. And one of the most important demographics for your pup to meet, and get comfortable with, is children. If you have well behaved children at home who are good at reading dogs' signals, you have a great advantage and you can probably already see whether your pup is good with kids. But some homes have only adults- and so do some neighborhoods. For example one of our customers recently joked that every house in sprawling new subdivision was owned by retirees. Often older couples here in Florida will raise their puppy for 6 months without seeing any children and then when they host a houseful of grandkids over the holidays they are shocked by how badly the pup behaves. To avoid lifelong problems with children it's essential that your puppy be exposed to them in a positive fashion before his critical window for socialization closes at approximately 20 weeks. If he meets children and has good experiences with them before then, happily accepting children should become a natural part of his personality. If his only contact with children comes later, you can still socialize him, but you may have to work much harder.

Children are not always perfect in how they behave towards puppies. All their natural inclinations-fast movement, shrill high-pitched voices, approaching at eye level and squeezing pups to hug them- are seriously negative signals for dogs. This is part of the reason children are the most frequent victims of dog bites, including many bad bites from small dogs. But if you separate a pup from children entirely, he will never receive the positive benefits of socialization with them.

To make socialization with children work properly the pup's owner should carefully supervise. Most children can learn the right ways to hold a puppy and show him attention if you take the time to explain it to them. We've seen 2, 3 and 4 year olds show great manners around dogs and we've been able to educate children this young in the proper- as opposed to dangerous- ways to touch dogs and puppies. But there are also cases of much older children who continue to handle pups in such a way as to hurt the animals and create bite risk. It all depends on the child. So the ideal way to have your pup get to know kids out in public is to strike a balance between enough contact and too much. **All pups should see children when they are as young as possible, starting at 8 weeks.** For example, you could practice obedience with your pup near a playground or you could pet him and offer him treats while he sits calmly beside your niece as she holds her infant.

If your pup has never interacted with young children before, carefully observe that his behavior is proper when he's just visualizing kids but not touching them. If your pup acts a little fearful, wild or overexcited, you can work on this behavior. Walk him around a bit or practice some obedience and then park him within view of the playing children at the closest distance where he stays calm. And then gradually move him closer, but never get closer than the distance where the pup can remain calm. To accomplish this, do as many repetitions as necessary, even if you have to return to the area thirty times.

Only when your pup acts completely calm seeing unfamiliar kids from a distance can he start safely meeting them. His first meetings should be without touching. With parents' permission, allow a mature-minded child to approach and give the pup a treat after the pup does an obedience command for them. With a very boisterous or rowdy pup, or a fearful pup, the children can start by throwing the treats on the ground in front of the pup until he starts acting more appropriate. Once the pup acts calm with the child near him, allow him to approach the child and sniff. If he continues to act calm you can allow the child to pet him on the side of the face or on the shoulder, while safely keeping their face averted. Praise the pup heartily for correctly greeting a child and never act nervous.

You should get permission from a parent before allowing any child to touch your pup. And you must stay alert, ready to calmly but quickly stop the interaction if either child or puppy acts inappropriate. **Never allow your pup to touch any child if he has ever shown even one second of unfriendliness to a human.** Very young puppies naturally tend to "mouth" people's hands, just like they put their little teeth everywhere else to explore the world, and this is the time for you to gently educate the pup in what is proper and what is not when he touches humans. But puppies of all ages aren't always playing when they use their teeth, and there is such a thing as a pup showing true aggression towards humans.

If your pup ever broke a human's skin and caused bleeding that required a bandage, bit a person's face, chased a person, knocked them down and bit them or bit a person hard enough to cause true pain or true fear, this was *not* an accident. **Dogs know exactly where they put their teeth. They never make mistakes with their teeth, just like wolves don't, and true puppy play never hurts people.** Trying to socialize a pup with a history of hurting people to unsuspecting children before you get professional assistance would be criminally negligent. You should seek professional help for aggressive puppies, or obtain an assessment from a high-level behaviorist, before attempting to socialize them to children on your own. And never expose innocent children to petting sessions with a pup that's growled or snapped at humans or tried to scare people off food or possessions.

We can't expect children to have adult judgment. No matter what you tell him, a young child may forget and suddenly hug and kiss your pup or even pull his tail. It doesn't matter whether a particular careless behavior triggered the dog to snap, because if he hurts a child, you will still be criminally liable- and morally responsible. **Every good dog should learn to like children.** And every dog should be able to tolerate a little silliness and irregularity from a little child, even if the child causes him momentary physical distress. Of course, **you should never allow children to manhandle or torment your pup- this could cause serious injury and lasting fears. However, if a toddler stumbles into a puppy by accident, the pup shouldn't bite.**

The best way to achieve this kind of acceptance is to let the pup meet children in positive ways when he's very young. And the more good experiences the better. It is up to you to keep child and pup interacting positively, whether this means physical petting or just saying hello from a distance. But if you know that your pup has ever hurt or threatened any person before, your window for having kids pet him is now over. Find a high level behaviorist (ideally with an advanced degree) to help you. The right behaviorist may be able to get your pup back on track for socialization while he's still young.

For "normal" socialization, the younger you start the better. **But keeping your pup "socialized" so that he remains comfortable around people doesn't end at 20 weeks. You'll want to make sure your dog encounters novel stimuli every day of his life** and, if you have children, they will probably want to help. They will start thinking creatively and they may suggest, "Oh, look, here's a field with cows. Can we stop so that the dog can see them?" or "Our puppy is a

Great Dane. Let him see that tiny Chihuahua, since he's never seen one before," or "Let's bring him into the city with us, so that he can see tall buildings" or "Let's walk past those housewives with strollers". Exposure to new stimuli like this is the same way young service dogs are socialized. Your pup will learn the proper reaction to different stimuli, different environments and different people and become a much more balanced adult. Your family's horizons will also expand as you interact with your pup in the larger world.

See Chapter 9 for a "List of New People, Places and Things Every Puppy Should Encounter" to introduce your pup to something new every day.

Hint: Socializing Your Pup to the Veterinarian: Since all new encounters for your pup should be positive, you may wonder how to keep him from getting upset at the veterinarian's office where treatment can be painful, and the office may reek of other dog's fear. The best way to get your pup to calmly accept the vet's office without fear is to take him to visit the office at random times when he's not scheduled for any medical procedures. Call ahead and then stop when he can get lots of attention, petting and treats from the staff. If you come at the right time, the staff may even let your puppy complete a "dry run" on the table in the examination room. Also interview veterinarians and choose one with a good bedside manner and plenty of time to spend with your puppy. Veterinarians who are dedicated dog lovers often have a healing manner that can comfort dogs even when they're in pain. But your pup should get to know, and like, your vet when he's young and before he needs any painful treatments. Sometimes discount shot clinics are the only way owners in financial distress can afford a pup's first vaccinations. But generally this is not a good idea because it's important to start a relationship between your puppy and your vet before there's ever a crisis. (Also see "#19 Mock Veterinary Exam", in Part 3 to rehearse vet exams at home.)

<u>Section C: Socializing Your Pup at a Pet Store</u>

Instructions:

Excursions to chain pet stores that welcome well-behaved pets (including Petco, Petsmart, Pet Supermarket and many small boutique pet stores) can stimulate your pup's mind and make him more comfortable with socialization with various types of people and animals in a real world setting. It's a good option in bad weather and your kids will enjoy coming with you. Letting your pup browse different toys stimulates his mind and builds his confidence. And you can save some money by letting him select toys he will actually play with.

Practice your training in a real environment:

As long as you and your pup don't bother employees or other shoppers, a pet store is an ideal setting to practice obedience commands in real-life. Teach your puppy to "sit", "look" and/or "stay" when you command him and to show restraint without leaping around while he encounters real-life distractions, like lots of different people and their dogs. Have treats available for occasional reinforcement, but don't depend on them. Your pup should reliably obey all commands *before* you ever bring him to a pet store.

In the pet store, you may get a chance to practice "Drop it" in a real-world situation if your pup picks up a toy or treat that's not appropriate- or one that you can't afford! At the conclusion of a successful outing you can buy your pup one toy he's indicated he wants as a reward. Keep the visit to the pet store short and casual, especially on busy days. And never make a scene of training an unprepared pup where he may disturb other animals or people.

You may bring your puppy to the pet store as soon as he's safely vaccinated, and with your vet's okay. While your pup is still under 20 weeks you should bring him to the store frequently for optimal psychological benefit. Increase duration and level of contact with people and animals a bit with each subsequent visit but too much at a time could stress the pup and defeat the purpose of socialization.

After learning to enjoy pet stores as a pup, your dog will continue to benefit from pleasant shopping trips when he matures. You can easily take your well behaved adult dog on regular shopping trips for continued bonding, training and socializing.

First introduce your pup to people without touching:

On your pup's first visit(s) start with him *looking* at people and dogs, but don't allow physical contact. **Delaying physical contact with strange dogs or people until your pup is comfortable seeing them from a distance will allow him to develop emotional balance at his own speed, rather than becoming reactive or snappy. No matter how cute your puppy is, don't let large numbers of people grab or fondle him at once. And don't let larger dogs roughhouse him, even if their intentions seem to be good. Instead, make all meetings gradual, and let your pup control the pace so he always remains relaxed.** Positive, stress-free experiences with every new dog and person when your pup's still a baby will shape his psyche to be trusting and positive.

Pet parents should first approach *near* store employees and shoppers with their pup either leashed or in their arms so that he can look at the new people without touching yet. As he visually checks out new people for the first time, offer him treats and/or praise and pet him if he remains calm. If he acts wild or agitated, walk away and then try showing him the new people at whatever distance is necessary for him to stay calm. When he remains calm; reward him with either praise or a little treat.

If the pup acts fearful when he first sees the people, don't make the mistake of petting him or cooing to him to try to comfort him. Instead ignore the fearful behavior, and move as far as necessary for him to again act confident and balanced. Once he does, reward him and approach just a little closer to the people, making sure he stays calm.

If you start with a very young puppy, he is at an optimal age for socialization, so your first visits to the pet store will likely progress smoothly. But older pups (especially those over 5 months with pre-existing issues such as puppy mill backgrounds) may have already learned to overreact to new people, places and dogs. So, on your first few trips to a busy chain pet store you may have to constantly back up to get enough distance from the action for your overexcited (or overly fearful) puppy to act appropriately. Waiting to introduce him to stimuli at higher levels until he's calm is necessary for the pup's psyche, and it's also kind to other shoppers.

We've worked with some dogs that had to spend their first half hour at the pet store in a shaded area down the plaza. Others had to start out under a tree at the far end of the parking lot. As long as your pup is not overheated or cold, you can wait with him as long as he needs until he's comfortable with a higher level of interaction. Even if your pup must remain at a far distance from the store in order to calm down on his first visit, this still represents progress. You can try again later that day or the next day, gradually bringing him closer until he's able to enter the store and start looking at shoppers and their dogs in a calm state.

After your young puppy acts appropriate on a few shopping trips where he does no more than *look* at people and dogs, you can initiate his first actual meeting with a human stranger:

This first person your puppy touches can be a friendly store employee or even an agreeable fellow shopper. Make sure the stranger approaches your puppy gently, offering a (safe) treat rather than immediately attempting to pet or grab. Allow the puppy to initiate physical contact at his own speed. If your puppy initiates contact, and if he seems completely comfortable and happy, it's okay for the stranger to gently pet him and/or hold him. **Even people who are dog lovers may not know that leaning over a dog, hugging a dog or petting directly on the head can be interpreted as signs of dominance, so advise anyone who pets your puppy to approach in a low-key manner.**

Even the best behaved dog or pup could theoretically bite, so people should always use reasonable caution. But the minute you invite someone to touch your dog, especially when you have brought the animal out to a public place, if he bites it's your responsibility. If you have any suspicion that your pup might not react to petting in a friendly, or at least passive, fashion, you are not yet ready to allow people to touch him. While socializing is necessary, you must progress at a speed that's safe for your particular pup. **If you don't fully know a pup's history, such as with many shelter dogs, you can't be sure he won't bite. So use extreme care the first few times**

you let strangers touch him. If your pup lashes out and hurts someone in a public place, you will be morally responsible for their injury as well as legally and financially responsible.

After a successful first meeting with a stranger, your puppy can now meet a few more people on his next trip to the pet store:

But never allow too many people to handle your pup during one session- two strangers in one trip is plenty. You may have to turn some admirers away if you notice your pup acting tired or burnt out. You might even want to bring a soft-sided ventilated carrier or even a stroller with a mesh covering that your pup can rest in if things ever get too intense. Or you can place your fur-baby up in a shopping cart if the store suddenly gets crowded with too many people and pets trying to touch him when he's tired.

It's also your social and legal obligation to never physically impose your puppy on strangers unless the encounter is consensual for everyone.

Be especially careful introducing your pup to children:

Your pup should learn to like children during his critical socialization period and, if you don't have kids in your household, the pet store may be the best place he meets them. But since kids sometimes handle tiny dogs roughly, you must carefully supervise.

Always check with the parents before allowing children to touch your pup and make sure your puppy doesn't jump on or nip children. It's tempting to let children play with your pup when they run up out of nowhere, but you should seek parental permission first.

By bringing your dog to a public venue like a pet store, you are guaranteeing that he won't ever hurt a person (or an animal), even when their behavior isn't perfect. If you aren't certain enough of your pup's temperament to face the potential cost of a multi-million dollar liability claim, then you shouldn't bring your dog among people until you *are* sure at that level, or until you get professional help from a behaviorist. And if all dog owners lived by this standard, there wouldn't have to be any dog bite claims…

Next start encouraging your pup to start looking at dogs and cats- but it's still not time for him to touch them:

To be completely safe around strange animals, your pup should have full immunity before he has his first physical contact. But even though your puppy may not be ready to *touch* dogs, he should start viewing strange dogs of all shapes and sizes at the youngest age possible. Before your puppy is 16 weeks old, you should start accustoming him to the *sight* of dogs of different dogs and reward him with treats and praise when he stays calm near them. Practice frequently with different types of dogs.

After your pup has full immunity, he's ready to physically meet friendly dogs:

At some point another shopper at the pet store will likely ask if their dog can sniff yours. Decide carefully when to agree to these requests because there is always a chance that a stranger's dog might carry disease or might bite your pup even if the animal acts friendly at first. And there's also a possibility that *your* pet could bite the other dog. Before the dogs greet each other, clarify with the other shopper how you'd like to see them socialize and agree to immediately separate them if they interact too roughly. If the other shopper isn't patient enough to negotiate the exact conditions of the dogs' meeting, they're not likely to act responsibly if their dog becomes rough or aggressive with your pup, so feel free to walk away!

You don't *have* to let your pup physically greet other dogs in public places if you don't want to, or if you sense he's uncomfortable. You can always let him play with other dogs in a more controlled situation on another day or another location. For example, you can arrange planned play dates with your friends' dogs as described in detail in the next section, and this will fulfill his need to practice physically interacting with dogs.

If your puppy acts shy around intense stimuli, you can still succeed with shopping expeditions if you visit the pet store when it's quietest. Avoid weekend visits to busy stores at first. Start at the slowest day or time of the week or in a smaller store, and increase distractions as your pup tolerates them.

Hint: Craziness can be catching, and dogs react strongly to energy, so all the dogs your pup meets and greets should be physically and mentally healthy and well behaved. If a stranger's animal seems nervous, hyperactive or highly dominant, keep your pup at a distance from the bad energy.

Section D: Play Dates to Socialize Your Puppy to Other Pups

Why you should arrange for your pup to play with other dogs:

Socialization during critical early development is vital for your pup to develop into a dog that doesn't get overexcited or aggressive when he sees other dogs in future. But for reasons ranging from busy schedules to behavior problems, owners often keep young pups isolated and don't take them out to encounter the world.

This can be a big mistake. **Young puppies during their critical socialization period before 20 weeks aren't yet wired to overreact and they still react to all new stimuli as benign and normal, just as human babies do. A young pup will naturally accept new stimuli as everyday parts of life. And this comfortableness carries into adulthood so that dogs that are properly socialized as puppies won't overreact every time they visit the vet's office or pass new dogs on the street.**

The idea of socializing your pup during this period is to let him see and, if possible, play with a variety of friendly dogs. In this way, your pup's neural development forms so he accepts dogs as an everyday part of life, rather than something that makes him act crazy.

One of the goals of socializing is to expose your pup to many new things when he's young so he'll be able to calmly accept them when he's older. But many dog people fail to mention the equally important fact that **socialization only works positively if your pup's encounters with the other dogs are positive.** As long as the encounters are fun, or at least neutral your pup will see the stimulus as undisturbing in the future. But if another dog hurts or scares your pup during his developmental weeks this can make him view other people's dogs as negative.

A single attack- or continued bullying- at the wrong time during puppyhood could even make your pup dangerously fearful and aggressive. And he may start to lunge at other dogs, trying to preemptively attack and scare them away before they can hurt him. If you let your puppy play with a dog that turns aggressive this could defeat the entire purpose of socialization and make your puppy nervous around other dogs for life. But neglecting to socialize your pup with new dogs when he's young isn't an option because this will also create problems with dogs in adulthood. So, **the best idea is to set up meetings where your pup can play with other dogs where you can guarantee the experience will be positive.**

Friends' well behaved dogs are an ideal way to help socialize your pup:

By letting the compatible dogs or pups play together on structured play dates, everyone can benefit.

Planned "play dates" with sweet dogs and/or puppies owned by trusted friends are also great for exercise and alleviating boredom. **"Play dates", are better than meetings between your pup and strange dogs because you can choose people you trust and the dogs or puppies that possess the best chemistry with yours.** To screen a friend's pup or adult dog as a possible buddy for your pup to play with, start with a few trial meetings in neutral territory with both dogs on leash. Study up on the subtleties of dog body language and then observe carefully to make sure the two animals are really getting along, not posturing in dominance.

Pups love to play, and sometimes doggie games can seem a bit wild to humans. But if a dog or pup ever squeals in pain or if one dog continually chases or jumps on the other while the other tries to get away humans should intervene. The time to redirect pups is the second their play starts getting rough. If you quickly intervene each time your pup plays too hard, this will encourage more polite behavior with other dogs for a lifetime. You should not allow pups to mount on each other, to push each other down with too much pressure on each other's back or to bite each other's faces or throats- even in play. These are all dominance gestures that can lead to future problems. When biting becomes extreme- with unpleasant displays of teeth and enough growling to make humans wince we immediately ask the pups to turn it down a notch. Gently redirecting behavior like this each time it happens and long before it becomes extreme helps us create dogs that never conflict as adults.

A good rule of thumb is that if you'd feel uncomfortable putting your hand between the pups when they're playing, it's time to stop and redirect them to gentler games. Just like kids, pups don't really mind if you tell them to tone down their play. And each time you gently intervene before things get too far out of hand, it easily brings your pup back on the right track and ensures your pup will mature into a gentle, well-behaved and well-balanced dog.

It's good for a pup to meet and play with other puppies, and he should also encounter adult dogs. Generally adult dogs like puppies and act patient with them, but we have seen some notable exceptions in dogs with emotional disturbances. Surprisingly, some adult dogs will bite pups in a truly malicious manner - bites that can cause bleeding, hidden internal injury and lasting terror of dogs for their victims.

If an adult dog, or an older or stronger pup that you invite to play with your puppy ever stiffens his body with baleful eyes, curled lip, growling, snarling or snapping- or if the visiting dog's behavior makes you nervous for any reason, then these dogs should NOT play with each other. Once you and the other owner notice a bad interaction you should quickly and efficiently separate the dogs. And if a large dog or pup constantly leaps up and lands on your pup's back during "play" your pup should not have to be around this animal. Dogs are tougher than humans, but **if you ever witness any "play" that might hurt your puppy, trust your instincts, ditch the offending dog for good and try a different one of the other 77 million dogs in the country as a playmate.** The only reason to have your pup play with other dogs is so he can have good experiences that will positively shape his personality. So you should arrange play dates so that every moment is always good for your pup. And offer the same courtesy to the other owner if your pup is the one that plays too rough.

Good games for pups to play together:

Some puppy play simulates hunting and fighting because this is how pups would play in the wild. Just supervise so there's no injury, fear or intimidation. **Letting pups chase each other is a good form of play (and exercise), especially if they play hide and seek around obstacles. And handing off non-food toys between each other is also okay as long as neither puppy acts domineering or possessive.** (Be careful because food-type toys like bones and rawhides could trigger aggression between dogs.) **An ideal toy for pups is a sturdy ball like a soccer ball that both dogs can chase but *not* possess with their teeth.**

For any outdoor play follow your veterinarian's precautions, don't let giant breed puppies run too vigorously and keep playtime brief and shaded in hot summer weather.

Games where the owners get involved are also important for puppies. The two pups can go on walks with both owners and practice obedience commands in tandem. Several pups can splash around in a kiddie pool together while their owner(s) play with them with pool toys. Or you could teach the pups how to play hide and seek with you or your children.

You can host puppy play dates either indoors or outdoors. Most people enjoy having their play dates outdoors, because another pup can encourage your pup to run around in circles and get a little crazy, burning off lots of energy. You can also schedule your play dates indoors on hot, snowy or rainy days, especially if the pups are small. And, if you can designate one room of the house with all hazards and breakables removed as a puppy playground, this is even better.

After the vigorous portion of each play date, spend some time with the owners and the pups relaxing together. This is a great time to practice obedience in tandem, offering treats and gentle petting. Practicing like this builds skills, respect for other dogs and self control. Your pup will also benefit from taking a nap with the other pup.

For everyday purposes, your pup doesn't have to play amongst large groups of dogs for him to be adequately socialized. Playing with one dog at a time is fine, although your puppy should have several varied playmates to get him used to a variety of dogs when he's young. The benefit of "play dates" is that you can carefully screen each prospective dog. And you can select the playmates that possess the best chemistry with your pup, rather than relying on luck to keep your pup safe in public venues. Once you've found some playmates your puppy loves, meet up with these dogs and their owners as frequently as you like.

As your pup grows, you will want to continue play dates, but some rules may change over time. With sexual maturity, most dogs' temperaments change. This change may be pronounced in certain dogs, especially protective breeds, that may start acting much more defensive in general, and not as accepting of other dogs. Always be vigilant for new dominance issues that might lead to conflicts as your pup reaches maturity, even with playmates he's previously gotten along well with. **Even though adulthood brings new challenges, starting your pup socializing positively with other dogs when he's young can make his future prospects getting along with dogs infinitely more successful, no matter his breed.** And good experiences with dogs during puppyhood can outweigh some of the natural tensions between dogs that develop with sexual maturity. **Many friendships your pup forms in his early months may last a lifetime, and most dogs will continue to enjoy positive socialization with many-although not all- of their favorite puppy playmates when they're adults.**

Attempting to socialize your pup with unleashed dogs in uncontrolled public settings can be dangerous:

People may assume, since we recommend socializing pups to other dogs during play dates, we'd also recommend dog parks. But, even though so many "dog people" heartily recommend dog parks, **for safety, the authors don't take our dogs to dog parks. And we recommend that our readers avoid unrestricted public dog parks because the risks outweigh the potential benefits.**

For everyday purposes there's no need for your dog to play amongst *large* groups of dogs for him to be adequately socialized. Meeting and playing off-leash with one, two or three dogs at a time works just as well, or better, for socialization than playing with larger groups. Even though there is no need for him to meet them all at once, your pup *should* play with a variety of different types of dogs off-leash. It's also vital that he *sees* (without necessarily touching) many different types of dogs on-leash in different real-life situations while he's maturing.

"Peer" type pups of similar size, age and breed and of the opposite sex are the safest everyday playmates for your pup. But a pup needs to encounter diversity as well, so he'll learn to be civil to all dogs and not feel alarmed by the unfamiliar in adulthood. Unfortunately many dog owners don't realize that it's okay if two dogs just see each other and relax fully in each other's presence. Dogs don't necessarily have to touch or play together for your pup to gain a good impression of stranger's dogs. Your pup and another dog could just wag at each other in a park where all dogs have to be kept leashed and this could be a positive experience. Or you could orchestrate a "chance" encounter with a dog belonging to a friend in a public venue. A dog can still be a surprise to your puppy even if you set up the meeting with the owner.

Screening dogs ahead of time can protect your puppy from disease or aggression while you cannot guarantee this if he encounters strangers' dogs by chance. Many people think that a well behaved dog must love and enjoy every new dog he meets. But the truth is that dogs' inherent nature is *not* to like every strange dog. In the wild, the canines that dogs enjoy socializing with are those in their *own* pack- a *limited number* of canines that they already know. Wolf packs go to painstaking efforts to mark their territory so that they never encounter wolves from neighboring packs. And, when they do, there is likely to be aggression.

While some dog breeds have been selectively bred for more friendliness around other animals than others, there's nothing in *any* dog's makeup that says he'll pine away if he doesn't get to romp with thirty new strange dogs a day in a public dog park. What your pup will thrive on most is some high-quality exercise and pleasant socialization with compatible playmates at an age when it will shape him into a more peaceable soul. Then he can follow up by socializing with some nice dogs that he likes throughout adulthood.

Although for safety reasons we don't advocate public unrestricted dog parks, we *do* believe that every dog of every breed should be trained to behave completely appropriately and non-violently in public situations. And every dog should always obey his owner's commands, even when he sees strangers' dogs and even when he's not leashed. And displays of aggression towards dogs in public places are not appropriate.

We say this as behavior specialists who've personally made our life with large defensive breeds and understand and respect their protective and reserved temperament. But no matter how protective our dogs feel about their home, we train them to always respect humans and dogs in varied public situations. And our dogs would no more lunge at a strange dog in public than a well-brought up human would violate the law.

If your dog is seated at a café near a dog at another table, he should never jump over your lap to try to attack, or try to play with, it. Nor should he disturb people by barking aggressively. Show dogs of every breed learn to stand on leash around hundreds of other strange dogs and act calm. And every pet dog that is obedient to his owner should react no differently, even if meeting new dogs is not his favorite thing.

Through play dates, your goal is to shape your puppy into an adult dog that acts calm, non-violent and unbothered around other dogs in general and that can become friends with a smaller group of nice dogs that he likes. This would resemble the behavior of most law-abiding humans. People don't love every stranger we meet, yet we don't attack them, and we all enjoy good times with a select group of friends.

Most free public dog parks don't have adequate controls on what dogs are admitted. Often dogs with internal parasites drop watery stools that cannot be cleaned adequately for the safety of other dogs. And frequently owners come to the dog park attempting to socialize dogs with unknown histories, or even histories of aggression.

Unfortunately, it can sometimes take months of intensive effort to rehabilitate emotional damage from a single bad incident that a pup suffers in an uncontrolled setting. Yet planning and structuring activities with other nice puppies during your pup's critical socialization period can lead to years of positive behavior when your dog grows up. And formal play dates also allow you a unique opportunity to socialize with trusted dog owners whose company you enjoy.

Hint: Some families think if their pup is in a home with another dog he'll grow up to like all other dogs the way he likes that one. And, for this reason they fail to introduce their pup to any new dogs during his critical socialization period. But the truth is that your pup's attachment with the dog in your home may actually make him behave *worse* around strange dogs. The two may start to feel that they are a pack that must fight off outsiders. And your pup will never get used to dogs of other sizes and breeds if he only sees one breed at home. **So even if you already have a dog at home, you should still take your pup out regularly to see the world and arrange play dates for him with other pups.**

Chapter 9:

List of 45 New People, Places and Things Every Puppy Should Encounter

1. Children

2. Infants

3. Elderly

4. People of different sexes

5. People of different ages

6. People in wheelchairs

7. People using walker/cane/crutches

8. Other puppies

9. Small adult dogs

10. Large adult dogs

11. Hairy dogs (like Pekinese) in full coat

12. People of all skin colors

13. Cats

14. Small animal pets

15. Small animals outdoors like squirrels, bunnies

16. Domestic birds

17. Wild birds

18. Large livestock (horses, cows)

19. Small farm animals (chickens, rabbits)

20. Bicycles

21. Skateboarders/rollerbladers

22. Kids bouncing balls

23. Kids on playground

24. Walking on busy city street

25. Veterinarian's office (practice "mock" vet exams and make visits just to meet the staff and get treats)

26. Dog groomer's (practice mock grooming, and visit grooming shop first just to meet the staff and get treats)

27. Sudden petting by multiple children or adults at once

28. Frequent rides in car (while safely restrained)

29. Having human guests visit the home

30. Visiting other people's homes

31. Going into dog-friendly stores

32. Eating out at dog-friendly cafes

33. Parks (when safely vaccinated)

34. Different streets and neighborhoods

35. Being lifted

36. Brief separations from owner

37. Walking on a close leash in varied situations

38. Children running away or playing

39. People suddenly hugging the dog, or containing the dog

40. People making sudden hand movements toward the dog

41. Eating and comfortably allowing people able to interrupt (teach with caution)

41. Surrendering toys, rawhides or other items to people (teach with caution)

42. People in uniform

43. People in hats/sunglasses

44. Large groups of people

45. Ability to do all commands without a leash around people & dogs (in safe area)

PART 5:

Housetraining

Chapter 10:

Instructions for Housetraining Your Puppy

Whenever people talk about puppies, housetraining is often the first subject that comes up. In this chapter we explain how to make this vital component of training and relating to your pup faster, easier and more comfortable based on communication between dog and owner and with no need for crates. And in the following chapter, you'll find a quick list of our favorite hints that have helped families resolve housetraining problems.

If you want to learn even more about housetraining, you can also read the housetraining chapter in our book *Dogs Hate Crates*, which is available in both print and ebook versions. Dogs Hate Crates, an expose based on years of research, describes many serious problems that result from crating dogs excessively- both in puppy mills and private homes. These days, many books and resources about puppies present crate-training (or caging a pup) as the *only* way to housetrain. But excessive crating can damage your future relationship with your dog, so we discuss more humane- and more effective alternatives for housetraining in our books.

Pet parents can often use the humane techniques we describe in this book to housetrain a pup in several weeks- or even several days.

Sometimes housetraining may take longer. Every individual pup reacts differently to housetraining based on many factors. But there is an optimal age to housetrain pups and pups under five months are usually easier to train than pups over 5 months that have existing problems. While very young pups of 8, 10 or 12 weeks have less physical control, older pups with existing behavioral problems are usually the hardest to train. Although some of the training techniques are the same, owners shouldn't confuse physical housetraining issues in young puppies with deliberate scent marking or other emotional/behavioral potty problems in more mature pups and adult dogs.

If your pup is older than 6 months and still not housetrained:

Today many families obtain full-grown (or almost full grown) dogs from shelters, rescues or Internet classifieds and then they're shocked to find that these dogs aren't housetrained at all! The roots of the problem often go back to the dogs being forced to spend their early lives in crates, with no chance for walks, so more crating isn't a solution.

A full-grown dog that soils in a house doesn't have immature bowels and bladder, like a younger pup but the problem may be due to lack of knowledge of proper behavior on the dog's part. If you have an older pup that comes to you without being housetrained, you can first try the same principles of puppy housetraining as detailed in this chapter. If the problem persists, however, your pup may have medical problems or serious behavioral issues. (And the house soiling problem may be why the dog was abandoned or surrendered.) Medical problems and even deep-seated emotional problems *can* be cured, sometimes easily. But you may need to put in additional effort and study or consult with a veterinarian or highly qualified trainer or behaviorist.

Regrettably dogs sometimes leave a shelter or rescue with house soiling issues because they were forced to urinate in their cage at the facility without ever being walked. Pups that come from pet shops and the Internet are also likely to have serious behavioral problems with housetraining. Almost all these dogs are bred in puppy mills- huge substandard breeding facilities, where hundreds of pups are left cramped in cages with no freedom to move around, no time outside and minimal encounters with humans. The breeders may deliberately conceal the truth from buyers with trustworthy looking websites and meaningless "pedigrees".

Puppy mill breeders are known to deprive pups of veterinary care and to abuse and neglect them in horrific ways. For example, pups commonly suffer extremes of heat and cold, and they're often deprived of clean water and food. Investigators who raid these breeding operations frequently discover horrors like pups living in cages with roaches, rats and the rotting corpses of dead littermates. These pups also receive no human interaction other than rough handling during transport.

Pups that originate in puppy mills often can't stay clean because of the weeks and months they've spent locked in tiny cages rather than living in the real world. These pups lose the desire to stay clean because they've already lived in their own urine and feces for too long. Ammonia in urine burns puppies' skin and, at first, they try to avoid it. But just like abused children feel they can't protect themselves from harm, these pups learn they have no power to stop their discomfort. Eventually they learn the habit of urinating and defecating where they live and this makes them quite hard to housetrain in their new homes without a lot of work and patience.

Many dog trainers tell families to crate-train these already damaged pups. But pups bred in puppy mills are resistant to learning to hold bowels and bladder in a crate because of their former upbringing in cages. These pups often mess on themselves day after day and month after month in their new homes. And additional cage time for these pups that have already been deprived of human contact for months further compromises their ability to live properly in a home and bond with people. Instead of additional time locked in a cage, these pups require careful behavioral interventions.

You also can't housetrain a puppy if he's sick. And pups purchased from pet shops, the Internet and irresponsible "backyard breeders" often come to their new families infected with diseases and parasites that cause elimination problems. If you suspect illness because your pup shows symptoms like loose stools, vomiting, listlessness, fever or poor appetite; or if he shows abnormal frequency, straining or odor when urinating, consult your veterinarian. **Almost every pup we've seen that families bought at a pet store or over the Internet has tested positive for some disease or internal parasite that affects elimination** (and some of these conditions could have been deadly without treatment.)

To cure older dogs or pups that are resistant to housetraining, owners often need to obtain veterinary treatment or use sophisticated behavioral interventions depending on the dog's former background. But families shouldn't confuse these more serious issues with simple "puppy" housetraining problems which have to do with physical maturity, environment and habit. The rest of this chapter focuses on housetraining pup without serious illness or behavioral imbalances.

How to housetrain a healthy young puppy:

Healthy young puppies have accidents in a home because their bodies aren't physically mature yet and because they haven't yet learned where they're supposed to eliminate. Housetraining a young healthy puppy should be quite easy and quick if you're gentle and consistently follow a few simple rules and you should never confuse younger puppies' physical elimination mistakes with behavior issues, defiance or attempts at dominance that you might see in older dogs or pups.

How long a young pup under 6 months can physically hold his bowels or bladder depends on his age, and a healthy puppy gains a little bit more control each day until he starts to approach physical maturity. An 8-week old puppy that urinates on your floor is most likely doing it for _physical_ reasons, like human babies mess in their diapers. Urine can just "slip" out of a pup's immature bladder after sleeping, eating, drinking or playing. And if this "accident" happens indoors, it truly *was* an accident because his human parents neglected to get him outside soon enough, and not because he was attempting to "mark territory".

It's a dog's inherent nature not to want to soil his house. So the point of housetraining is to make your pup understand from the first day he comes to your home that voiding in the house immensely displeases you. He should also realize that you feel filled with joy and love for him whenever he potties outdoors! Your skill, timing and finesse, along with how much time you can spend with the puppy when he first comes to your home will determine how quickly you can teach him. Repetition also aids learning. You may have to tolerate a few accidents. But don't be upset about this. Appropriate corrections speed housetraining, and your responses to a few accidents when your pup is tiny will help teach him the difference between desirable and undesirable behavior.

The best way to both housetrain and bring up a puppy you can live with is to spend time to do it right and teach the dog what you want. Many people buy or adopt a puppy on Saturday or Sunday and then go back to work for a full day on Monday, immediately leaving the pup alone for 8-10 hours. But brining a new puppy into your home is like bringing a new baby home from the hospital. And parents wouldn't bring a baby home, leave him alone in his crib two days later and expect him to potty train himself.

Yet many dog trainers use a similar theory and tell families to lock their pups up all day in small wire cages where they can barely move so, if they soil themselves, they'll have to suffer by lying in urine or feces. These pups are also deprived of water. And, because they are not physically mature enough (or because of illness or a history of abuse and neglect) many of these pups *do* soil themselves. They then lie immobile with urine and feces covering their entire bodies for 8-10 hours. When their owners come home each evening they hose the pups down. All of these experiences are needlessly traumatic, and this daily trauma can manifest in future behavior problems.

Other pups eventually learn to hold their bowels and bladder in the crate, but then they have problems generalizing to their owners' homes in the larger sense. So owners may have to go through the whole process of housetraining again in the house- even though they simply could have started training in the house for quicker results.

Obviously, living in a cage with minimal interaction with family is not the ideal quality of life for a beloved pet. And most families would prefer to have their puppy available rather than always caged so they can socialize with him and show him love. Instead of crating, we teach families to train a pup to respect every area of the home as his own and always maintain appropriate bowel and bladder control. **Puppies, just like human babies, take time to develop bladder and bowel control, so total housebreaking takes time**. Give your pup frequent opportunities to relieve himself outside. And don't get angry if he has a few accidents, because anger has no place in training. Healthy young pups *want* to please their owners and each accident can serve as a learning experience if you handle it right.

Note: If you buy your new puppy from a trustworthy breeder and you don't have time to housetrain, you can ask the breeder to housetrain for you. Just make sure they housetrain using gentle methods, ideally without crates. And any pup that comes to you older than four months should be reasonably housetrained.

If you housetrain your pup on your own, the best thing you can do is to spend enough time with him the first few weeks to teach him where to relieve himself- and how to act in your home in general. Any investment of time in your first weeks with your pup will have tremendous implications for his overall behavior in the coming years. And, if there's ever a time to invest large amounts of your time and attention in your pup, the first week is that time.

Try to bring your pup home during vacation or when someone can watch him most of the time for several weeks to teach him how to behave in the home and get past the initial hurdles of housetraining. A few weeks might seem like a lot of time to put into a pup. But those two weeks will pay off manyfold and can make the difference between living with a wonderful dog versus a problem dog for the next ten to fifteen years.

The first, and perhaps most important, step in housetraining starts with the way you introduce your pup to your house:

The worst mistake many people make is to bring their new puppy home and immediately set him on the floor to smell his new environment while everyone in the family meets and greets him. This adds so much excitement that, within minutes, the new puppy suddenly squats and pees. As soon as everybody notices, they start to yell and the whole scene erupts in confusion...

Instead, **before your pup ever steps into your house, you should bring him outside to a designated spot and wait for him to eliminate; then give him lots of loving praise. This will immediately set a lifetime precedent that outdoors, not indoors, is the correct place to relieve bowels and bladder.**

If you clearly show your puppy a particular spot where you want him to eliminate outdoors, he'll keep going back to that spot- because you praised him and also because he marked the spot with his scent. **At first, teach your puppy only one designated area to relieve himself to prevent confusion.** Many families designate one corner of their back yard as a toilet area. If you don't have a backyard, you could use a particular spot on your street near your apartment or condo. But never expose a young pup with immature immunity (and incomplete vaccinations) to the droppings of other dogs- consult with your veterinarian for the safest plan in your particular situation.

How to supervise a young puppy so he doesn't damage your home:

When you first bring your pup home, keep him in a small enough area that you can watch him. It may be easiest to stay with him in one room at first. Provide some safe teething toys, a safe dog bed and a small bowl of fresh water. Some pups will stay very close to you on their first day while others will start wandering the room to explore and others will play with the toys. **Watch your pup and, if he gets too far away from you or tries to put something inappropriate in his mouth, interrupt him by whistling, making a repetitive sound or slapping your hand on your leg, and then call him to you.** When he gets to you, praise him, pet him gently and/or offer him a safe treat or toy. Then let him wander away again.

Frequent gentle redirections like this each time your pup interacts with specific items in your house work like the game of "hotter and colder" to teach your pup the difference between proper versus improper behavior in your home. This is why a pup that is brought up interacting with people grows up to show better manners and sensitivity than a pup that was raised isolated from people in a cage or a kennel.

When you leave your young pup completely alone in your home at first, you'll have to completely "dog proof" the area he stays in until he starts to physically mature and learn the rules of the home. But if you stay in a room to supervise your pup, you don't have to totally "strip" the room of furniture, rugs, lamps, computers, remotes or other everyday items when you are only a few feet away. You also don't have to close your pup in a cage. *As long as you can actively supervise and keep him safe*, you can allow the pup to wander a real room, watch what he does and gently correct any mistakes. This is how he'll learn to live safely and properly in the home for the rest of his life. But even if you are watching, you should still remove highly dangerous items from any space the pup will occupy even for a second.

A pup is just like a baby and so you must protect him. **Never leave household poisons or chemicals where the pup could reach them. And clear the home of sharp items like pins, tacks or fishhooks.** A good trick when baby-proofing a room for an infant is to get down to his level to look for possible hazards. You should do the same thing in your entire house before bringing your puppy home. And remember that pups can jump surprisingly high. Lock any true hazards away in high cabinets, closets or rooms like garages or workshops. Even when you're in the room with your pup, he could rapidly swallow dangerous items like poisons or tacks before you could stop him, so clear away deadly hazards entirely. You can find lists of hazards, poisons and dangerous foods and plants online, or ask your veterinarian's office.

As long as you protect your pup from serious hazards, we do *not* believe a pup should always be locked away from general household items when his family is there to watch him, because he must someday learn how to live in this home among the same items. For example, a pup that pulls a throw blanket down off your sofa is not going to really hurt himself or seriously damage the item in the few seconds that he plays with it. But this might be a good learning opportunity to tell him to "Drop" the throw and then "Go to his place" on his dog bed to play with an appropriate toy instead. (Find the instructions for teaching these commands in Part 2).

Likewise you can teach your pup that he should never stand up on your glass coffee table or squat to urinate behind an ornamental basket in a corner. **Allowing the pup to walk around your living room and gently correcting mistakes for a few weeks or months- just as you might with a child- can make the difference between an adult dog that "intuitively" knows good house manners and one that you will constantly have to chase after and correct, year after year.**

Remember, however, that a young puppy is like a baby or a toddler, and mishaps will occur as he is first getting used to life in your home. Your pup's wagging tail might knock a delicate glass sculpture off your coffee table, he might try to eat from a plate of food you set down during a commercial break or take a quick chew on the edges of your leather wedding album, not understanding how valuable it is to you. So, when your dog is a baby- especially in his first few days in your home- you can deal with these situations in one of two ways. The preferable way is to put all breakables, valuables, jewelry, antiques away or up on high shelves, where he absolutely can't reach them. Or you can contain the pup to certain areas that don't contain these vulnerable items, but where he can still relate to his people. Family members can stay in the room or rooms where the pup is contained to work with him and keep him company.

We hope that every home where a puppy needs to be housetrained will avoid wall to wall carpet if at all possible, because even the best puppy has an occasional elimination accident. Confining a pup to a crate for months just to avoid one or two accidents can have dire consequences for the dog's future relationship with his family, so it's advisable to just plan on cleaning up an occasional accident while separating the pup from carpeted areas as best you can. You can contain your very young pup in uncarpeted rooms like a kitchen or a designated playroom spaces when you leave the home and whenever you can't supervise him.

When you are home and have free time try to stay in the room with him or close enough that you can interact with him. For example, you could contain him in a spacious exercise pen or in an adjoining room behind a baby gate where you can see him. **Every moment and everything you teach your pup during his first days in your home has enormous consequences for his behavior for the entire rest of his life**, so you should plan ahead of time how you can stay close to him for these vital hours and days while still keeping him safely contained.

Avoid accidents the first day(s) by taking the pup out at brief regular intervals:

After about twenty or thirty minutes when your pup has had time to wander and play in your home, *even if he does not give an indication that he has to potty*, call him over to you and take him outside to a designated spot and then wait until he relieves himself. By taking him on out at regular intervals on his first day(s) you will avoid accidents and teach the pup that he will always have regular opportunities to go outside. Keep taking the pup out at regular intervals until you become familiar with his particular patterns. **You should also walk your pup outside at particular times of day, and any time he gives signals that he needs to relieve himself, as listed below.**

Times of day when puppies generally have to relieve themselves:

    a. **after waking up in the morning or waking from naps**
    b. **around 30 minutes after eating**
    c. **around 10 minutes after drinking**
    d. **after playing and**
    e. **just before bed.**

Take your pup out at all these times. If you neglect to take a young puppy out at these times, he's likely to have an accident.

Signs a puppy has to relieve himself:

Puppies always give noticeable signs that they need to relieve themselves, even though the signs may be subtle. If you can catch the signs and get your pup outside, you will avoid an accident. He'll also learn that, whenever he feels the physical need to void, he always goes outside.

When your pup needs to go outside, he might show any of these signs:

a. **sniffing**
b. **spinning**
c. **pacing**
d. **looking antsy**
e. **whining**
f. **squatting or**
g. **staring at you oddly or intensely**

Take your pup out immediately if he shows any of these signs, or he is likely to have an accident. Some pups show completely different signs. **When you learn to recognize your pup's unique cues that his bowels or bladder are full, this will take much of the mystery out of housetraining.**

<u>Until your pup is fully housetrained, you should always take him outside on leash to observe that he actually relieves himself, rather than just letting him go free so he can sniff around the bushes:</u>

As you wait for your pup to eliminate, don't walk him around to see the sights, and don't give him any privileges or let him lead you by pulling.

Just remain in the spot you have designated as the pup's toilet and wait. When the puppy squats to urinate or defecate say the elimination command you have selected. Examples include: "Go Potty", "Go Pee-pee" or "Do your business". Once he's completed his movement, reward him with praise and petting, a play session off leash in a fenced area or a pleasant leisurely walk. Your puppy should make the connection that you feel ecstatically happy whenever he relieves himself outside.

Don't rush back inside your house as soon as your pup relieves himself. There are two reasons for this. The first reason is that you want to reward your pup with a little time to play and sniff around the yard after he relieves himself. If you deny him this, he may think the only way to gain some time outside is by delaying his movements.

Another reason you don't want to rush your pup back in immediately is because he may have to go more than once. Giving him a few more minutes to void again will greatly reduce his chance of having an accident when he gets back inside the house.

If you know your pup has just gotten through sleeping, eating, drinking, stress, excited play, or any combination of these factors, then you know he's "full" and has to go. So don't budge from his designated potty spot until he eliminates! **If you get tired after a while, bring the pup inside, but watch him even more closely.** If you're unable to watch him at this time, you can humanely contain him, for example, in a spacious playpen or a small blank room. Then try taking him out again in ten or twenty minutes.

If he tries squatting indoors again before twenty minutes is up, interrupt him with methods described later in this chapter- such as sudden sound- and then *immediately* take him outside.

If your pup has an accident, you have either left him too long or failed to notice the signs that he had to go out.

Until your pup is completely housetrained, you should always go out with him on a leash to watch that he relieves himself rather than just wandering around. A pup that comes back inside "full" after wandering around in the yard and not relieving himself may have an accident seconds after you call him back indoors. So, when you first start housetraining, you should always hold your pup on a leash in one spot outdoors so you can observe him actually emptying bowels and bladder.

Short leashed walks around the neighborhood can be good for exercise and bonding. But your pup should learn to relieve himself *before* he starts a walk. If you don't make him relieve himself before walking, he may learn that, the longer he waits to relieve himself, the longer you'll walk and he might start delaying his movements to prolong walks. So take him to one designated spot, either in your yard or near your home, and wait for him to relieve himself before starting a neighborhood walk.

After your pup voids outside, bring him back to a small enough area that you can watch his every move. You can allow him to play with toys and explore a little, but redirect him if he tries to chew on inappropriate items or starts sniffing as though he's thinking of using an indoor area as a toilet.

After twenty or thirty minutes, take your puppy outside again. Then repeat the process throughout the day, progressively adding ten minutes of time between walks as you learn his patterns. In a few days you can have your pup reasonably housetrained. But remember that you have to give a young pup many opportunities to void outside until his bowels and bladder physically mature.

Eventually, when the pup matures, he may be able to go out to relieve himself as infrequently as three or four times a day. This is the absolute minimum for adult dogs and you can't expect any adult dog to hold his bladder longer than this. (Some adult dogs, especially small breeds, older dogs and those with health issues, may have to go more frequently). Adult housetrained dogs may do anything to please their owners, so sometimes they will hold their bowels and bladder past the point where it feels painful for them, and past the point where it starts to do physical damage. Even some puppies may try to wait past the point where it hurts them. So it's the responsibility of the owner to either come home frequently enough to give their dog adequate bathroom breaks or to make other arrangements.

Some options include providing wee-wee pads, installing a doggie door, hiring a dog walker or even taking your dog to work with you. Adult dogs should get a potty break at least once every eight hours. A working person with a large breed dog and a short commute might be able to stretch this a tiny bit longer to accommodate their average workday. Although it's not ideal for the dog, this arrangement seems to work out all right in many households as long as the owner has a backup plan of someone they can contact to take the dog out if they are delayed any longer.

Young pups need to relieve themselves much more frequently. And you can't expect pups under 6 months to make it eight hours at a time without physically needing to urinate. Often one noontime bathroom break is often all your young pup needs to make it successfully through a workday.

If you catch your pup having an "accident" in your house:

Ideally you should get your puppy outside the moment he feels a pressing need to evacuate, but before he loses bowel or bladder control. **If, however, your pup starts having an accident and you catch him in the act, you can make it a priceless lesson.**

Anytime a family member catches the puppy squatting, immediately interrupt him with a loud noise, like hard hand clapping. Or you can make a sharp "uh-uh!" noise, say "no!" or shake ten pennies inside a taped-up soda can behind your back. Noise aversion contracts a pup's sphincter muscles and stops elimination momentarily. It also marks inappropriate voiding as the behavior that caused the unpleasant sound.

After you stop him with the noise, immediately get hold of the pup. (But never call him to you in an unpleasant situation like this, or he'll learn not to want to respond to the "come" command later in life.) **Quickly lift or lead him away mid-accident, hook him onto a leash and immediately rush him out to the area you've designated for elimination outdoors.** Move fast! Have shoes, keys and leash right by the door so you can get your pup outside in an instant or you'll miss this critical moment for learning.

If you discover an accident after it has already happened:

Pet parents who keep up with progressive thinking about dogs have probably already heard that you can damage your pup by attempting to correct him for an accident that happened when you were away. This is because the pup cannot make the connection between your displeasure and the action that happened hours before.

If you discover that your pup has had an accident somewhere in your house, don't get mad at him. It is okay to show some displeasure when cleaning up the movement (we actually think this helps a pup understand). But never aim any anger at the puppy. **Don't hit the puppy, shake the puppy or throw items at him.** Physically punishing a puppy like this could seriously hurt him and it could make him distrust humans for life, possibly creating fears and aggression. And forget the old-school advice about swatting the pup with a rolled up newspaper or rubbing his nose in the movement. These actions could terrify your pup so much that he won't understand what you want of him. And **never scream at your pup when you discover a movement that may be hours or days old.**

There is never a place for punishment in housetraining. And the only time for (humane) correction is when you catch your pup actively relieving himself in the home. Even then, you should not do anything to hurt or terrify the pup. Just make a sudden sound to interrupt the movement and then rush the pup out to the designated toilet area.

For any bowel or bladder accident, new or old, clean the area with enzyme cleaner specifically formulated to remove dog pheromones. (Don't use regular household cleaners which are ineffective at fully removing scent). Then give the pup less freedom to prevent him from going back to the area where he voided. Once a dog urinates or defecates in one place, his natural instinct is to want to keep using that spot as his toilet, so it's vital to remove all the scent. **Also completely remove any scents from other dogs that ever had accidents in your home, whatever this takes.** If another dog soiled repeatedly in one area years ago and it soaked through carpeting, padding and subfloor, your pup could still smell it and be naturally attracted to mark the spot.

Containment during housetraining:

Since your young pup's bowels and bladder are not fully developed during housetraining, you must expect some accidents. In order to protect your home, you can

safely and humanely control the pup's environment when you can't supervise. But there's no need to confine him cruelly. When your pup is very young, start out with a comfortable, yet relatively small, space. As he achieves success, you should gradually expand the area he's loose in. Containing pups in a safe, yet sufficiently spacious and stimulating area whenever you can't watch them cuts down on accidents. It also keeps pups safe from household hazards during teething.

But extended crate-training- or confining your pup for many hours in a cramped wire cage just big enough to turn around in is not humane. **When you humanely contain a pup, it should be only: 1) for short periods, 2) when necessary, 3) in safe and comfortable rooms or areas with space to move and varied stimuli and 4) where the pup can see and be near his human family when they're home.**

You should never cage your pup for long periods with nothing to do during the critical months of his development, or you will also restrict the development of his mind, his senses, his personality and his emotions. Ideally, the area you choose for your pup to stay in when you're away should provide space for him to wander and play and access to safe toys, safe bedding and fresh water. Just make sure he won't ingest bedding or parts of toys.

We suggest using a baby gate and gating off a nice, totally dog-proofed, area with safe bedding, unbreakable toys, enough space for the pup to run around and play and easily cleaned flooring. **Leaving your pup** contained in a bare, climate controlled room **is often a good solution when owners go out.** For nighttime hours some pet parents get good results bedding their puppy down behind a baby gate in a comfortable, hazard-proofed master bath, so they can hear him if he cries to empty his bladder during the night, while others use a puppy playpen near their bed.

Not being able to physically make it through an entire night without urinating is normal for most extremely young pups. **Owners should expect that very young pups will need approximately one bathroom break in the wee hours, just like babies.** The good news is that most healthy pups will quickly mature enough to be able to make it through an entire night at a time, although small breeds often have more problems.

Until he physically matures, to keep his training consistent, it's best to take your puppy outside to relieve himself if he cries in the middle of the night. But, if you feel too tired to get up in the night, you could also give your pup a wee-wee pad in case he can't hold his bladder all night long. And remember, just like a baby, your pup needs some time to fully develop, so try not to get mad.

An open master bath with a baby gate across the doorway or an exercise pen near your bed that leaves your pup room to get up and change position during the night are more comfortable alternatives than small crates. However, if you own an 8-week old Chihuahua, and you also own a Great Dane sized crate, it could be fine to keep the puppy in the crate overnight if you feel this is the only way to keep him safe and secure in his early weeks. If you want to contain your pup like this, provide safe toys and bedding, and give him sufficient socialization and stimuli during waking hours. Crates at night become a problem when they're too small for the pup to move around in, and when eight hours crate time at night is combined with 8, 10 or 12 hours crate time during the day. Crates at night are also inappropriate for adult dogs- especially guardian breeds- that could save the family's lives by patrolling the home each night and signaling danger.

But it's usually not safe for an extremely young puppy to have complete run of an entire house during his first days and weeks with his new family (unless the family has been able to dog proof 100% or close off most of the doors). Pet owners should use common sense and kindness and always keep safety in mind when they decide how to house a pup. And always make sure large breed pups have the space they need to move their bodies, even during the night.

Young puppies (especially those under four months) can only hold their bladders several hours at a time. So until your pup's bladder matures, if you can't come home to give him a midday potty break, you should ask a friend to do it or hire a dog walker. If there's no one to take your young pup out midday, you may have to leave papers or wee-wee pads in your pup's room. Some people worry that giving a pup a wee-wee pad can confuse him during housetraining. But sometimes there's no choice.

Unlike many dog professionals today, we believe it's cruel to force a young pup to feel pain holding his bladder/bowels in a tiny crate just because he dreads lying in his own mess. If you give your young puppy a spacious room to stay in and you're away too long (for example, more than 4 hours at a time for pups under 4 months), the pup *will* likely soil on the pad in a corner you designate. And while this may confuse him a bit, it's not likely to ruin housetraining. As your pup matures and starts holding his bladder for longer periods, you can decrease the number of wee-wee pads, eventually eliminating them entirely.

Instead of a crate, you can contain your pup in a puppy playroom:

If you don't wish to crate, but fear leaving your pup free in your entire house when you go away because of other animals or valuables, you can contain him in an individual room. Designating one room in the home as a safe playroom allows you to contain your pup while still providing him all the room he needs for play and mental stimulation. This will be a room where your pup can play to his heart's content and where your kids can play with him when the weather's not ideal.

Most homes have some climate-controlled space without carpet that you can prepare for this purpose by removing all hazards and valuables, for example, a rarely used game room. If the area does not have its own door, you can use a baby gate in the doorway. Ideally, the area should give the pup some room to run and play.

Even if you don't have a lot of extra space in your home, if you think creatively you can multi-purpose a room like an infrequently used guest room as the pup's playroom. Just furnish the area to be flexible; leave some of the better furniture and breakables like table lamps out of the room when your pup stays there alone, and move these items back in when guests arrive. While it might seem like a sacrifice at first to give up space, having a safe place where your pup can run around whenever you leave the home or don't have time to supervise can improve quality of life tremendously, both for the pup and the entire family.

Your pup should never feel imprisoned in his playroom. Provide treats, toys and soft bedding in the room and leave the door open when you are home. The puppy can go in for a nap whenever he feels he needs some "quiet time" away from people and you should praise him for going there voluntarily. **When you have to leave him alone when you go out, if he's not mature enough yet to stay free in the entire home, you can leave him in the playroom with the door closed.** An arrangement like this may be a necessity while you are housetraining and/or when your puppy is teething.

Prepare your doggie playroom by covering outlets and removing any poisons, chemicals, hanging cords, electric wires and media and any small or sharp objects that might be ingested. Use only overhead lighting and remove breakables and furniture that might not be safe.

The other two necessities for a doggie playroom are that it must be climate controlled and the floors must be easy to clean and sanitize if the pup does have a bowel or bladder accident (don't ever use carpet). Ideally the room should allow your pup adequate floor space for a little running, or at least space to walk around.

But if you have other alternative for exercise, then you could temporarily contain your pup in any small room like a dining room, office or bathrooms, as long as the room is climate controlled and well ventilated and all hazards are removed.

Chapter 11:

List of 12 Tips to Prevent Housetraining Mistakes

1) **You may want to keep a log book** of every time your puppy eats, drinks, plays and relieves his bowels and bladder for at least three days. This gives you insights about your pup's habits and helps you housetrain more quickly. (Keep the data and if you notice the pup's habits ever suddenly change, it might mean he's sick.)

2) **Until your pup is fully housetrained, you should always take him outside on leash to observe that he actually relieves himself, rather than just sniffing around the bushes.** People often make the mistake of thinking a pup relieved himself just because they let him outside. Then they're surprised the pup immediately has an accident when they let him back in. But the pup may have never relieved himself outdoors at all.

3) **Don't rush back inside your house as soon as your pup relieves himself, because he may have to go more than once.** Pups having to move their bowels or bladder a second time minutes after their first movement is extremely common, and it often frustrates and confuses owners.

4) **Try to spend at least a little time outside with your pup after he relieves himself.** If the pup thinks you'll immediately bring him back into the house after he voids with no time to explore and stretch his legs, he might start holding his movements just to stay outdoors.

5) **If your pup has an accident, you've either left him too long or failed to notice signs he had to go out.**

6) **Puppies always give signs that they need to relieve themselves, even though signs can be subtle. When your pup needs to go outside, he may: sniff, spin, pace, look antsy, whine, squat or stare at you oddly or intently.** Some pups will also show their own unique signs.

7) **There are certain times of day when puppies usually have to relieve themselves. The times you should take your puppy outside to avoid accidents include:** after waking; around 30 minutes after eating; around 10 minutes after drinking; after playing; after waking from naps and before bed.

8) **If your pup has had an accident somewhere in your house,** don't get mad at him. **Clean the accident thoroughly with an enzyme cleaner like Nature's Miracle (not regular household cleaner),** give the pup less freedom and prevent him from going back to the area.

9) **Feed your puppy meals at set times (according to your veterinarian's recommendations); and avoid leaving food down all day. But you should always leave water available for puppies,** especially in hot weather. Many dog trainers advise owners to limit their pups' water during housetraining. But, unfortunately, on this advice, a good number of owners are now leaving tiny pups for 8 or 10 hours at a time with no water. And this can seriously damage a puppy's health. Keeping your pup adequately hydrated may mean you have to take him out more, but you should never dehydrate a pup, and potentially cause lifelong damage, just to keep him from urinating.

10) If you want to supervise your pup so he won't have an accident, but you don't have any small room where you can contain him because of an open floor plan, you can also keep him on a leash close to you until you know he has "emptied" outside. (See "Umbilical Cord" in Part 3, Activities). Whenever you can't supervise your pup, you can also contain him using a baby gate or a doggie playpen.

11) **Nighttime with your puppy**: If your young pup has been doing well with his housetraining, he can sleep in your closed bedroom with you on a dog bed or a puppy playpen beside your bed or in a safe adjacent room like a master bath with a baby gate across the doorway. If you want your pup to have the run of your bedroom thoroughly "puppy-proof" the room, removing all hazards. Accustom the pup to the room, nicely correct any inappropriate behavior, and then take him outside, making sure he completely empties bowels and bladder just before bed. When your pup is very young, you can't expect him to make it through an entire night without having to urinate. You may want to set an alarm so you can take him outside once each night.

Other pups will cry and wake their owners to let them know they have to go out and some pups can learn to ring a bell to make their needs known (see "Ring a Bell" in Part 3, Activities). Rarely young pups physically make it through eight hours at a time without waking their owners at all. But the good news is that if your pup is healthy (and if he doesn't drink a vast quantity of water just before bedtime) he will soon mature enough physically to make it through the night.

12) One well known rule of thumb is that pups under 6 months can't hold their bladders longer than one hour for each month of age. This rule is good because it gives novice dog owners some framework and keeps people from thinking that a 10 week-old pup can wait ten hours. But, in truth, each pup is unique when it comes to their physical maturity. Typically large dogs can hold their bladders longer then small dogs, yet we've seen unusual cases where a young small-breed pup sleeps comfortably through the night without needing a bathroom break. In other cases, an active small breed pup might have to go out several times an hour if he plays vigorously. By following all the hints on this list, you can get a good idea of your pup's normal pattern.

Chapter 12:

Why Crate Training is Not the Best Way to Housetrain

The best and quickest way to housetrain a puppy while avoiding future behavioral problems when the dog grows up is by consistently following the simple training methods and hints in this book.

But, in the past decade or so, a highly vocal segment of the dog industry has begun advocating the use of crates (or small wire cages) as the preferred method of housetraining. If you're like many new puppy owners, someone in your life has probably already pressured you to use a crate to train or house your puppy. Based on this advice, many families begin crating their pups. Unfortunately, many families that start crating for convenience can easily start to lose track of how many hours a day their puppy is actually in the cage. For example, many families where two parents work now crate their pups for as much as 18-23 hours total per day and as long as 8-12 hours at a stretch. This kind of isolation from exercise, human contact and everyday stimuli can cause devastating damage to the pup's long-term health, emotional well being and bond with their family.

But excessive crating is becoming a dangerous trend that's spreading. Today, very many dog owners use crates for housetraining, and many continue crating for the remainder of their dog's life! Meanwhile dog professionals who support crating theory don't tell people when the justification for keeping the dog in the tiny crate for housetraining has passed and that, if they wish to enclose their dog, they could do it in a much larger sized kennel. Some naturally active breeds suffer physically from the cramping of their bodies in wire crates that are intentionally kept so small that the dog only has room to turn around in. In average suburban homes today, many full grown dogs spend as much as 23 hours a day total with no chance to run and play, no chance to wander and sniff around, and no chance to even get a good long stretch.

Obviously, dogs cannot tell us how they feel, but scientific research documents how pups' senses can be damaged by early confinement away from natural stimuli. And pups of active breeds need exercise, so time in the crate only builds frustration, contributing to dogs that act like "tornadoes" when they're let out of the crate for the first time all day when their owners return at 5:30.

In our book *Dogs Hate Crates: How Abusive Crate Training Hurts Dogs, Families & Society*, we cite case studies and scientific research on the dangers of crating taken to extremes in private homes. And we show owners how to recognize common physical and behavioral symptoms of overcrating that range from excessive barking to fears, aggression and aversion to human touch. Often these problems start with the breeder. *Dogs Hate Crates* also tells the story of the approximately 10,000 puppy mills operating in America. These large-scale substandard breeding facilities sell 2-4 million dogs to the public each year and despite recent public outcry, for political and sociological reasons, extreme cruelties in puppy mills are allowed to continue.

Pups suffering from the hundreds of disturbing symptoms listed in *Dogs Hate Crates* may come from abusive puppy mill backgrounds without their new owners ever knowing. And excessive caging at a breeder, puppy store or pet dealer during early life often causes lasting housetraining issues. **While normal healthy pups coming from healthy upbringing can often be trained in several weeks or less, pups that were excessively crated and deprived of proper stimuli in early life may require many months of careful effort to get the same results.** But almost all physically healthy pups *can* be housetrained.

If you, like us, never thought of crating a puppy to housetrain it- or if you never heard of the concept of crate-training before reading this book- you'll probably agree there's no reason to risk caging your pup. But many caring owners have already been convinced to crate by people they like and trust ranging from family members, to well known and well-liked dog experts, breeders, trainers and even certain veterinarians. Some proponents of crating cite "den theory"- the fact that wolves whelp in dens and that the young pups feel safe there. Unfortunately, using this rationale is scientifically flawed, since the wolf pups are already out of the den and starting to explore the world by 8 weeks to learn all the skills that make them extremely intelligent, alert and athletic hunters. And, even though dogs do sometimes like to curl up and de-stress in a safe private spot like a dog bed in a quiet corner, no healthy animal in the wild would willingly live 8-23 hours of each day locked in a tiny wire cage. Yet one of the most popular sayings of the crating movement is "dogs love crates".

Awesome Puppy **is written in particular for those pet parents who consider dogs family members and who wish to develop their pup's highest potential.** If you do choose to use a crate, remember that there is a huge difference between confining a pup 4 hours a day total and confining a pup 22 hours a day total. The less hours a day total that a pup spends caged the better, both for his physical and mental well being. And never crate a pup for too many hours consecutively. This is painful and needlessly cruel and it can defeat the purpose of housetraining to ask a pup to "hold it" longer than he's physically capable of.

Personally, we don't use crates. When we leave the home, however, we do keep teething puppies safely contained in certain areas to protect them from chewing on or ingesting potentially deadly hazards like chemicals, electronics and small, sharp or brittle items. Usually the best way to safely contain a pup is in a thoroughly dog-proofed room (or rooms) using the door or a high, solidly installed baby gate. (For tiny toy puppies, a playpen or exercise enclosure may sometimes also be effective.) Eventually, as a pup stops teething and demonstrates more trustworthiness in the home, we start expanding the areas he's free in, as tolerated, until he has free run of most of the house.

Ultimately, the choice of whether to use a crate at all for housing or training is yours. And it is a serious decision that will have a huge impact on your pup's future. Pet parents who do *not* **use a crate must be especially careful and keep their pup away from hazards while he is young, especially when he is teething; and they must remember that pups require supervision, just like babies. And owners who** *do* **use a crate must be careful to confine the pup only for short stretches of time, and give him extra exercise, attention and training at other times to compensate for the hours he spends confined.**

Some dogs have serious issues when they come into a new home that can make owners distrust them. And we always stress safety above all for both dogs and families. But we'd never tell a family to sacrifice their dog's entire quality of life and damage his bond with people by caging him the majority of every day of his lifetime, just because they feared he'd soil their carpets.

Dogs can be housetrained easily, with no need for extreme methods like extended caging. **And a healthy emotionally balanced adult dog that grows up without being crated would no more soil in your living room than a human would.** The only reason a dog would soil in a home is if he is a physically undeveloped puppy, if he has serious physical or emotional problems that require treatment or if he's left too long with no opportunity to go outside. But there are housing and training alternatives that can keep everyone safe and comfortable at every stage of your dog's life, while offering much better outcomes than caging.

If you train your pup with consistency from a young age and always give him positive and productive activities to fill his days, he can assist you in real ways when he matures. And a well trained dog by your side for all the years of his life can bring you a thousand times more joy than he could have if you attempted to train him by leaving him locked up in a little box!

About The Authors:

Canine psychology specialists and authors of *The Cure for Useless Dog Syndrome. Ray & E*mma Lincoln have had unique opportunities to observe dog behavior while treating complex canine issues in suburban environments. Long term advocates for environmental preservation and animal rescue, the authors learned that excessive crating is a poorly understood problem affecting a huge number of dogs, so they made it their personal mission to raise public awareness. The authors' previous education is in psychology, philosophy, biology, animal behavior and social trends. Ray & Emma are wide-ranging travelers who spend most of the year on Florida's East Coast, and now offer telephone consultation for canine behavior issues.

The authors can be contacted through Awesome Book Publishing at awesomebookpublishing@gmail.com

Printed in Great Britain
by Amazon

36145267R00136